RELATIVE STRANGERS

RELATIVE STRANGERS

Italian Protestants in the Catholic World

Frank Cicero Jr.

ACADEMY CHICAGO PUBLISHERS

UNCORRECTED PAGE PROOFS

Published in 2011 by
Academy Chicago Publishers
363 West Erie Street
Chicago, Illinois 60654

© 2011 by Frank Cicero Jr.

First edition.

Printed and bound in the U.S.A.

Library of Congress Cataloging-in-Publication Data

Cicero, Frank.
Relative strangers : Italian Protestants in the
Catholic world / Frank Cicero, Jr.
p. cm.
Includes bibliographical references and index.
ISBN 978-0-89733-615-4 (hardcover : alk. paper)
1. Cicero, Frank. 2. Italian American Protestants—
Illinois—Chicago—Biography. I. Title.
BR563.I8C53 2010
284'.4092—dc22
[B]
2010053281

CONTENTS

For my grandparents
Margherita Balma and Giacomo Balma
Antonina Panepinto and Giuseppe Cicero

Exemplars of the courage and industry of millions of
immigrants who forged the American dream

PROLOGUE

Are All These People
Really Italian?

ON CHRISTMAS EVE WE WALKED the block down the street to Uncle
Benny's house in the dark and cold. We were loaded down with pans of
food and shopping bags full of gifts. Christmas Eve celebrations with my
father's side of the family were always at Uncle Benny's house. My father
and his older half-brother had made a big move in the 1930s from the old
Italian neighborhood at the edge of downtown Chicago. They shifted as
far west in the city as they could, buying vacant lots on adjacent prairie-
covered blocks on Neva Avenue, the last street in from the city limits.
Their two houses were identical, built at the same time from the same
plans, except that Uncle Benny's, on the opposite side of Neva from ours,
was flipped so that the screened porch off the dining room would be on
the sunny south side, just like ours.

When we entered the front door, the house was already crowded. I
think my mother delayed our arrival as long as she could. The house was
always hot, the windows steamed and dripping. The fire in the fireplace
was blazing, the Christmas tree in the living room was lighted with large,
candle-shaped, colored lights and surrounded by brightly wrapped packages, and the card game was in full swing straight ahead on the dining
room table. All the uncles and older cousins were in the game. The table
was covered with poker chips, platters of antipasti, beer and wine bottles,
glasses, and rapidly filling ashtrays, the room cloudy with smoke. The
aunts hustled around refilling the drinks, preparing the feast, trying to
control us younger cousins.

And the noise. The card game proceeded with raucous laughter, shouts
of triumph or wails of outrage, and loud accusations of fraud. The play of

the younger cousins usually involved running all over the house, down to the basement, up to the second-floor attic, into every bedroom and closet, and back down through the kitchen, where we were sternly chased out by the aunts. Our play was loud when it was happy and even louder when it was rancorous. There were always arguments. There was always crying.

We younger kids were fed in the kitchen while the dining room table was cleared and reset for the potluck Italian dinner. Then we were moved off to sleep—three or four crossways on each bed. When the older folks' dinner was over, we were awakened to see what Santa Claus had brought. Protecting our eyes against the bright lights, we shuffled sleepily from the bedroom toward the Christmas tree, past the dining room table that was again covered with glasses, beer and wine bottles, empty food platters, and full ashtrays.

The gift opening was subdued by our sleepiness and accompanied by the coming and going of adults packing up to leave. Then we bundled up and walked the block back home in the dark and cold, loaded down with leftover food and shopping bags full of gifts.

Christmas Day was spent with my mother's family in the house on Narragansett Avenue in which my mother and her three younger siblings had lived a good part of their lives. When we arrived—usually well before noon—the house was quiet, the air fresh, and the dining room table neatly and fully set with its lace-edged tablecloth and my grandparents' Sunday-best dishes and glasses. No one would have dared smoke. There was no wine or beer and certainly never any card playing. We opened presents around the tree. The cousins—many fewer in number—ran around the house and up and down the narrow stairway to the second floor, but we knew we shouldn't make noise.

On this side of the family, my grandfather and grandmother were still living. They were nice. I liked them. But they were stern—especially Grandpa—and protective of the house.

Grandfather took the lead in the Christmas religious observances. Before the midday Christmas dinner, we listened to the reading of the familiar Christmas story from the New Testament. We sang hymns and Christmas carols. We prayed.

We all ate Christmas dinner together, after praying again to bless the meal and those who had prepared it. After dinner, while Grandma and the aunts cleared the table, did the dishes, and cleaned the kitchen, the cousins played with our new toys or ran around in the backyard as Grandpa and the uncles watched and talked. Darkness came early, of course, so we went in the house for more play on the stairs until supper was ready.

Supper also was early, for the men had to be at work the next morning or everyone had to be at Sunday school if the twenty-fifth was a Saturday. We prayed before supper. We ate leftovers from dinner with a couple of additional Jell-O salads. The kids were cranky from being up late Christmas Eve and early Christmas morning to see what Santa had brought. There were squabbles and crying. We all packed it in early and departed for home.

There were weddings—lots of them—and they were as different from each other as the Christmas celebrations. On my father's side, I heard, the wedding masses were on a Saturday morning followed by a luncheon—events my family never attended. In the evening there was always a reception—a boisterous one—at a hall, usually above a tavern, with a band, dinner, dancing, toasts, much drinking, a clamorous cake cutting, garter and bouquet throwing, and more music and dancing that went on late into the night. How late, I never knew: we always left long before the party ended.

The wedding celebration in my father's family that I remember most clearly was on June 22, 1946, shortly before my sister, Nancy, was born. My cousin Elaine was marrying Frank Kolovitz. My mother, who knew from experience and, I think, with some distaste, that the wedding celebration would be raucous, feared her labor would be induced and she would have to rush off to nearby St. Elizabeth's Hospital, where I and my brother had been born and where she planned to deliver Nancy. To be ready, she packed a suitcase to take along to the party. There was nothing extraordinary about that; she often packed a suitcase to be prepared. The wedding party was in a large dance hall and bar on the second floor above a tavern. When we arrived, after climbing the long, straight flight of steps, Mom took me by the hand, walked me to the rear of the building, opened the exit door, and assessed the fire escape down to the alley where she could make a hasty exit when nature was sure to summon. To my disappointment, we returned home that night with the suitcase.

Weddings on my mother's side were often in the large sanctuary or a smaller chapel at Moody Church, the huge, historic, nondenominational house of worship near Chicago's lakefront that served as a sort of mother church for our conservative Protestant faith. We attended all the wedding services, usually held early on Saturday evenings. The marriage ceremony was followed by a reception in a parlor at the church, usually a dinner or buffet supper, and a program in the same hall. There were nonalcoholic fruit punch and cookies, hymns and blessings. A solo musician or small ensemble played religious or popular classical works. There were readings and recitals of poems or limericks by friends of the bride and groom and some of us cousins. There was never dancing; there were no toasts; there was very little noise. Everything ended soberly, sedately, and early.

Other differences marked our lives as well. My Catholic aunts, uncles, and cousins did not eat meat on Fridays. We did. We did not dance or smoke or drink alcohol. They did. We attended Sunday school and church services every week at a Baptist church. They went to mass, and some of my male cousins were altar boys; I was never clear exactly what their duties involved. My Catholic cousins all had to go to confession on Saturdays—an obligation they complained about every week. At some point in their lives, they attended something called catechism; whatever that was, it was a mystery to me. They mostly went to Catholic schools, and some traveled a considerable way by bus and streetcar to do so. We, of course, attended public schools in our neighborhood.

My mother was the only one of her family to marry an Italian and a Catholic; her two sisters and brother all married non-Italian Protestants. My father was the only one of his siblings to marry someone who was not Catholic.

As a child, I was mystified by our family gatherings. Could all these people really be Italians, I wondered. Could I really be related to all of them?

I always had a vague feeling with each side of the family that my brother, sister, and I were some kind of strange crossover cousins. I felt that the Protestant families on my mother's side regarded us as having an alien, dark connection out there somewhere, while the Catholic families thought of us as somewhat peculiar sectarians.

I was well into adulthood before I understood how the marked religious differences between the two sides of my family were the legacy of a protestant reform that goes back almost 850 years. It was even later, however, before I understood the religious, social, cultural, and political differences—going back millennia—between my mother's ancestors, from the high mountain valleys of the Piedmont region of northern Italy, and my father's, from the ancient island civilizations of Sicily.

The gulf fostered by those differences existed not only in Italy but in Chicago as well. In 1904, my mother's parents, Margherita and Giacomo Balma, arrived in Chicago from Italy. They moved into a basement apartment on West Ohio Street at Halsted Street. Later the same year, my father's parents, Antonina Panepinto and Giuseppe Cicero, arrived in Chicago with their large family, including my father, then six years old. They moved into a basement apartment on North Peoria Street at Grand Avenue. The Cicero home on Peoria was one and a half blocks from the Balma home on Ohio.

Immediately upon their arrival, my mother's parents became worshippers at the First Italian Presbyterian Church of Chicago. The church met in the same tenement building they lived in on Ohio Street. My father's parents became worshippers at Santa Maria Addolorata Roman Catholic Church, on the corner of Peoria and Grand, next door to the tenement building in which they lived—and a block and a half from the Balma's Presbyterian church. The Balma children became involved in activities at the Erie Neighborhood House, a Presbyterian institution a block from their home. The younger Cicero children were active at the Chicago Commons, a determinedly nonsectarian neighborhood house a block from their home.

Over a period of almost thirty years, members of the two families crisscrossed the same streets, frequented parks, schools, churches, and numerous other places in the same neighborhood, but never met. Their separate worlds never touched until Mary Balma, later my mother, and Frank Cicero, later my father, went to work in 1933 at the same wholesale produce seller at the Randolph Street market a few blocks from their childhood homes. When they courted and resolved to marry, a bitter family reaction was provoked—a reaction rooted in those ancient religious and cultural differences.

As a child and youth, I had a simple and incomplete impression of these two worlds and how they came together. I understood that my mother's side of the family had emigrated to America from northern Italy while my father's came from a mysterious island called Sicily. I understood further that we were Protestants and not Catholics because in some unusual way my mother's parents—who called themselves Waldensians—brought with them a vehement antipathy toward the Roman Catholic Church and the pope.

I became more aware of the origins of my grandparents' faith in a remote corner of northwestern Italy during my work in Paris on the *Amoco Cadiz* litigation. On one of my walking excursions, I stumbled upon a small religious bookstore on Boulevard St. Germain, just east of the St. Germain church. There I found a small paperback book by Georges Tourn, a contemporary author whose work I would come to know well.[1] Tourn was an Italian Protestant minister from the Waldensian valleys in the Cottian Alps along the frontier between the Piedmont region of Italy and the southeastern corner of France—the very valleys from which my grandparents hailed. He wrote about those valleys, even mentioning the villages in which my grandparents had lived. And he wrote about the Waldensians' beliefs in simple, non-intellectual terms with a strong emphasis on personal faith, persecution, isolation, heroism, perseverance, and survival. It was exciting to read this history, helpfully translated from Italian into French but more importantly recounted by a writer still living this ancient faith.

I decided I wanted to learn more about the Piedmont valleys my mother's parents had left and the faith they brought with them. I also wanted to know more about my father's origins on the mysterious island of Sicily. I determined to explore both, and set out to do so.

Descendants of Giacomo and Margherita Balma

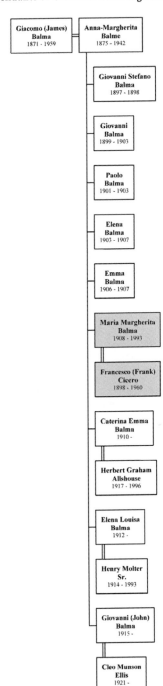

DAVID SOKOL/AUTHOR

Descendants of Carmelo (1824) Cicero

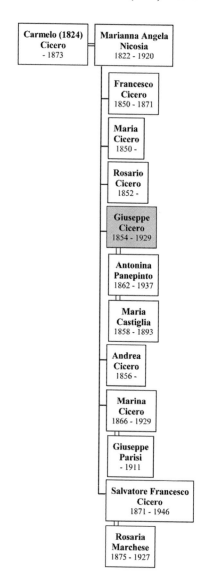

Descendants of Giuseppe Cicero

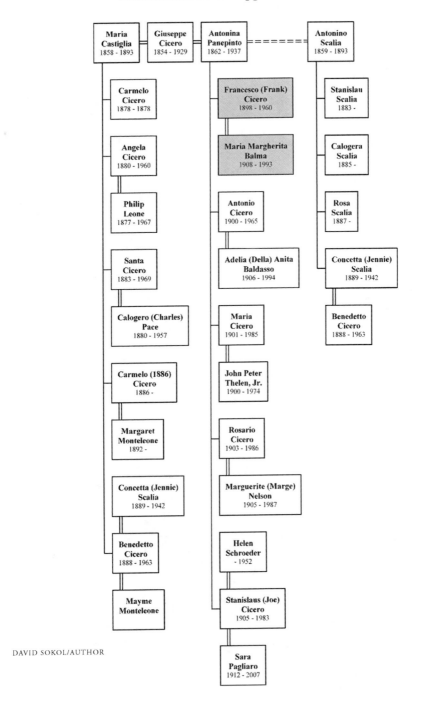

DAVID SOKOL/AUTHOR

Piedmont Waldensian Valleys

Turin

Sestriere
Rodoretto
Balma
Prali
Briancon
Pinerolo
Bobbio
Torre
Pellice
Pellice

France

Sicily

Messina
Trapani
Palermo
Cefalu
Taormina
Montermaggiore
Marsala
Belsito
Valledolmo
Catania
Agrigento
Siracusa
Ragusa
Ispica

Maps not to scale

Switzerland
Austria
Hungary

France
Slovenia

Milan
Venice
Croatia

Turin
Bologna
Bosnia–
Herzegovina

Piedmont Waldensian Valleys

Florence

Italy

Corsica
Adriatic Sea

Rome
Sardinia
Bari

Naples
Brindisi

Tyrrhenian Sea
Gulfo di
Taranto

Mediterranian Sea
Palermo
Messina
Reggio di Calabria

Sicily
Catania
Ionian Sea

Algeria
Tunisia
Siracusa

DAVID SOKOL

PART I

PIEDMONT

1

Emigration

At first light on the morning of April 13, 1904, Giacomo Balma said good-bye to his wife and five-month-old daughter and began the long trip to America. Joining in the tearful farewells were a few neighbors who shared the cluster of stone huts perched high above the headwaters of the Torrente Germanasca, a turbulent mountain river. Winters were harsh and long in the upper Alps of remote northwestern Italy. The deep accumulation of snow still filled the meadows and covered the mountains down to timberline a few dozen meters above Balme, the small hamlet where Giacomo had lived with his wife, Anna-Margherita, for eight years.

Giacomo loaded his wooden trunk and a few other possessions in the back of his old horse-drawn farm wagon and began the last trip he would ever make from Balme. He bumped slowly down the rutted and rocky pathway to Rodoretto and then down the switchbacks of the gravel road that descended the steep sides of the valley a thousand feet to the Germanasca River. At the junction of the Rodoretto road with one from Prali, he was joined by other young men and women from that hamlet, nestled further upstream on the edge of the river.

Giacomo transferred his baggage to the larger wagon and horse team that carried passengers on the valley road, said good-bye to the friend who would return with the farm wagon to Balme, and resumed the trip with this new group the dozen miles down the Germanasca River valley to the Val Chisone, where they would catch the train. By midafternoon, they were aboard for the two-hour ride to Turin. There, early that same evening, they boarded the overnight train to Paris. From Turin, the train followed ancient routes, crossing the French frontier through the Tunnel of

Frejus, traveling across Savoy through Chambery, on to Lyon, and from there to Paris, where they arrived on the fourteenth.

Paris at that time was home to many recent emigrants from Prali and neighboring communities.[1] After staying the night with friends, on the morning of the fifteenth the group moved by train on to Le Havre, the major French port in Normandy west of Paris, where they would board the ship for America the next day.

Giacomo was thirty-three years old. He and Margherita, then twenty-nine, had married in 1896. They had lived the eight years since in the small hamlet of Balme,[2] a cluster of half a dozen stone huts two miles by foot up the mountain trail toward France from the small village of Rodoretto, where they were married. Balme was home to no more than fifteen people.

Life was hard in these mountains. Prali and Rodoretto were at the upper end of the Val Germanasca in the Alps west of Turin, just below the divide at the summit ridge that defines the French-Italian border. It is beautiful and rugged country of steep mountain valleys formed by rushing streams. The Germanasca valley is one of the steepest, made up of sides and summits of mountains with few bottomlands. The wildest and most barren of the communes in the valley is the area of Prali and, above it, Rodoretto.[3] Families farmed where they could to raise sustenance crops in the summer. They kept sheep, goats, and, if prosperous, a few cows, all of which were sheltered in stables beneath the open-spaced floorboards of stone huts, the families living above. Winters were very cold and snows were deep.

Families struggled to survive and raise their children. Giacomo and Margherita were not successful. In the span of a little over four years, they buried their first three children in Rodoretto's little cemetery. Their firstborn, Giovanni Stefano, died weeks before his second birthday. Their second child, born four months later and also named Giovanni, died just days after his fourth birthday and weeks after the death of his two-year-old brother, Paolo. With Giovanni's death, Giacomo and Margherita were left childless for the third time in their six and one-half years of marriage.

They decided to strike out for America, as had others from these alpine valleys. For more than a decade, many neighbors and acquaintances, known to each other from their Waldensian churches, had emigrated to the United States. Hundreds had settled a new community called

Valdese in the Piedmont foothills of western North Carolina.[4] Others settled in New York, Chicago, and other places in North and South America. Giacomo and Margherita had decided to go to Chicago, where a small colony of friends from Prali and neighboring communes in the Germanasca valley had settled beginning in the 1890s.[5] There Giacomo also had a close friend from home, Francois Peyrot, who shortly before had emigrated to Chicago and now could offer the promise of employment.[6]

With their arrival at Le Havre, Giacomo and his friends began the arduous experience of poor immigrants crossing the oceans. Le Havre was a crowded, busy port. Third-class travelers in "steerage"—such as Giacomo and his companions—were herded into the warehouses of their shipping line from the time of their arrival. Many lived in such company warehouses for days, awaiting the departures of their vessels. There was no privacy. Families and groups worked to keep their members together. All struggled to manage their baggage and protect their belongings.

The waiting areas on the quays were a noisy crush of people. Hawkers and sellers of all kinds loudly plied food and other wares. Children were crying. Parents and grandparents were shouting. When time came to board the ship that loomed above, gangplanks were jammed with people and baggage as the passengers pushed ahead and scrambled for accommodations.

On Saturday, April 16, 1904, Giacomo and six of the friends who had departed the mountains with him boarded the French steamship *La Savoie* in Le Havre. Giacomo and one other friend, Giacomo Pons, were headed for Chicago. The other three young adults and two children were bound for New York, where they also intended to join friends and relatives.[7]

La Savoie was built in France in 1901 specifically for the huge North Atlantic immigrant traffic. At 1,168 gross tons, it was 580 feet long and 60 feet wide. It carried 1,055 passengers: 437 in first class, 118 in second class, and 500 in steerage.[8] A modern transport ship, the *Savoie* typically made the crossing from Le Havre on the western edge of Europe in only seven days, contrasting with the ten to fifteen or more days frequently required by other ships departing European ports.[9]

The rigors of the crossings in steerage class have been well documented. Indeed, they have become the stuff of legend, dramatized for well over a century in literature, film, and fable. The vessel rolled and tossed in adverse weather, causing sickness and discomfort for all classes. In still or calmer conditions, the smoke and noxious fumes from the ship's two huge stacks enveloped the passengers. The noise of engines and other machinery, of lifeboats swinging on their davits, and of other fittings and equipment was a constant presence. Common to all passengers, these conditions were much worse in steerage. In the lower reaches of the ship, the noise and motion were louder and inescapable. The crowded, airless hold made the sickness of many a misery for all.

Typically, a steerage berth was an iron bunk with a mattress of straw and no pillow. Sometimes in large rooms, sometimes in smaller cabins, the space was cramped and there was little privacy. With no room for storage of hand luggage, travelers lived and slept with it in their bunks or hanging from any available support. Floors were normally of wood, which was swept every morning and sprinkled with sand. Few washrooms were provided; all were used by both sexes. Passengers were issued tin plates or bowls, utensils, cups, and some cans for washing, food service, or laundry. Floors were wet and littered. The number of vessels to use for seasickness was always inadequate. Even without serious seasickness, by the end of a crossing everything was dirty and disagreeable. On rough passages, the floors were often filled with vomit. Passengers would spend as much time as possible above on the open—but also crowded—decks.[10] There the steerage passengers could observe the relatively spacious and luxurious surroundings of the first- and second-class travelers.

La Savoie reached New York on Saturday, April 23, 1904, a week after departure from Le Havre. Arrival day was always busy, turbulent, and exciting for steerage passengers. They arranged their luggage for the last time, washed in their basins with cold salt water, and made themselves as clean and tidy as possible for the fearfully awaited inspections at Ellis Island. Then they pushed up to the deck—which became nearly impassible with baggage—to witness the New York arrival. As the vessels passed into the Narrows, the passengers could celebrate the famous and awaited view of the Statue of Liberty. They could also take in the panoramic scene of the New York skyline and the many ships from all over the world docked at the Battery and around the tip of Manhattan. The impression on Giacomo and his companions, who just ten days earlier had departed the hamlets and stone huts of their sparsely populated, remote mountain valleys, can only be imagined.

It is interesting to me now to reflect on the fact that I never, ever heard my grandfather refer to the huge contrast between his homeland in the Piedmont mountains and the surroundings he experienced and settled into in the New World. Grandpa Balma died two years after I graduated from college. For some fifteen years after he gave up the family home, he lived with us several months at a time as he rotated among his three children who lived in the Chicago area. I recall no conversation about the mountains in which he grew up, his passage to America, or the contrast between life in America and his prior life in Italy. Of course, I never asked—nor knew to ask—either, and that is now a great regret.

When the arriving liners slowed on the approach to New York, steerage passengers experienced in a new way the class distinctions they had endured in their travels to Le Havre, at Le Havre in their sorting and separation, during the voyage, and probably through much of their lives as the poor classes in their homelands. In the grand era of immigration through New York, arriving ocean transports did not go directly to Ellis Island. Indeed, they did not go there at all. The vessels docked at the Battery on the tip of Manhattan. There first- and second-class passengers disembarked and were expedited on their ways. To speed up the process, small cutters bearing uniformed immigration officers often came out to the ships. Inspectors boarded the ships, reviewed the list of first-cabin passengers, conducted perfunctory interviews of second-cabin passengers—who also were observed by medical officers for obvious signs of illness—and asked the ship's doctor if there were any contagious diseases on board. If the answer was positive, the entire vessel was isolated at the quarantine station. Absent the need for quarantine, the ship docked and the first- and second-class passengers departed.

Steerage passengers also debarked, but they immediately were loaded onto ferries that took them to Ellis Island. There the immigrants dragged their luggage ashore and proceeded to the vast reception hall. They were examined for disease or other infirmity, and their baggage was inspected. If they cleared the process, they were taken by ferry back to Manhattan or to New Jersey to continue on their ways. If they were not cleared, they either were interned on the island for observation or for time to cure their medical condition or they were transported back to the ships on which they had come to return across the oceans to their ports of departure.

During the peak years for immigration—particularly in the last two decades of the nineteenth and the first two decades of the twentieth centuries—arriving transports often had to wait offshore for days before a berth became available to discharge their steerage passengers. Frequently in those cases, cabin-class passengers were taken ashore by small ferries while steerage passengers were left to wait in their squalid accommodations.

Giacomo and his companions were fortunate to have an expeditious passage through the New York arrival procedures. *La Savoie* docked promptly. They were taken by ferry to Ellis Island and passed through the immigration processing quickly. Then the weary travelers were met at Ellis Island by New York City friends, including the husband of one of the women on the voyage. A number of Waldensians from the Piedmont valleys, including three ministers, one of whom was from Prali, were living in the New York area. They had organized a Waldensian church that held meetings at the Church of the Strangers at Eighth Avenue and Fifty-seventh Street. Church members regularly went to the Battery and to Ellis Island to meet and welcome immigrants and visitors from their home communities in Italy, help settle them if they were staying in the New York area, and assist them on their way if they were traveling on to other places in the states.

From Ellis Island, Giacomo, his immigrant traveling companions, and their New York friends returned to Manhattan, where several of the newly arrived intended to stay. The two Giacomos heading for Chicago visited with friends from the Waldensian community, attended Sunday services at the Waldensian church, and on Monday were assisted onto the train to Chicago.

* * *

Six months later, my grandmother Margherita followed, making the long journey from Italy to Chicago with their eleven-month-old daughter, Elena. In the spring of 1904, shortly after Giacomo's departure, twenty-eight-year-old Margherita had left the remote and isolated mountain community where she had lived her entire life. She first relocated some twenty miles down the valleys of the Germanasca and Chisone rivers to stay with friends in the larger community of Pinerolo. That historic city, some forty miles southwest of Turin and less than thirty miles from the French border, had for centuries been a fought-over stronghold in wars between the kings of France and the rulers of the House of Savoy. In 1904 Pinerolo was the prosperous center of economic life for the rugged and sparsely populated Valdese valleys southwest of Turin. In later years, as transportation improved, many residents of the small mountain towns—towns like Prali and Rodoretto, from which my grandparents emigrated—passed some or all of their winters in Pinerolo and their summers at their old family homes high in the mountains.

Later in the summer of 1904, Margherita and baby Elena relocated to Turin, the capital city of the Piedmont region, where she resided with friends until she left for America in October. By then, Giacomo had settled into his work in Chicago and had established his earning power in a reliable job. After an initial period of loneliness and depression that had caused him to consider moving back to Italy, he had become fixed emotionally on staying in America and had sent money back to Margherita to pay for passage to Chicago.[11]

Margherita made the trip alone with her eleven-month-old baby. Leaving Turin the first week of October, she and Elena also traveled by train through the Alps and across France to Lyon and on to Paris and the port at Le Havre. In Paris, she had the comfort of staying with friends from the city's sizeable Waldensian community, including many émigrés from the same valleys she had called home. Early on Saturday, October 8, 1904, her friends assisted her to the port at Le Havre. Thereafter, she was left alone with Elena to find her way aboard the ship, establish them both in a bunk, and prepare for the long voyage.

Margherita and Elena sailed on the French Line passenger steamship *La Lorraine*, a sister ship to *La Savoie*.[12] During the week-long voyage, Margherita endured all the usual privations of steerage-class passengers, compounded, of course, by the fact that she—undoubtedly like many other young women on the vessel—was a nursing mother with an infant to care for.

Margherita and Elena Balma arrived in New York on Saturday, October 15, 1904, almost six months to the day after Giacomo's arrival. They also were met at Ellis Island by friends from the Waldensian church in New York. After a short stay in the city, Margherita and Elena left by train for Chicago.

2

Childhood and Youth

My grandfather Giacomo Balma was born on May 28, 1871, in the hamlet of Coste di Rodoretto. Coste was a cluster of three or four stone houses clinging to the steep side of a mountain about a mile up the Germanasca River valley from the small village of Rodoretto. Rodoretto had a population of about fifty at that time.

Baby Giacomo was baptized in the small Waldensian church in the village. The baptism was recorded in the church records in French as *Jacques Balme*. His birth was also registered in the civil records in the commune's town hall.[1] Civil records were kept in Italian; there his name was recorded as *Giacomo Balma*.

The simple fact that key records, such as births, baptisms, marriages, and deaths, were registered in French in church records and in Italian in civil records reflects the ancient duality of the region's history, as does the fact that Giacomo was baptized in the Waldensian church in Rodoretto, a Protestant church located just a few meters away from the village's Roman Catholic church.

The region that is now Piedmont in Italy was for centuries part of the domains ruled by the House of Savoy.[2] At its greatest extent, the Savoyard state straddled the ridges of the Alps across what is now the French-Italian border. It was composed of four principal regions: the county of Nice and the duchy of Savoy on the French side, and the Val d'Aosta and Piedmont on the Italian side.

The Savoy dynasty, of vague origins, is generally credited with having its first ruler in the person of Count Umberto I (c.980–c.1048), who was given the mysterious appellation of Biancamano, or White-Handed.

Over the centuries, the status of the heads of the House of Savoy grew in rank and prestige. They were counts until Amedeus VIII was named duke in 1416. They became kings when Vittorio Amedeo II attained that title in 1720. Although the economic and political heart of the Savoyard state was Piedmont, the capital was at Chambery in Savoy until Duke Emanuele Filiberto moved it to Turin in Piedmont in 1560. From its base in Piedmont, the House of Savoy led the struggle for Italian unification in the nineteenth century and gave to the resulting Kingdom of Italy four kings who reigned from 1861 until June 13, 1946.

French, Italian, and the Piedmont dialect were official languages of the Savoyard state and were spoken by the king and other officials. In the Waldensian valleys southwest of Turin, however, French and at least five different patois generally were the spoken languages, although much of the population also spoke Italian. Both Giacomo and Margherita spoke, read, and wrote French and Italian.

In my family, the legendary blame was put upon officials at Ellis Island for the claimed fact that the family name was spelled as *Balme* in Piedmont but later was changed to *Balma* in America. In reality, parallel records in Piedmont going back to the 1860s display the same events and names in both French and Italian, depending on the record keeper. Many documents in Italy record the name as *Balma* and show that Giacomo himself used that spelling and his Italian name.

As a child growing up in a sparsely populated and isolated area high in the mountains, Giacomo found playmates and companions where he could. His immediate family was small. His father, Jean-Jacques Balma, was forty-three years old when Giacomo was born; his mother, Anna-Catherine Baral, was thirty-five. Although Giacomo was the fifth of six children, the records I have seen show that only two siblings, his ten-years-older sister Marie and five-years-younger sister Caterina, lived beyond infancy. Several aunts and uncles lived in the Prali/Rodoretto area, however, and young Giacomo undoubtedly knew many cousins well.

The only significant fact that distinguished Giacomo and his family from the others in their valleys is that he was raised in the Waldensian faith. The protestant Waldensians were a minority but believed passionately—even fiercely—in their faith and the conviction that they were an isolated and embattled minority of true believers in the Word of God, different from the dominant Catholics and their pope. Giacomo and his family attended services regularly at the small but beautiful Waldensian church that stands on the up valley side of Rodoretto with splendid views of the surrounding mountain peaks and valleys.

Children were put to work early. Giacomo helped tend the livestock—perhaps even remaining away from home many nights in pursuit of suitable pasture—and assisted in cultivating the family's subsistence crops. He was educated in Rodoretto's small schoolhouse.

Older boys were expected to try to find work. It was no easy task, for there was no gainful employment in the mountains. Young men had to go elsewhere. From the time he was fifteen years old Giacomo traveled regularly to nearby communities and into France to try to earn a living. He followed this path until he was twenty, when he joined the Italian army.[3]

More than fifty years later, he succinctly described those times in a recorded interview: "When I was about fifteen years of age, I have to go out to earn my bread. I went along in and out until I was twenty-one years old [sic] when the government took care of me and feeded me for three years straight."[4]

The source of these recollections is a recording made in 1947 by one of my uncles, Herb Allshouse. Uncle Herb was an early technical geek and a dedicated ham radio operator. Immediately after World War II, he bought a wire recorder, one of the very early versions of portable audio recording equipment. On a Sunday afternoon in April 1947, he sat Grandpa Balma in front of a microphone and recorded an eighteen-minute interview guided by gentle questions asked of a reluctant witness. The recording is a cherished memento, the only source I know of recollections—oral or written—by any of my four grandparents.

Matters concerning my grandparents' lives before they came to America, or my parents' lives growing up as children of immigrants, never were discussed in anything but the most general and infrequent ways. Like many other children or grandchildren of immigrants, I now wish, of course, that I had asked more questions.

When I began my history search a few years ago, I knew of no records within the family of my grandparents' lives. The 1947 tape recording was the first specific information I obtained. I later learned about a scrapbook of correspondence and photographs gathered by my uncle John, my mother's youngest sibling, and his wife, Cleo. It proved to be a valuable trove of information.

An especially remarkable document in the scrapbook is Giacomo Balma's *Libretto Personale,* issued to him when he joined the army. The *Libretto* is the personal manual and handbook that he was required to keep with him at all times while in the service. In addition to printed rules, regulations, standing orders, and other such matter of general interest, there is in handwriting a great deal of personal data, such as vital statistics, illnesses, medications, issues of equipment and clothing, and other details of life.

Twenty-year-old Giacomo entered the Italian army at Pinerolo, a larger city down valley from his home, on June 23, 1891, after signing papers of enlistment two weeks earlier on June 11. He was assigned to the Third Alpine Regiment based in Pinerolo. The first page of personal information in his *Libretto* describes him as unmarried, occupation farmer, of the Waldensian religion. He was five feet, six and one-half inches tall, weighed 148 pounds, and had straight chestnut-colored hair and eyebrows, gray eyes, pink coloring, and healthy teeth. Further identifying physical attributes included a high forehead, large nose, medium mouth, regular chin, and good eyesight.[5]

The section concerning his education is only partially filled out. There is no entry on the line asking whether he knew how to read and only an ambiguous handwritten mark or sign on the line asking if he knew how to write. His discharge papers three years later in 1894, however, state that he could do both.[6]

As a rifleman in the Third Alpine Regiment, Giacomo apparently enjoyed the soldier's life, doing his service in the mountains, traveling up and down the valleys, training, and patrolling the frontier. By all appearances, he wore the uniform proudly. He also suffered disabling illnesses that twice required lengthy stays in military facilities. Thus he spent twenty-nine days in October and November 1892 in the military infirmary in Pinerolo. It is difficult to read the army doctor's handwriting describing the malady, but the note appears to refer to an infection under the arm and in the armpit. Five months later, beginning in April 1893, he was hospitalized for sixty-three days, until mid-June, in the Turin Military

Hospital because of a subcutaneous bacterial infection and abscess in his left foot.[7]

His service time appears to have gone smoothly thereafter. Giacomo was promoted to the rank of corporal on February 28, 1894. He was discharged honorably from active duty on September 9, 1894. The discharge papers record that he was recalled twice for training, once in the summer of 1899 and again in the summer of 1902.[8]

Years later in Chicago he summarized his service, discharge, and return home: "[T]he government took care of me and feeded me for three years straight. They sent me home. Not penniless because they gave me seventeen cents to pay my expenses home. There was rejoicing when people see me coming home. My mother, father, sister who was five years younger than me."[9]

After his welcome home, Giacomo remained in Rodoretto for a short time. A few companions from army days joined him there. Once again, however, they could not remain in their home valleys because "there was no way to make a living."[10] Accordingly, he and his friends went to France, where they stayed with occasional visits to Italy until 1896. That year he "decided I had to change my life," so he returned home.[11]

* * *

My grandmother Anna Margherita Balma was born on December 5, 1875, in Prali, the same commune in which Giacomo had been born four and one-half years earlier. She was the only daughter of the eight children born to Jean Balma and Marie Madeleine Genre. Her baptism in the Waldensian church in Prali was recorded in French as *Anne Marguerite Balme;* in the civil records of Prali it was recorded as *Anna Margherita Balma.*

The choice by her parents of the name *Margherita* was not uncommon: thousands of girl babies in Italy were named Margherita in the last thirty years of the 1800s and on into the 1900s in honor and admiration of Margherita of Savoia. In 1868, Margherita married the royal heir of Savoy who in 1878 became King Umberto I, the second king of Italy. Margherita was a hugely beloved figure—beautiful, charming, educated, cultured—in contrast to the kings themselves and to many past queens and princesses. She reigned for twenty-two years, until Umberto's assassination in 1900, and remained the beloved queen mother until her death in 1926.[12]

It is not clear exactly where Margherita was raised in Prali. The commune, then as now, covered a broad area at the upper end of the steep Germanasca River valley. Within the commune were a number of small villages and hamlets. Some, such as Rodoretto, Balma, and Coste, where Giacomo was born, were high up on the side of the valley. The town of Prali itself, the seat of the commune, was almost a thousand feet below in the valley bottom, nestled on the banks of the river at the forest's edge.

As the only girl in her family, Margherita learned the skills and tasks of a woman, helping with household chores, caring for her two younger brothers, assisting with the livestock and garden and farming chores, and generally engaging in the customary activities of her gender. She attended school for at least a short time in the small local schoolhouse.

Margherita and her family also were active participants in worship services and other activities at the Waldensian church in the center of the town of Prali. The Waldensian faithful in these valley communities shared opportunities to fellowship with others from nearby villages. Giacomo and Margherita became acquainted in the normal course of church and family activities. They attended fairs, church conferences, and other activities in the summertime and shared mutual acquaintances and a family relationship by marriage: Margherita's brother, Jean, married Giacomo's younger sister, Caterina.

Margherita and Giacomo knew each other and liked what they knew. In his wry fashion, Grandpa Giacomo described how they got together and married: "In 1896 . . . I decided I had to change my life so I went home and meet a girl that was known to me anyway because she was a sister-in-law of my sister and we get hooked together and we live happily for awhile forever anyway."[13]

Margherita and Giacomo were married in the spring of 1896, on April 6, in the Waldensian church in Rodoretto. If Giacomo indeed had returned home in the year 1896, the process of getting "hooked together" was not a long one.

Giacomo bought a Bible for the occasion, as was the custom. Destined to be the family Bible, it was with him to the day he died sixty-three years later. He also began a practice that he continued until his death in October 1959. He prepared a small insert, a handwritten page, that would be part of the Bible for reference and commemoration. It stated, "This copy of the Holy Bible was bought by Giacomo Balma married to Margherita Balma April 6, 1896, the day of the blessing of their marriage in the Church of Rodoretto." Other handwritten inserts were added in due time: a listing of birthdates of Marguerite and their children; on a separate sheet, a listing of death dates of each of the same people—completed in a different handwriting with a final entry, October 11, 1959, for Giacomo's death.

The newlyweds made their home in a small stone hut that was part of a cluster of such structures two miles up valley from Rodoretto, the nearest village. There they struggled for eight years to make a living and raise a family.

One can only imagine the long winters at their exposed site high above the valley bottom. They, with their few neighbors, were on their own, confined in a small stone hut, the livestock sheltered beneath the house floor, without fresh food, required to go out for water and other needs.

In such an environment it is not surprising that infant mortality was high and that childbirth was dangerous and not infrequently fatal to the mother. For this young couple, however, infant mortality exceeded all reasonable expectations. As noted before, Margherita gave birth to three sons between February 1897 and July 1901. She and Giacomo helplessly watched all three die between December 1898 and February 1903.[14]

Married seven years, having struggled to build a life and family, Margherita, age twenty-eight, and Giacomo, about to be thirty-three, were childless. Margherita, however, was also pregnant. On November 17, 1903, their first daughter, Elena, was born. Thus, in a period of ten months they had suffered the deaths of two sons and enjoyed—no doubt very poignantly—the birth of a daughter.

They decided the time had come to change. They would to go to America. For Waldensians from their valleys, this decision was not unusual. Indeed, it was even more common of their neighbors in the Germanasca valley. Hundreds from the Waldensian communities in Prali and neighboring communes had emigrated to America in the previous decade. Indeed, within a few months in 1893, more than three hundred neighbors from those communes had sailed to establish a new Waldensian community in the Piedmont area of North Carolina. Moreover, the travel and communication were not all in one direction: emissaries and mail went back and forth between families or churches in the New World and those in the Old.

Nor was it unusual that people of the Waldensian faith would make such a choice. Their history, their beliefs, the tribulations they had endured, and the insularity, independence, courage, and desire for free expression that those experiences fostered had prepared them to try a new world.

3

Waldensians

As I learned more about the geographical origins of my mother's family in the isolated valleys of northwestern Italy, I also wanted to learn more about the faith that was such a distinctive aspect of life there. I determined to learn Italian, something I had long wanted to do. The two objectives seemed compatible; I believed that much of the history I would want to read and the research I hoped to do would be in Italian and not in English. Indeed, that turned out to be true.

In a short time I learned a great deal about the Waldensians, their beliefs and history, and the religious and political context in which this faith—often described as a heresy—had survived for some 850 years. I discovered that theirs is a rich but small and somewhat obscure history. Much of the writing about them has been by medieval history scholars or a cadre of religious historians and theologians. I also learned that there are few written records concerning the early years of this movement. The oldest writings about Waldensian beliefs date to a hundred years or so after the founding. These early accounts, however, mostly were written by their enemies—the priests and monks who had conducted inquisitions— and were based on their interrogations. Frequently the accounts were not written down until much later. Often they were polemics by writers on a mission to make a case against people they thought of as heretics. I also learned much that surprised me, particularly about early Waldensian beliefs and practices and about Waldenses' relationship to the Catholic Church before the sixteenth-century Protestant Reformation.

ORIGINS

There is agreement on a great deal. The founder was a rich merchant of Lyon named Valdesius. In 1173 he suddenly decided to abandon his trade and his wealth and seek a life of perfection through apostolic poverty. Valdesius, it is said, had heard an itinerant preacher describe a fifth-century Roman patrician, a Christian, who had left his wealth for a life of preaching and almsgiving. After speaking to local theologians, Valdesius apparently took the example literally: he left his real property to his wife, settled an amount of his money on his daughter, made restitution to those from whom he had charged usurious interest, and gave the rest to the poor.[1]

Valdesius undertook a mission founded on the belief, first, that the means of grace were to be found by personal knowledge of the scriptures and strict adherence to its teachings and, second, that, in accordance with the teaching of the scriptures, he and his followers were called to be poor apostolic preachers of the gospel who honored obedience to God over any authority of the church. He and his followers rejected the church's claim that its clergy alone—who they believed were a sink of vice and avarice—had the authority to control and direct saving grace.[2]

Being able to read the scriptures directly was important to Valdesius. So that others could do so as well, he paid two clerics of his hometown to translate the Bible into the French vernacular. This translation is the oldest certain vernacular translation of significant parts of the Bible, described as "an epoch-making achievement" and a "prime cause for the use of the Romance vernacular in imparting knowledge of the basic text of all religious writing."[3] Valdesius's action soon was widely emulated elsewhere, with hundreds of translations made in the first half of the thirteenth century.[4] The Waldensian preachers and their followers attained an unusual degree of literacy: future leaders were trained to read and write;[5] Waldensian brethren and clerics wrote high-quality texts and letters.[6] Although ordinary Waldensians were peasants, "they were distinct from others in their greater concern with reading and writing."[7]

Conflict with the Roman Catholic hierarchy came early when Valdesius and his followers sought clerical approval for their mission, claiming that their teaching and way of life supplemented those of the church and should be an example to the clergy. Rejecting that assertion, Catholic bishops initially, and later the pope, forbade them to preach and teach, maintaining that teaching the gospel was a function of the Catholic priesthood, not the laity. The Waldenses' persistent disobedience to the hierarchy's orders, rather than wrong doctrine, caused them to be marked as heretics.[8]

The way of life Valdesius and his followers observed attracted at least as much attention as the beliefs they preached. Early on he gathered a followers who included both men and women. They traveled in pairs or small groups, at times comprised of both men and women. They had no fixed homes, no possessions, and no work besides teaching the gospel. They relied on people whom they met to house them and provide for their living. They gathered clandestinely in homes, barns, or other private places. In time the Waldensian preachers and pastors became known as *barbes* (derived from the dialect word *barba,* a term of respect meaning "uncle"). The appellation persisted for centuries.[9]

The doctrines and practices of Valdesius and his followers evolved over time as the emphases within Catholic belief and worship shifted. Among the most important was rejection of the Catholic doctrine concerning the purgation of souls after death and the consequent importance of offerings for the dead. Additionally, there was to be no prayer to or worship of saints. In rejecting the idea of masses or indulgences for souls in purgatory and in preaching that there was no period after death when souls could still be the subject of saving grace or intercession by saints, Waldensian beliefs struck at the heart of the growing and highly lucrative medieval Catholic Church practice of selling indulgences. This reality further stimulated the view that Waldensians were dangerous heretics whose ministry must be suppressed. Two matters of personal conduct and practice—that they should neither swear nor take oaths—also came to the fore in the course of the twelfth century.[10]

These core teachings—personal knowledge of the scriptures, preaching and evangelism by lay persons and not by a hierarchal priesthood, the uselessness of indulgences or prayers for the dead, no worship of saints, no oaths and no swearing—continued for centuries to be cardinal beliefs of Waldensianism. Knowing the strength of these convictions, and the fact that thousands of Waldenses in France, Savoy, and elsewhere died because of them, I was personally surprised to realize that until the sixteenth-century Protestant Reformation Waldenses also continued to be faithful participants in Catholic services, practices, and sacraments. Thus, to varying degrees in different locations, they lived dual lives. They practiced their Waldensian beliefs secretly: they attended clandestine meetings, listened to sermons, and confessed to their barbes and other religious leaders. At the same time, they also attended masses, had their children baptized, confessed to their parish priests, and generally performed the duties required of Catholic faithful by canon law.[11]

* * *

In perhaps overly broad, general terms, three phases summarize the Waldensian saga over almost 850 years, a saga that gives them the distinction of being the oldest surviving Christian reform movement. In the first phase, during the half century after the founding in the 1170s, Valdesius and his followers sought to be welcomed by the Church for their example of devotion and spirituality. They were met by hostility and efforts at suppression, retraction, or excommunication, but not by violence and physical retribution. However, the second phase, over the following three centuries, was a period of inquisitions, burnings, and other mortal punishments initiated and executed by clergy and monks against individuals or small groups. The third phase was characterized by violence, armed force, massacres, mass punishments, and relocations, generally carried out by political or civil authorities motivated by papal and civil politics and pressure.

A HOPE TO REFORM

In the beginning, the call to poverty in obedience to God and the impulse to preach not only compelled Valdesius, he also thought his example of devotion should be welcomed by the Catholic Church. Some of his followers, perhaps including Valdesius himself, attended the Third Lateran Council in Rome in 1179. They hoped to persuade Pope Alexander III and the Church's ruling hierarchy that their preaching and example should be welcomed. The pope did in fact appear to show understanding and appreciation of their advocacy of a life of poverty and evangelism. He did not, however, approve of their request to be preachers of their beliefs. Shortly after the council, Valdesius and his followers were directed by the church hierarchy not to engage in preaching unless given permission to do so by their local priests. Some of the Waldenses attempted for a time to cooperate with this edict and refrain from preaching unless authorized. However, when their efforts to cooperate and seek permissions were met with widespread and general prohibitions on preaching, they resumed their evangelism.[12]

The Church reacted strongly. On November 4, 1184, the Council of Verona under Pope Lucius III decreed that those who preached publicly or privately without the permission of the pope or a bishop were excommunicated. The decree specifically referred to and anathematized the Poor of Lyon, a name for the followers of Valdesius that had only recently come into use but would become a standard appellation for the Waldenses for centuries.[13]

Although a very short period of reconciliation with Rome occurred in the years 1208 to 1212, when Pope Innocent III not only accepted the Dominicans and Franciscans but also endorsed the efforts of the Poor of Lyon to evangelize, in short order those benevolent attitudes changed and the response of local church hierarchies again became repressive.[14]

EXPANSION AND INQUISITION

The papal condemnation did not deter the expansion of the Waldensian movement. The movement as it grew and spread comprised preachers and teachers, who took religious vows, preached, traveled, and evangelized, and their followers, who received Waldensian instruction and participated in secret meetings but who also lived settled lives, generally within the Catholic church. The movement achieved an extraordinary geographical spread. In the thirteenth, fourteenth, and fifteenth centuries, Waldensianism expanded into large areas in southern France, the north of Italy, and various regions of Germany.[15] In many areas it was met by efforts at repression that became deadly as the Inquisition sought to convert or exterminate the Waldensian preachers and believers.[16] Inquisitioners ranged throughout the territories peopled by Waldensian believers. Motivated by their own zeal or directed by church rulers, the inquisitors' attention and their torture and murders were directed at individuals or small groups who almost everywhere made up only a small percentage of the population.[17]

Waldensian preachers evangelized and gathered followers in several areas of Occitan France in the thirteenth and fourteenth centuries. Waldensian settlements were established in Languedoc, Gascony, Burgundy, and other areas. Efforts at repression there, by the celebrated inquisitor Bernard Gui, based in Toulouse, and others sought to stamp out the spreading heresy.[18] As will be discussed below, there were also large-scale massacres in the Luberon in 1545 that wiped out communities of Waldensian believers.

Waldensianism quickly spread to other regions of Europe outside central and southern France. By the early 1200s, significant groups of Waldensians as well as other dissenters and heretics lived in Lombardy (today the region centered in Milan). The Lombard Poor went well beyond the teaching and preaching mission of the Waldenses in Languedoc. They acquired buildings and schools, created institutional structures, held religious debates, and may have celebrated their own eucharist. While Lombardy Waldensianism continued to be strong into the early and mid-thirteenth century, and probably continued beyond that date, evidence of it is very sparse thereafter.[19]

Waldensianism very early spread into Germany, where it survived broadly from 1200 to the end of the Middle Ages, with adherents numbering in the scores of thousands. During the first thirty years or so, when Waldensian evangelists were expelled from one town for their teachings, they simply moved on to another. Around 1210 the pattern changed. Penalties for heresy were imposed—at first penances, and then death at the stake for recidivists. In 1211, eighty Waldenses were said to have been burned alive in one day in Strasburg. Thereafter, Waldenses went underground and proselytized by stealth.[20] German Waldensianism reached its three-hundred-year mark in the early sixteenth century. In the decades that followed, the Waldenses who remained in Germany were absorbed by Lutheranism.[21]

The history of Waldensianism as it was generally presented into the second half of the 1900s described the movement as it existed in these varied locales as a single coherent one that continued into the first half of the 1500s, when it was largely absorbed by the Protestant Reformation. That view has been challenged in recent years by some historians who contend that there were various Waldensianisms in different areas and times, not the single one that the term implies. In turn, of course, that "deconstructionist" view has been questioned by other scholars.[22]

The debate as it involves Waldensianism in its various locales need not be decided here. Insofar as the faith of my maternal grandparents and my own heritage are concerned, it is clear that followers of "the" Valdesius established their faith in the Piedmont valleys in the 1200s and that a community of adherents to that faith has continued there to this day.[23]

Thus, from the mid-1200s onward, the Waldensian faith was established across a swath of mountainous territory in the southwest of the Alps, particularly in valleys of the Cottian Alps, an area that extends roughly from Turin in the east to Grenoble in the west. That region, which now straddles the French and Italian frontier, was then primarily in the Duchy of Savoy. On the Italian side these are the Piedmont River valleys that were home to my grandparents and also to most Italian Waldenses who emigrated to the United States. The Val Perosa (now the Val Chisone),[24] the Val San Martino (now the Val Germanasca), and the Val Luserna (now the Val Pellice) were the principal strongholds of the Waldenses in Italy and, after 1848, the sole refuge and bastion of the Waldensian church. The region and the people retain their distinct identity as the Waldensian valleys (Le valli valdesi) and as Waldenses (Valdese) even today.[25]

When I first learned about the Waldensians, I assumed that over centuries they had fled east from Lyon into these remote alpine valleys in response to persecution and repression in Languedoc and other areas of southern France. The records of inquisitorial prosecutions confirm, however, that there were Waldenses in the Val Perosa by the early 1200s. One scholar states, "there is no . . . evidence to suggest that the Alpine Waldenses were 'migrants' from another part of France or Italy. Their names, their culture, their knowledge of the terrain, above all their language, suggest that they had firm roots in the Alpine Valleys well before 1300."[26] The same writer adds that the ideals of the Waldensian protests may well have been transported to these alpine regions by missionaries from outside and then adopted by the locals as their own.[27] In any event, well before the 1330s the movement was solidly established in the Piedmont valleys.

VIOLENCE, SUFFERING, AND MARTYRDOM

Waldensian writers in the twentieth century, and others long before, put great emphasis on the martyrdom and suffering of the Waldensian people over centuries at the hands of the pope, the Roman Catholic hierarchy, and civil authorities.[28] Several years ago, when I began seriously to study Italian language and history and the particular history of the Waldenses, it was immediately noteworthy that yet today the Waldenses of the Piedmont valleys celebrate key events in their history going back to the fifteenth century. When I first explored the website of the Waldensian Church headquarters in Torre Pellice, a significant chapter was entitled "The Places" (*I Luoghi*). This chapter commemorates events in the valleys dating to over six hundred years ago, into the 1400s. It describes locations of massacres or martyrdom but also commemorates contacts with Calvinist reformers from Geneva and, later, schools and churches established in the nineteenth and early twentieth centuries. It even offers detailed directions for self-guided visits.[29]

Shortly thereafter, my wife and I visited the area to see firsthand the valleys and sites I had been studying. The historic town of Torre Pellice, earlier named Luserna, has been the center of the Waldensian Church since 1832, when a boarding school and hospital were built there with financial support from the tsar of Russia and the king of Prussia. Today, the Tavola Valdese—the headquarters complex of the Waldensian Church—occupies much of the town center. In addition to the nineteenth-century church (*il Tempio*), there is a boarding school and seminary, a museum, a library, a large conference center, residences for visitors, and an archives that is an invaluable source of original documents and other reference materials.

On our first visit to Torre Pellice, I arranged for a guide to conduct my wife and me to the various historic places. The young woman, Sasha de Bettini, was born and grew up in the valley. Sasha's mother, Jean, who joined us for much of the day, is an English woman who had met a local Waldensian, married, and settled into the pastoral life of a small subsistence farm a mile climb into the mountains above town. Traveling with them was a most interesting way to learn the history, the geography, and the relationship of sites in the valley, to see the venerated sites themselves, and also to gain an understanding of how strongly people of these valleys feel about their history.

The commemorated events from the long history of Waldenses in the Piedmont valleys illustrate well the tribulations and the successes that the Waldenses have experienced over the centuries. First, there was the

Inquisition. From the earliest days, Waldensians in the Piedmontese Alps maintained a clandestine existence. Inquisitors were abroad in the 1200s and 1300s. The first burning at the stake occurred in Pinerolo in 1312; the victim was a woman condemned for "Waldoism."[30]

A considerable number of times during their history the Waldenses, who generally have tried to live secluded and peaceful lives, took up arms to defend themselves against inquisitors or others seeking to conduct religious crusades against them. Indeed, at least once in each of the last several centuries the Waldenses were either the victims of significant armed repression and massacres or fought off such attacks. They were not always alone. At times, the Waldenses found supporters among the local aristocracy. In the 1370s, Pope Gregory XI several times complained to local bishops and secular rulers about the abundance of Waldenses sheltered in the Alps. On one occasion, the pope protested to Amadeus VII, the Count of Savoy, that heretics in the count's dominions were being protected by local nobles who were frustrating the moves inquisitors were making against them.[31]

In mid-December 1387, a prominent inquisitor, Antonio Settimo, abandoned his campaign in the Piedmont Waldensian valleys because the people of the Val Perosa, on the advice of the chancellor to Count Amadeus VIII, had agreed to pay the count's treasurer some five hundred florins annually on condition that he would prevent the inquisitor from entering their valleys to investigate their religious allegiances. Settimo left Pinerolo and returned to Turin in disgust, denouncing the contumacy of those who had blocked his work.[32]

Across the border from Piedmont, in the French area of Dauphinè, earlier in 1321, again in 1335, and several other times later in the fourteenth century, the Waldenses took up arms against inquisitors, repulsing their efforts to enter communities to interrogate alleged heretics. Similarly, a century later, in what came to be known as the Waldensian Crusade of 1487–88, Waldenses in the French Dauphinè fought against the archbishop of Chrimona and others who tried to carry out a bull issued by Pope Innocent VIII in April 1487; the pope authorized the local hierarchy to proceed against heresy in the Dauphinè and Piedmont. In March 1488, Savoyard soldiers of the duke invaded the Val Chisone to carry out raids. Although the Waldenses tried to hide in mountain caves, they were overwhelmed by superior arms and numbers. The figure representing Waldenses killed in each repression has been exaggerated over the years, but authorities believe that several hundred men, women, and children suffered violent deaths as a result of this incursion.[33]

While numerous skirmishes, repressions, uprisings, and other violent conflicts are commemorated to this day by the Piedmont adherents to the faith, a much larger assault, instigated by a storied French king, resulted in annihilation of entire Waldensian communities in southern France. The massacres occurred in the middle of the sixteenth century in the isolated region of the Luberon near Aix-en-Provence. King Francis I of France, who lived a significant part of his life in the Piedmont (Turin) and Lombardy (Milan) regions of Italy and became known—ironically, in the view of my Waldensian hindsight—as the king who loved Italy, expended considerable effort trying to eradicate Protestant heresies. In the 1530s he directed attempts to coerce Waldenses and reformed Catholics in the Luberon to abandon their faith. After sporadic conflicts over almost fifteen years, in February 1545 Francis I ordered that his earlier decree to stamp out the Protestants, long in effect, finally be implemented by the destruction of villages and the extermination of believers. For three days in April 1545, the French army staged a series of destructive and murderous raids along the southern edge of the Luberon, leveling numerous towns and killing some three thousand inhabitants. Many of the survivors were taken prisoner; more than six hundred men were sent to the galleys and numerous others were banished into exile. Large numbers migrated to Geneva during the 1550s and joined with the Calvinist reformers in Switzerland. The military leader of the massacres was praised by the king and honored by the pope.[34]

CONFRONTING THE REFORMATION

Conspicuous among the battles, victories, and suffering commemorated by the Waldenses is a site that celebrates meetings in 1532 between the Waldensian leaders of the Piedmont valleys and reforming churchmen and theologians from Switzerland, France, other parts of Italy, and elsewhere in Europe. In the first decades of the 1500s, reform movements spearheaded by Swiss evangelists were making inroads on both sides of the Italian-French frontier, including various areas in Piedmont outside the Valdese valleys. Others were breaking out across central and western Europe. News of the spreading Reformation reached the Piedmont Alps as early as 1526. The Waldenses in the valleys, however, initially kept themselves separated from other Protestants due in part to their geographic isolation but also to their view of themselves as an ancient reform movement going back at least many centuries and perhaps even to apostolic times.[35]

The year 1532 is remembered by the Waldenses as the time they became involved with the broader Protestant reform movement. For six days in September 1532, William Farel, Antoine Saunier, and other leaders of the Swiss movement that would later bear Calvin's name met with Waldensian leaders on a hillside meadow at Chanforan in the Angrogna valley not far from Torre Pellice. At the time Calvin was still a Catholic student in France. The Swiss reformers' objective was to have the Waldenses split from their continued affiliation with Catholicism and the Catholic Church and form their own church, as had occurred in Switzerland.[36]

A monument erected in 1932 in a pasture at Chanforan celebrates the meetings that occurred there four hundred years earlier; in several languages it states that a "synod" resulted in "solidarity" of the Piedmont and Swiss churches. The implied outcome of the proceedings suggested by the monument is an overstatement, however. The meetings at Chanforan did not induce the Waldenses to break openly with the Catholic Church and join or establish a Protestant church.[37] The assembly, though significant, was only the first step in a thirty-year process that eventually resulted in major shifts in the religious practices and culture of the Piedmont Waldenses.

Changes began to occur by the mid-1550s as a result of several factors. One thrust came from the Waldensians themselves. Although they were fiercely proud of their 350-year dissent, the openness of the European reform movement contrasted with the clandestine nature of their own worship practices. While they held services in secret and stressed piety, honesty, good works, and virtuous lives, for cover and security they also attended their local Catholic churches, had their infants baptized by priests, participated in masses, including services for the dead—which contrasted with their own beliefs about the value of post-death prayers and deeds—and looked to their local priests for counsel and guidance. In short, they lived double lives, a circumstance that caused uneasiness on the part of many Waldensian barbes and others.

The ongoing contacts and discussions with reform movements attracted the Waldenses to the idea of more open worship. They were further stimulated by a missionary offensive in the years 1555–57 by the Company of Pastors of Geneva that sent preachers into the Valdese valleys. The Waldenses in the Piedmont received a disproportionate amount of attention and support from the Church of Geneva. Of the eighty-eight ministers dispatched by the Company of Pastors to the whole of France between 1555 and 1562, at least nineteen were committed to "the extremely uncomfortable, dangerous, and often lethal posting of the Piedmontese Alps, [a fact that] testifies to the seriousness with which Geneva took the . . . Waldensian communities."[38]

The preaching of the Swiss pastors generated such enthusiasm among the Waldenses that they began to conduct worship services publicly, despite warnings that to do so was exceedingly dangerous; Calvin and his colleagues wanted the Waldenses to continue for the moment to remain clandestine.[39] In 1555 two Waldensian "temples" were constructed in the Angrogna valley. Later the same year churches were built in the valleys of the Pellice and the Luserna, and in March 1556 another went up in the Val Germanasca.[40] The Swiss pastors also prevailed on the barbes to abandon their itinerant ways and settle in local communities in order to nurture their believers.

The cultural and practical changes did not all occur quickly. In time, the Piedmont Waldenses abandoned their duplicity. They stopped holding secret meetings. They ceased participation in their local Catholic parishes and terminated their reliance on priests. They established new parish churches. The formerly itinerant barbes became pastors in local temples. Young people became more formally trained for the ministry by attending academies in Switzerland. The new churches became presbyteries of their own; the community of churches in effect became a synod.[41]

The public practice of their Waldensian faith that was stimulated by interaction with the Swiss Calvinists met a strong reaction from the Duke of Savoy and the Savoy Parliament. The result was the war of the Edict of Nice, waged between the Piedmont Waldenses and the Duke of Savoy in 1560–61. In 1559, Duke Emanuele Filiberto—who had been restored to his duchy by major European powers after some years during which he had been dispossessed and living in exile—began to organize against his Protestant subjects in Piedmont. He deeply resented Protestantism, believing that Protestant soldiers serving in French occupying forces had weakened the Catholic Church in Piedmont and his hold on the duchy. Determined to purge his lands of the heretics, he promulgated the Edict of Nice in 1560, which forbade listening to "Lutheran" preaching in the Val Pellice or elsewhere in Piedmont. The Duke marshaled his forces to enforce the edict.[42]

For months the Waldenses attempted to negotiate with parliamentary authorities and tried to resolve the matter peaceably by persuading the duke's representatives that they were good Christians. These efforts failed. The Waldensians also prepared for an armed resistance.[43]

Fighting broke out when landlords in the valleys—allies of the duke acting on their own initiative—attacked the Waldenses. The duke's armies followed. The Waldenses defended fiercely and turned the tide of the fight, repulsing the duke's soldiers. By early summer Emanuele Filiberto decided that he had had enough. An accord was reached by which the duke, in June 1561, issued the Edict of Cavour, which conceded to the Waldenses the right to practice their reform religion in the confines of the valleys.[44]

For the first time in their history, the Waldensian communities had defended themselves against a threat to their religious identity, had fought for their position, and had won the right to public profession and practice of their dissenting beliefs. The war of the Edict of Nice caused a sensation in Europe, reinforcing the solidarity of the Protestant community by showing that resistance to a ruler was possible.[45]

Along with the Luberon massacres, these two events in the middle of the sixteenth century, occurring as the printing press enabled broader publication and as Protestant historical writing became widespread, projected the Waldenses onto the European stage. Protestant historians throughout Europe began to celebrate the Waldensian heresy. Their sufferings and martyrdom became part of a body of literature that built a sense of Protestant solidarity across Europe.[46]

The accord with the duke that resulted in the Edict of Cavour was criticized by some as "ghettoization" from the outside world. However, it permitted the Waldenses to continue the process of openly establishing their own reform church.

New forms of worship were instituted. The "synods of Waldenses," in 1563 and 1564, introduced to their services the order of worship and hymnals of the Geneva churches. Music and the singing of hymns became an important part of the worship service. The Bible was emphasized as the basis of their faith and the sole source of their moral principles; Bible reading became an important part of services.[47] The key confessions of faith of the early church—the Apostles' Creed and the Nicene Creed— were recited.

Waldensian beliefs and doctrine shed their links to Catholic practice and became a form of reformed Protestantism. In the lands of the crown of France, Waldensians were incorporated into the French reformed church. In Germany and Eastern Europe, Waldensian people lost their identity entirely. However, in the Alps, particularly in Piedmont and Dauphinè, Waldensian identity continued "as generation after generation of people, some bearing the same surnames as their medieval forebears, maintained their distinctive communal identity, embodied in a non-Catholic religious practice."[48]

The Waldensians in the southwestern Alps formally adopted a Confession of Faith in 1655. Published originally in French, it expressed their understanding of the true principles of Christianity. The Confession of Faith of 1655—now published in French and Italian—is cited to this day by the Waldensian Church headquarters in Torre Pellice as the Confession of Faith of the Waldensian Church.[49]

The majority of historians describe this process as the adoption of Calvinist Protestantism and the end of medieval Italian Waldensianism, but the Waldenses at the time did not regard the changes in this way. They considered themselves to be "reformers before the Reform" and believed that the sixteenth-century Protestant reform constituted acceptance of teachings they themselves had faithfully preserved for ages.[50]

It should be noted that while the Waldenses in the Piedmont Alps largely agreed doctrinally with the Calvinist, Lutheran, Hussite, and other sixteenth-century reform movements, and while there were in the sixteenth century and since many interactions among Waldensian Protestants and the other groups, the Piedmont Waldenses never achieved the majority position in their communities and never converted the political and civil status of their towns or nation from Catholic to Protestant, as the reform did elsewhere in Europe in the sixteenth and seventeenth centuries. In the Piedmont Alps, although the Waldenses may have attained a majority of the population in a few towns, usually they were a minority that pursued their dissenting religious customs alongside the Catholics. Indeed, in most villages in the Waldensian valleys there are both a Waldensian church and a Catholic church. In small communities like Rodoretto, from which my grandparents emigrated, the churches are similar in size and at times side by side. In some towns each faith has a separate consecrated cemetery. In other towns—as in Rodoretto—there is a communal cemetery. Waldensian faithful are buried on one side; Catholic faithful on the other.

* * *

In the middle of the seventeenth century, the Piedmontese Waldensian Church endured several serious crises that could have resulted in its obliteration except for the support of the Swiss reform church. In 1630 the clergy and the inhabitants of the Waldensian valleys were nearly decimated by a savage plague that devastated Europe. All the high mountain villages were abandoned and left to become pasture. As many as 8,500 to 9,000 people died; entire families were killed. The church was virtually eradicated: eleven of the thirteen Waldensian pastors in the valleys died. Help was urgently sought from the Calvinist Church in Geneva, which sent ministers to replace the deceased pastors. The newly inserted clergy, trained in the Geneva Academy and without time or means to become integrated in local traditions, profoundly altered the patriarchal Waldensian society. Church governance was modified; the office of moderator assumed more prestige; ministers were called *Monsieur* or *Mademoiselle* and no longer *barbe*. The broader cultural world was also changed. The new pastors did not speak the Italian that was the language of the Piedmont church and community. Instead, French became the official language of the Waldensian churches and would remain thus until the middle of the nineteenth century.[51]

The second devastating event was a dreadful massacre that came to be known as " the Piedmontese Easter." From the time the young Duke of Savoy, Charles Emanuel II, came to power in 1650, repressions were instituted against the Waldenses to compel them to become Catholics or to isolate them in remote valleys. In this climate, in April 1655, a powerful local aristocrat set out with a large army against the Waldenses. Destruction and death were widespread. More than a thousand Waldenses were said to have been put to death in the Luserna and Angrogna valleys. News of the barbarism and brutalities spread quickly throughout the European Protestant world. Protests denounced the cruelty of the persecutors, collections were made to help the survivors, and the Duke of Savoy was assailed by the embassies of several countries for allowing such conduct.[52]

The events surrounding the "Glorious Return" some thirty years later illustrate well, in one small corner of the world, the way the politics and cynicism of civil rulers affect the lives of the poor and innocent. For nearly a hundred years, going back to the Edict of Nantes issued by Henry IV of France in 1598, freedom of worship had been permitted in France. The result was relative tranquility in the mountains of Savoy on both sides of the France-Savoy border. However, in 1685, Louis XIV revoked the Edict of Nantes and sought to expel or exterminate his Huguenot subjects.[53]

The Piedmont area under the Duke of Savoy, including particularly the valleys of Rora and Chisone and their tributaries in the Waldensian valleys, had long been the subject of wars between the Savoyards and the French rulers. Louis XIV, to help carry out his extermination plans against his Huguenot subjects, put great pressure on his nephew, Duke Vittorio Amedeo II of Savoy, to repress the Protestant worship of the Waldenses and other reformers. Giving in to his uncle, Vittorio Amedeo II on January 31, 1686, issued an edict that banished the Waldensian pastors and schoolmasters, ordered the cessation of Protestant worship that had been formally permitted in Savoy since the Edict of Cavour in 1561, and imposed Catholic baptism on all infants. The Duke's forces rounded up thousands of the Waldenses. Several thousands died in prisons. Those who could escape and flee to Switzerland did so. A small group of self-described "invincibili" stayed in the mountains, however, fought off the ducal forces, and eventually emigrated to Genevan territory in Switzerland in early 1687.[54]

The next year the balance of international politics was altered drastically, based primarily on changes on the English throne. The strength and influence of Louis XIV diminished sharply. An anti–Louis XIV coalition was formed. Against this background, a group of the Savoy Waldensian émigrés in Switzerland, led by Pastor Henri Arnaud, fought their way back into their homelands in August 1689. They reached Bobbio Pellice in the Val Pellice after a series of skirmishes in which they repulsed the ducal forces. They spent the winter recruiting others and preparing to defend their valleys.[55]

In the meantime, however, even as the Waldensians were preparing for battle with Duke Vittorio Amedeo II, he had changed sides and, in the spring of 1690, joined the forces fighting against Louis XIV. The Waldenses were not only given back their rights of residence and worship but, because of their renown as fierce mountain fighters, immediately were recruited by the duke to join in the fight against Louis XIV. On May 28, 1690, the Duke's envoys contacted the Waldensian fugitives and offered a truce: the Waldensians would join forces with the Savoyard troops in the valleys in the fight against Louis XIV; in return, their freedom to worship on the old conditions would be restored.[56] Thus, in four years' time the Waldensian people went from being victims persecuted by the duke and killed, forced into prison, or driven into exile, to sought-after allies given permission to return to their homes and worship.

Foreign assistance and support for the Piedmont Protestants from the Swiss, English, and Dutch that had been so important in restoring the Waldenses in the valleys following the disastrous plague of the 1630s continued to be crucial to the survival of the isolated Waldensian minority throughout the eighteenth century and well into the nineteenth. Although Vittorio Amedeo II had agreed in the Treaty of 1690 to restore the Waldenses to their former legal and religious status, he delayed putting this clause into effect, knowing that concessions to the Protestants would cause trouble with the pope and with his Catholic subjects at home. Pressure on the duke from King William III of England and envoys of other allies became irresistible, however. In May 1694, Vittorio Amedeo issued an Edict of Toleration granting to the Waldenses the limited rights they had enjoyed before 1686. The edict regularized the position the Waldenses had conquered for themselves in 1689–90 and defined their legal status within the Savoyard state for the next century. It did not, however, eliminate disputes, pressure, discrimination, and persecution against the very small and isolated minority within the overwhelmingly Catholic state.[57]

The Glorious Return is perhaps the most famous chapter in the long epic of the Waldenses. I remember well going to lunch with our guide, Sasha, and her mother, Jean, at a small restaurant in the center of the village of Bobbio Pellice and being reminded there by plaques and the locals of Bobbio's significance as the place where—more than three hundred years earlier—the "invincible" exiles to Geneva finally reached their home in the valleys.

The Glorious Return is celebrated by an imposing sculpture of the exiles' leader, Henry Arnaud, on the grounds of the Waldensian Church headquarters in Torre Pellice. Said to be unique among statues of Protestant clerics, it conspicuously shows Arnaud with sword unsheathed, defiantly ready for battle.[58]

ALPINE GHETTO

Treaties at the end of the seventeenth and the beginning of the eighteenth centuries shifted the battle lines among the major powers and altered the conflict between the Duke of Savoy and Louis XIV. Following the Treaty of Utrecht in 1713, religious disagreement diminished and the Waldensian bastion in the valleys lost its importance as a front line of the battles among the major powers. It became simply a Protestant enclave in a Catholic country.[59]

Pressures by the House of Savoy against the Waldensians did not cease, however. In fact, Tourn describes the period from the beginning of the eighteenth century as a dreadful time during which Protestants in Italy were pushed back into a small area in a few mountain valleys: "[I]n this period . . . the last act of the tragic epic of reform in Piedmont played out. What decades of war had not succeeded in doing . . . the House of Savoy accomplished now: in a little more than twenty years the protestant world in Italy lost more than 50% of its territory and about 60% of its population."[60]

This major shift occurred with the forced ouster of Protestants from other areas of Piedmont, leaving the Waldensian valleys west of Turin "with the aspect of a miniscule ghetto in the Piedmontese mountains."[61] The surviving communities in the valleys were burdened and oppressed in various ways by the Savoyard government. They were subject to extra taxes and to the "full weight of institutionalized intolerance" from the legal system and the Catholic officials who administered it. This included prohibitions of work on Catholic feast days, restrictions on the numbers who could attend worship services, and many other discriminations.[62]

Anglo-Dutch sympathy for the Waldenses had pressured Victor Amadeus into concessions to the Waldenses in the last decade of the seventeenth century; diplomatic intercession by the Protestant states continued to be the communities' chief recourse against official and clerical intolerance in the decades that followed. The Waldensian communities also relied heavily on financial and other aid from their foreign friends. Funds channeled to them by British, Dutch, and Swiss charities supported pastors and schoolmasters, assisted the poor and indigent, and in other ways helped the communities survive.[63]

Finally, in 1848, the Waldenses of Savoy were given full civil and political rights. The Edict of Emancipation issued by King Charles Albert conferred the same civil rights as other citizens to study, to practice professions, and to own property. It did not, however, change religious practices: Catholicism remained the state's official religion, and principles of religious freedom were not put into practice. Nevertheless, with the year 1848 and the beginning of the Risorgimento,[64] the Waldenses were not the only Protestants in Italy. Groups of exiles spreading out from Piedmont or returning to Italy from elsewhere in Europe created a Free Italian Church. Waldensian missionaries and others coming from abroad opened missions and schools in all sections of the country.

The Risorgimento, of course, wrought immense changes on Italy in just a few decades. In 1860, large portions of northern and north-central Italy, as well as Sicily, were annexed to Piedmont to create the new Kingdom of Italy, with the kings of the House of Savoy becoming the kings of Italy. In 1870, the French and the pope were ousted from Rome and the Papal States as well as the remaining areas of central and southern Italy, thus creating a unified Italy covering the entire peninsula, with the capitol at Rome.[65]

In a move fraught with both symbolic and practical importance, on September 20, 1870, when royal troops breached the gates of the Porta Pia and entered Rome, Waldensians and other missionaries also entered the city and set about founding Protestant churches. Waldensian pastors and lay workers promptly established a small church in rented facilities in the city's center. In 1878, property was purchased on which an imposing Waldensian church was built. Inaugurated in 1883, that church, on the Via IV November, not far from the Piazza Venezia, continues to prosper.[66]

I had an interesting surprise at the Via IV November church a few years ago. I was just beginning my research concerning the Balma side of the family. I wanted to see if I could find any trace of Guido Balma, my mother's cousin, whom she and Nancy had visited in Rome some thirty years before. I called the IV November church. The publicly listed number was that of the pastor's apartment. As with many Waldensian churches, the pastor and his or her family live at the church in an apartment that also serves as the church and pastor's office and as a meeting place. When I called, the pastor himself answered. After a short time listening to my then rudimentary Italian, he asked—in what was clearly a perfect American accent—if I preferred to speak English. We did so. I explained who I was and why I was calling. He said he might be of help and invited me to meet him at the church the next morning, a Saturday. He also told me that his name was Thomas Noffke, obviously not an Italian name.

The next morning, Pastor Noffke explained that he was indeed an American. He was born and raised a Catholic in Neenah, a small north-central Wisconsin city on the shores of Lake Winnebago. While serving in the U.S. Army in Pisa, Italy, he had met his wife, a descendant of a long line of Waldensian ministers. They married; he joined the Waldensian Church, graduated from the theological seminary, and became a pastor.

Pastor Noffke was generous with his time that morning. He dug out the registers and other church records, from which he determined that Guido Balma, his wife, and three children had been members into the 1960s. He also located their home address and telephone number from that time. Unfortunately, my efforts to reach them, including a visit to the apartment address, were not successful.

A second Waldensian church was constructed in Rome beginning in 1910 and inaugurated in 1914. The church is located on the Piazza Cavour, across from the imposing seat of the Ministry of Justice and not far from the Vatican and the Basilica of St. Peter. The Waldensian Theological

Seminary, a library, and a bookstore were also built alongside the church. The seminary is the principal education center of Waldensian clergy.

In 1979 the Waldensian Church joined with the United Methodist Church of Italy, a denomination that has been in that country since the nineteenth century. A Covenant of Federation went into effect, uniting the two churches into a single organization. They share a common administration—known by ancient tradition as the *Tavola Valdese*—based in Torre Pellice, a faculty of theology, and the synod, a decision-making assembly. The members of the Waldensian and Methodist churches in Italy and South America number about forty-five thousand people. One-third live in the group of eighteen communities in the western Piedmont valleys that are centers of the Waldensian faith. Another third are scattered over the Italian peninsula. South American churches comprising about fifteen thousand Waldensians in Uruguay and Argentina make up the third group.[67]

THE NEW WORLD

Following the Piedmontese Easter massacre of 1655, several hundred Waldenses fled the valleys and took refuge in Holland, England, and Switzerland. They joined many other Protestants in those countries who earlier had escaped their homelands.

Many of the Waldensian exiles moved on to the new world of the Americas. On Christmas Day, 1656, three shiploads comprising some 167 refugees, many of them Waldenses, sailed for the Dutch colonies in America. The expedition was arranged by the City of Amsterdam, which had been providing financial assistance to distressed Waldensian exiles for many years. In early 1657, these settlers touched on Long Island and, according to legend, went on to establish a colony on Staten Island. While those settlements were abandoned within a decade, others founded soon after at White Plains, New York, and later in other communities continued into the next century.[68]

In 1700, four ships loaded with refugees sailed from London for Virginia. There were some former dwellers of the Waldensian valleys among them, as was the Reverend Benjamin de Joux, who had been pastor of the church of Fenestrelle in the Val Perosa from 1659 to 1662. These immigrants settled along the James River. Early settlers to Georgia and South Carolina, arriving from England in the 1730s, included Waldenses from Piedmont.[69]

New York City. As noted above, Waldensian history in New York began with the arrival from Amsterdam of the *Prince Maurice,* the *Bear,* and the *Flower of Guelder* in March 1657, with the short-lived settlement of Waldensians on Staten Island, and with later settlements in Westchester County.[70] Little is known of Waldensian activity in New York during the eighteenth and early decades of the nineteenth centuries, although the early settlers may well have prospered in and around New York City.

During the late nineteenth and early twentieth centuries, many of the Waldensian émigrés who came to America passed through New York City, among them my grandparents in 1904. These immigrants were met and welcomed by the local Waldensians and, if their journeys were not yet complete, assisted with their onward travels.

During the first decade of the 1900s, three pastors of Waldensian origin were conducting services in the New York area. They were joined by a fourth—the Reverend Pietro Griglio of Prali, my grandmother's home village—who arrived from Italy in October 1910. From 1903 until 1912, the Waldensians held their meetings at the Church of the Strangers at Eighth Avenue and Fifty-seventh Street. They next met at the Holy Communion Protestant Episcopal Church at Sixth Avenue and Twentieth Street until March 1916, when they moved to the Knox Memorial Dutch Reform Church, later constituted as a Presbyterian church. It and another Waldensian church, later named the First Waldensian Church of New York, served Waldensians in the area at least into the 1940s.[71]

Chicago. Professor George Watts of Davidson College in his significant book *Waldenses in the New World* describes the Waldensian immigration to Chicago: "During the last decades of the nineteenth century many Waldenses emigrated to America in search of better living conditions. Among the most important groups to come was that of Chicago. The first to settle there were from the two highest parishes in the Waldensian valleys, Prali and Rodoretto. They came in the 1890's and 1900's, following a Waldensian pastor from Prali, the Reverend Filippo Grilli, who became pastor of the Italian Presbyterian Church of Chicago."[72]

Prali and Rodoretto were, of course, the villages from which my grandmother and grandfather had come to Chicago in 1904. Interestingly, my grandfather, James Balma, is one of the Waldensian immigrants specifically named in the Watts book.[73] James and Marguerite Balma joined the First Italian Presbyterian Church immediately upon their separate arrivals in Chicago and continued to worship at that church—which was renamed the Waldensian Presbyterian Church in 1927—into the 1930s.

Watts, writing in 1941, also described the role that the First Italian Presbyterian Church played in the creation of other Italian Protestant churches in Chicago:

> Not all of the Chicago Waldenses have remained in the Italian Presbyterian Church. Several other Italian churches of the city have had as their organizers those who had first been members of Grilli's congregation. The West Taylor Street Mission, now the St. John's Presbyterian Church . . . was founded and directed for many years by Grilli. Several of the former members of this mission are now influential leaders in the First Italian Methodist Church. The Moody Italian Church . . . has among its members former parishioners of Grilli. But the Italian church which counts the largest number of Grilli's former members is the Italian Pentecostal Church.[74]

Valdese, North Carolina. The largest Waldensian colony in North America is Valdese, North Carolina, whose first settlers arrived from the Waldensian valleys on May 29, 1893. According to Watts, "In the early 1890's the Waldensian valleys [in Italy] were again becoming overcrowded and many families were desirous of emigrating. Some went to South America, others came to the United States. A number wished to locate in some undeveloped area where the cost of land would be less."[75]

The motivations of these families fit well with the ambitions of a North Carolina land promoter, Marvin F. Scaife, who had business contacts in Turin through which he arranged to meet with Waldensian leaders—all ministers—in Rome, in the Piedmont valleys, and in New York. After their favorable response, Scaife bought a tract of more than one hundred thousand acres of land in western North Carolina and contracted with Waldensian leaders to form a colony there. The land was promoted as heavily timbered, for which there would be a ready market, with abundant water, and suitable for cultivation.[76]

The settlers arrived in three groups in 1893. The first detachment of twenty-nine reached New York on May 26 and arrived in what is now Valdese during the afternoon of May 29. During the week of August 20, the colony received twenty-five new members, fifteen from Italy and two families from Utah. On November 23, the largest contingent, comprised of 178 people, arrived from Italy.[77]

Life was hard for the settlers in the early years. For the first eighteen months, the colony was operated as a cooperative enterprise run by the Valdese Corporation, which was organized on June 8, 1893. Meetings were held nearly every evening to divide up the property, to organize the colony, and to assign work.[78]

Organizing and building a church was the matter of prime importance to the colonists. The first pastor, the Reverend Enrico Vinay, arrived in July 1893. A manse was built in 1894–95. In 1896 the colony turned its attention to the construction of a church building. Excavation started in December 1896. The building was completed in October 1898 and dedicated on July 4, 1899.[79]

The Valdese church prospered and grew rapidly. It was supported by the Congregational Church the first two years but affiliated with the Presbyterian Church on July 9, 1895, with the name Waldensian Presbyterian Church. The church and the Presbyterian affiliation have continued to this day.[80]

The settlers survived, and many prospered, but not primarily by cultivating the land, which, they found, was poorly suited to agriculture. Instead, Valdese immigrants found success because of their entrepreneurial spirit, turning to manufacturing, such as furniture and textiles, baking, and other lines of business.[81]

The languages used in services and activities of the Waldensian Presbyterian churches reflected the traditions and origins of the members. The First Italian Presbyterian Church of Chicago used Italian in its services and in official records. The North Carolina church, founded by and comprised of Waldensians from the same communities in the

Piedmont valleys, primarily used French. At the outset, in July 1894, the board of the Valdese church adopted a resolution for the regular holding of Sunday services with one each month in Italian and the rest in French. After twenty-seven years, in 1921, English began to be used in the Sunday school, and on June 4, 1922, twenty-nine years after the colony's founding, a congregational meeting voted to have the morning service on the first Sunday of each month in English and the evening service in French. The morning services on the other Sundays would be in French and the evening services in English.[82]

In 1923, when skilled Italian workers were imported from Rochester, New York, to work at the Valdese Shoe Corporation, Pastor Pons organized a third preaching service for them in Italian. Thereafter, he preached on Sundays in three languages: at morning service in French, during the late afternoon in Italian, and in the evening in English. During Reverend Verreault's pastorate, from 1926 to 1931, the church had services the first and third Sundays in English and the other services in French. As late as the 1940s, services were held on the second Sunday of each month in French.[83]

The change in the 1920s to the use of English in some services was deplored by many older members. That was, of course, only one of many changes in this once close-knit community. One from the initial group of settlers, Francis Garrou, Sr., died November 24, 1937. He was the first mayor and first citizen for many years. In 1933, he offered a wry summation of the changes that had occurred: "We are no longer a Waldensian colony. When we came to this country we were all good Waldensians. We were members of the Presbyterian Church and voted the Democratic ticket. Now many of our workers are native Americans. We have married into native families until our identity is almost lost, and we have become so fully American that some of us even go to the Baptist Church and vote the Republican ticket."[84]

SUMMATION: THE MAN AND THE FAITH

At the outset of his book, the Waldensian minister and historian Georges Tourn encapsulates the attitudes of faith, rebellion, pride, and distinctiveness that have characterized the Waldenses over the centuries: "It is important to mention because it is significant: contrary to the Franciscans, the

Waldenses have not embellished the legends and miracles of the life of the founder of their movement, they have not made a saint of him, they have limited themselves to never losing sight of two important facts: the choice of faith that he made and the experience of his life."[85]

I saw the same attitudes of singular faith, pride, and faith-based distinctiveness play out in my own family.

* * *

James and Marguerite Balma arrived in Chicago in April and October 1904, respectively. Each reached Chicago after traveling some ten days from their lifelong home in Piedmont. They traveled across more than geography in those ten days. The contrast in societies and living conditions could hardly have been greater than between the remote, sparsely populated mountains they left and the city in which they would live the rest of their lives.

PART II

SICILY

The search to understand the disparate worlds of my ancestors inevitably also led to Sicily, my paternal grandparents' much-maligned place of origin. It always had seemed a distant, exotic, and unreachable place. I wanted to go there.

4

The Road to Sicily

THE ROAD WAS ROUGH AND ROCKY. The holes and ruts were becoming so deep I thought the car might get hung up. On the map, the route north from the south coast of Sicily seemed the most direct. I was learning, however, that the warning signs *non asfaltate* and *non sempre praticable* not only meant "unpaved" and "not always usable" but in fact meant virtually impassable. Just as I began to fear I would have to turn back or, worse, get stranded and have to walk out, I topped a rise and glimpsed Montemaggiore Belsito nestled into the hillside just a few miles ahead.

The anticipation I had been feeling all day increased. All my life, Sicily could have been the moon. To my knowledge, our family never had any communication whatever with anyone in the "old country"—no correspondence, no calls, no visits, no messages through others. If there were any relatives there, living or dead, they were unknown to me.

Although I had four immigrant Italian grandparents, I had been raised to be "American" by a mother and father who both seemed to want to forget our Italian ancestry. I had been homogenized into white, Protestant, middle America by five moves before my fourteenth birthday, from my birthplace in Chicago at the edge of the city's second-largest Italian neighborhood, through much less ethnic areas farther west in Chicago, through working-class western suburbs, finally to settle before high school in a leafy, white, middle-class suburb on the western edge of Cook County. Along the way, we were consistently diverted from any Italian consciousness.

Now, on my first visit to Sicily, a trip I had never been certain I would make, I was about to reach the village from which my father's father had emigrated almost a century earlier. No one knew I was coming; there was no one I knew to tell. Able to read some Italian but speak little, I had no idea whether I would be able to communicate in rural Sicily. I was about to find out.

My visit to Sicily followed a business trip to Genoa and Naples. I was leading the defense of Standard Oil (Indiana) and its subsidiary, Amoco Oil Company, in multinational litigation over the huge oil spill that followed the grounding and destruction of the supertanker *Amoco Cadiz* on the rocky shores of Brittany, France. Testimony of the ship's Italian crew was being taken in Naples over a period of several weeks. I attended the key depositions, including that of the master of the *Amoco Cadiz*, Captain Pasquale Bardari.

During a recess in the schedule, I seized the opportunity to travel to Sicily. Early on a Saturday morning, I departed Naples in a rented car to drive the three hundred miles south to Reggio di Calabria, ferry across the straits of Messina, and drive on into Sicily.

For several days, breakfasting on the balcony of my hotel I had enjoyed a splendid view of Mount Vesuvius across the Bay of Naples. Now, I began my trip on the highway around the bay, skirting the lower slopes of the famous volcano, to stop at the spectacular ruins at Pompeii.

The guidebooks give graphic descriptions of the events of August 24, AD 79, when life in this rich resort and commercial city with a population of twenty-five thousand ended abruptly. First, there was "a cloud, remarkable in size and appearance," followed by a rain of cinders that quickly covered the ground to more than three feet deep.[1] Then, as inhabitants tried to flee or take cover, a second rain of molten lava and cinders began to fall, burying the town under a layer twenty to twenty-three feet deep that solidified into a crust of volcanic rock.[2]

Two hundred fifty years of intermittent excavations have exposed remarkable ruins; columns, walls, baths and other structures, mosaics and frescoes, art objects and furnishings, streets with stepping-stone blocks for pedestrians to cross and deep wheel ruts in the cobblestone roadbeds—all give a vivid picture of the beauty, wealth, and ambience of a vibrant city. The overall impression, however, is well described by one of the guidebooks: "The ruins of the city are deeply moving, for the Romans seem still to people it in the deep silence."[3]

The day was bright and clear. The silent volcano loomed to the northwest. I spent most of the morning walking freely on my own, as one could then, through the deserted streets. There were surprisingly few other visitors.

Almost reluctantly, I left behind the calm and quiet splendor of Pompeii. Moving beyond the turbulence and congestion of the Naples metropolis, bypassing the busyness of the Amalfi Coast, as one heads south of Salerno the highway passes into country that appears much more remote and isolated. Although it was July, near the peak of the vacation season, there seemed to be relatively few vehicles traveling on the highway.

Aided by the concierge at the hotel in Naples, I had made a reservation for the night at a resort hotel in the mountains beyond Eboli, the isolated village made famous by Carlo Levi's book—and later the movie based on it—describing his exile by the fascists in 1939–40.[4] Arriving around seven o'clock on Saturday evening, I was surprised at how few cars were in the parking lot. Although the area was remote, the hotel was large, perched on west-facing lower slopes of the mountain. The evening was still bright. The sea was visible in the distance to the west, glistening in the late-afternoon sun.

I walked through the extensive gardens and a short way into the neighboring forests before returning for dinner. To my surprise, the large, high-ceilinged dining room, with an expanse of windows looking out toward the sea, was almost unoccupied. Guests were dining at perhaps a dozen tables of the sixty or more in the room. The dinner was good, but an eerie feeling predominated because—for reasons I did not learn—so few people seemed to be staying at the hotel.

I retired early. The night was cool and quiet. Sunday morning I took a long hike through the nearby forests before breakfast, packed up, and left. My destination that day was Pizzo Calabro, a small southern coastal town in Calabria. Pizzo was Captain Bardari's home. I had learned a great deal about it from him. I looked forward to seeing it and wanted to arrive by early afternoon.

I took the autostrada. Most of the way to Pizzo, the highway twists and turns as it passes through the rugged mountains. Farther south, closer to Pizzo, the road descends to the coast and passes near the sea. The sparkling blue waters of the Tyrrhenian, shining off to the right, excite and inspire.

Shortly before noon, I drove close to the beach and entered Pizzo Calabro. Pizzo was a town of about nine thousand inhabitants, unremarkable in appearance itself but in a beautiful location on a promontory with a spectacular view of the volcanic island of Stromboli across the Gulf of St. Eufamia. Founded by the ancient Greeks, it boasts two events of historical significance. The first was the erection in 1492 of the imposing Castello di Pizzo by Ferdinando I of Aragon. The second, ironically involving Ferdinando IV and the Castello, occurred on October 13, 1815. On that date, Napoleon Bonaparte's brother-in-law, Gioacchino Napoléon Murat, was executed by firing squad in the courtyard of the Castello for attempting to lead an insurrection after Napoleon's second fall.[5]

Pizzo today is known as the site of one of Italy and Europe's leading nautical institutes for the training of merchant marine officers. Graduates of the school go on to distinguished careers sailing the world on merchant vessels, among them the most famous cruise ships.

Many of these merchant mariners continue to live in Pizzo. Among them was Captain Pasquale Bardari. Bardari had achieved international notoriety as the master of the *Amoco Cadiz* supertanker after it went aground on the Brittany coast of France in March 1978. I had spent time with him in Brest, France, where he was confined to house arrest in the Hotel Continental for several weeks after the incident before finally being allowed to return to his home and family in Pizzo. When we were together in Naples for his deposition, he had invited me to visit with him and his wife in Pizzo on my way to Sicily.

I remember particularly well that Sunday afternoon. I met Bardari at a small trattoria. After a light lunch, we made a walking tour of the town; he showed me in particular the nautical institute from which he and several other of the *Amoco Cadiz* officers had graduated.

Captain Bardari and I spent hours sitting in the Piazza della Repubblica, with its beautiful terrace overlooking the sea and the Castello, watching the *passeggiata*—the traditional leisurely walk that Italian townspeople in great numbers so love in the late afternoon and early evening. This one was remarkable for the strolling lineup of masters, pursers, chief engineers, mates, and other officers of various types employed by leading cruise and transport lines. The senior officers of the ocean liners and cruise ships were particularly notable in their white loafers—sans socks, of course—cream slacks, and cream pullovers draped upon their shoulders. Bardari recited their names and positions as they passed by—chief purser of the Queen Elizabeth II, masters of cruise ships on other lines, and so forth. Many gave Bardari a cheery wave. Some stopped by with a word of encouragement for him—and also for me when Bardari introduced me as the principal lawyer for Amoco.

We drank Campari sodas and watched the passeggiata until the sun began to settle toward the sea in the west and the brightness of the day became tempered. Then we walked the several blocks back to the Bardari apartment to meet his wife and young son before going to dinner.

About 9:30 in the evening, the captain, his wife, and I drove across town to a seaside restaurant that Bardari had described as one of his favorites. It quickly became one of my favorites as well. The restaurant's large indoor dining room was empty: all of the diners were at tables on an outdoor terrace sheltered under a red and white striped awning with views over the sea. The evening was warm, with mild sea breezes. There was lively chatter at all the tables. We were joined by friends of the Bardaris. Dinner continued at a leisurely pace until past midnight. This, I understood, was a typical Sunday evening in Pizzo.

My room at the Hotel Grillo was in a wing directly over the beach, perhaps ten meters from the sea at high tide. French doors and a fenced terrace opened to the sea. The night was peaceful. I slept with the doors open to the breezes and the sound of the gently lapping waves.

Monday morning I woke early, stimulated by the anticipation of reaching Sicily at last. After a swim in the sea and breakfast on the terrace above the beach, I drove south on the autostrada for about two hours. For several miles on the approach to Reggio di Calabria, the highway points directly at Sicily. Rising in front of me was the profile of the island basking in the sun. As the highway turned south to proceed down the toe of the Italian boot, Sicily lay four miles across the Straits of Messina. I did not continue to Reggio but instead turned toward the docks at the much smaller town of Villa San Giovanni. There I waited in a long line of vehicles for the ferry to arrive from Messina, unload its cargo of cars, trucks, and people, and load us to cross to Sicily.

All morning, from the time Sicily first came into view, its mountain profile was dominated by the summit of Mount Etna. Although the famous volcano is some thirty miles south along the coast of Sicily from Messina, its snow-capped slopes were visible as we crossed the straits. I stood on deck and watched the island draw nearer as we steamed toward Messina. Sicily was still in my mind an alien place. I was excited and expectant, but I wasn't sure what to anticipate from the land or the people.

Apart from the fact it was the first place I landed on Sicily, Messina had no attraction for me. We arrived at a typical commercial seaport: docks, cranes and heavy equipment, warehouses, and, beyond, high-rise tenements. I drove off the ferry through narrow lanes, turned one way, then another, then turned some more as directed by waving workers, and finally drove onto city streets that were well marked to get through the city as quickly as possible and onto the highways west or south.

I chose south, toward Taormina. Mount Etna loomed closer and closer. As always, the volcano is a dramatic sight with a long plume of smoke blowing horizontally from its mouth in the westerly wind. The largest volcano in Europe, Mount Etna is a constant presence for all in Sicily who live, work, and play within well over fifty miles of it.

The highway from Messina past Taormina and on south to Catania and Siracusa is a busy one, crowded with cars and trucks hurrying in both directions. The road from the highway up into Taormina has many tight switchbacks, with the straits of Messina on one side and the cliffs on the other, as it climbs the face of the rocky plateau to the ancient town, several hundred feet above the sea. I knew of Taormina only as a beautiful resort city that is the first stop for tens of thousands of visitors to Sicily every year. For many tourists, and especially for many Americans, it is one of the few places in Sicily, if not the only place, that they ever visit.

Taormina is indeed a spectacular place to explore. But I soon learned it is much more. Through this introduction, I also began to understand that Sicily offers more than the poorly educated, poverty-stricken, backward land I had been accustomed to expect.

Sicily is the largest island in the Mediterranean. From a thousand years or more before Christ, it has been dominated by many foreign cultures and civilizations. The ancient Sicani, Elymi, and Siculi came first, from other parts of the Mediterranean. They were followed by the Phoenicians, who settled in the western and northwestern parts of the island, establishing magnificent temples and cities: their spectacular ruins can be seen to this day at places like Selinunte. In the east, the Greeks founded a colony in the eighth century BC on the beaches below the plateau on which Taormina sits. The Greeks dominated Sicily for several hundred years, building temples and other structures at Agrigento and elsewhere that were far grander than those in their home country. They prospered quietly for centuries until they were conquered by Dionysus, the tyrant of Syracuse.

Sicily became a province of Rome in 227 BC. Ruins of Roman villas, with their magnificent mosaics, are among the most often visited sites on the island. After centuries, the Byzantines, followed by the Arabs, arrived and dominated Sicily for almost eight hundred years. Their rule was ended by the Normans. When William the Conqueror famously was establishing dominion over England in the second half of the eleventh century, another branch of Normans went south, marching down the Italian peninsula and on to Sicily, conquering Palermo in 1072 and ousting the Arabs from the rest of the island in the 1090s. The Normans ruled Sicily for more than two hundred years. Their cathedrals, chapels, castles, and palaces—many adorned with exquisite mosaics—are still among the most beautiful structures on the island. Sicily was ruled later by the Spanish and the French before finally becoming part of a unified Italy.

Taormina has been a popular destination for travelers since the 1700s—Goethe in 1787 and numerous others later wrote books celebrating its glories. Its location and landscape are superbly beautiful. The views of the Gulf of Naxos below, the landing point for the first Greek settlers, are remarkable, as is the scene toward nearby Mount Etna and across the straits to Italy. Its cultural history is reflected in the magnificent ancient amphitheater above the town that was originally built by the Greeks and later reshaped and enlarged by the Romans.

In the last half of the nineteenth century, Taormina's popularity soared. Many English and German tourists built villas in the city. Celebrities, industrial magnates, artists, and writers such as D. H. Lawrence and others were drawn there.[6]

In addition to being graced by the magnificent Greco/Roman amphitheater and by beautiful piazzas, villas, churches, and gardens with views from hundreds of meters above the sea, Taormina also has one of the more interesting hotels in the world. The San Domenico Palace Hotel is a former Dominican monastery with magnificent views down the Sicilian coast past Mount Etna and across the straits to Italy. The spacious formal gardens and a beautiful long wing of rooms that are the former cells of the Dominicans are among the splendors that make the hotel special. After two days and two nights in Taormina, I departed to head down the coast toward Siracusa and then on to Agrigento. The ancient city of Siracusa, first colonized in the eighth century BC by Greeks from Corinth, was the site in the next centuries of furious conflicts between Greeks, Phoenicians, and, later, Romans, Byzantines, Arabs, and Normans. It is notable for its native son, Archimedes, and for its archeological sites.

Siracusa is a small place. I spent half a day visiting the principal archeological attractions, including the Greek Theater, the large, sound-magnifying cave called the Ear of Dionysius, the Tomb of Archimedes, and other sites. Then I drove in the late afternoon to Agrigento.

Agrigento is renowned for its magnificent collection of ancient Greek ruins that grace its famous Valley of the Temples. The valley in reality is a ridge with spectacular views over the south coast of Sicily. I well remember the first time I saw the temples. I had arrived at the Hotel Villa Athena, located on the edge of the valley. Dusk was falling. From the hotel parking lot and from my room's windows facing the ruins, one could see the lighted, orange-tinted temples against the darkening deep blue sky as the sun set. Throughout the evening—at dinner on the hotel terrace and later walking through the hotel grounds—the lighted temples were a constant presence. The next morning, I experienced firsthand their grandeur as I ran close by along the long row of ruins. Later, when the park opened I could enjoy them from within.[7]

Coastal Sicily, whether along the east coast from Messina south past Taormina and Catania to Siracusa, the south coast past Gela, Agrigento, and the Phoenician ruins at Selinunte, or around the west coast past Marsala and Trapani and on to Palermo, is a spectacular and oft-visited area. Every year thousands of tourists see only coastal Sicily as they go ashore for day trips from anchored cruise ships. It is historic and it is beautiful. It is not the Sicily of many Sicilians.

The dramatic differences between the hot but temperate climate of Sicily along the coast and the burning, dry interior became immediately apparent as I drove north from Agrigento toward Montemaggiore. In the summer, as soon as one turns inland from the coast, the landscape shifts from green to straw colored. Even as the road ascended into more mountainous country, it was still searingly hot.

The highway passes near many small towns, most unheralded and unheard of. One exception for me, and for many Americans I am sure, is the town of Lercara Friddi. Nestled in a beautiful broad valley, about two-thirds of the way from Agrigento to the north coast, Lercara Friddi became famous in the decades after World War II to readers of the American press, and particularly those who were fascinated by stories of the mafia, because it was the hometown of Lucky Luciano.

Luciano was a notorious mafia capo who is said to have been one of the mafia chieftains dispatched to Sicily by the American army in 1943 to pave the way, probably with dollars, among their Sicilian contacts for the landing of the American invasion forces seeking to oust the Nazis and their Italian Fascist allies from the island. Luciano was released from a New York state prison to undertake this secret mission. Following the war, he was paroled in 1946 on condition that he go into exile in Italy. He died in Naples in 1962.

Following my map, I drove northeast from Lercara Friddi to the small town of Alia. Perched on the side of the mountain above the highway, Alia is the gateway through which one must pass in taking the only road—a minor interior highway—north to Montemaggiore.

The drive took an interesting turn—or several—in Alia. As one enters the town from the south, the streets become quite narrow. The road snakes back and forth several times through the residential heart as it climbs to exit toward the north. The two- and three-story stone houses form a solid wall along the narrow streets. The several steps from the front doors come down to the curb, a few feet from the wheels of passing cars. During the daytime, women gather in small clusters chatting on the stairways; children play in or run along the streets.

The distance from Alia to Montemaggiore on the winding mountain road is about ten miles. The road lies along the side of the steep hills, in most places dropping abruptly off to the left as one heads north. Herds of mules were grazing in many pastures along the way. The fields were often so steep that I had the sense that with one misstep, the animals would roll down the hill onto the road.

The route is higher in elevation; it is cooler; it is greener. The road on my first visit also was poorly maintained, rough, and precarious. On my recent travels over the same road, it is wider, better in many places, but still precarious and rough in some.

Along this interior stretch of Sicily, from the hills above Agrigento into the mountains as one approaches Montemaggiore, my longtime sensibility that Sicily was a different place—that it was remote and isolated—came to the fore.

As I reached the point where the road tops a rise and the city of Montemaggiore appeared in the distance, the drama of at last approaching the place from which my ancestors had emigrated became very real. It was exciting to wonder what the people and town were like.

The excitement dissipated suddenly when I reached the point where the pavement ended. Much of the road's surface had washed away. There was a drop of almost a foot from the pavement onto gravel and stone, which extended several tens of yards ahead. I wondered whether my rented car would be able to pass over this stretch or whether I would get hung up and have to walk the several miles into town. To my relief, slowly, roughly, rocking back and forth, the car did reach the end of the broken-up stretch. It succeeded in climbing the abrupt step up from the stone roadway to the asphalt roadbed, at which point I could resume my journey. As I drew closer to town, the road showed more signs of maintenance and, shortly, at the edge of Montemaggiore it became relatively smooth.

5

Montemaggiore

DISCOVERY

Benvenuto a Montemaggiore Belsito. Brightly painted at the beginning of
the asphalted road, the sign was the first indication of civilization. In less
than a mile, I was entering the built-up center.

Although I had long wanted to go to Montemaggiore, and had initiated this trip eager to see the town, I had done nothing to prepare for
what I might find. At that time, there were no websites and few research
tools concerning places like Montemaggiore. I knew no one who had ever
been there.

I slowed to stop at the first bar for information. As I was getting out
of the car, I saw a sign farther down the road with an arrow pointing to
an uphill street to the right—*Gendarmerie.* I quickly decided the police
headquarters promised more information than the men lounging in front
of the bar—perhaps even in English. I got back into the car, drove directly
there, and parked at the empty curb in front of the building.

The gendarmerie headquarters was a squat three-story stucco structure located on the corner of a residential block. It was about 10:30 on a
weekday morning. The mid-July heat was rapidly becoming oppressive.
No one was in sight in any direction.

I entered the building. It was difficult to see in the darkness after
the dazzling sunshine outside, but I soon became aware of a uniformed
gendarme sitting tilted back in a swivel chair in the center of the room.
Cap pulled forward over his eyes, hands clasped across his large belly, he
seemed to be sleeping. Hearing me enter the room, however, he stirred

and leaned forward, popping the spring chair erect, pushed back his cap, and looked up with an air of annoyance at the interruption.

I tried English, saying I was looking for information about my family. He did not understand. Instead, he held out his left hand, saying, *"Documenti, per favore,"* and *"Che si chiama?"* I handed him my passport, saying as I did, "Cicero, Franco," pronouncing the *ci* and *ce* with a soft "sh," thereby using up nearly everything I knew about Italian. He took the passport, opened it slowly, looked carefully at the photograph, then at me, the passport, then me, and finally said quizzically, "Signore Frank?" He appeared to be confusing my last and first names, perhaps misled by their first-name-first arrangement in my American passport; last name first is the normal usage in Italian documents. I tried to clarify matters. We got nowhere. Finally, he shook his head, gave an elaborate sigh of exasperation, held up his hand, palm forward, to silence me, rose from his chair, and walked out the door, motioning for me to follow.

The gendarme stood for a few moments in the middle of the street. He tipped his head slightly toward the sky as if seeking guidance from the heavens. Then he nodded, beckoned me to follow, and led me purposefully across the street to a house at the corner of the next block, attempting conversation as we went.

All I was certain I could understand of his rapid Italian was something about *signora* and *parla inglese.* Great, I thought. We're probably going to see a villager who has had a high school course in English, can't really communicate or understand, and will simply involve us in a fruitless effort to get me where I'm trying to go. Still I followed—there was nothing else to do.

Our destination was an attractive four-story yellow stucco townhouse. It was well kept, with boxes of blooming flowers in the windows, colorfully painted shutters, windows, and doors, and a low-walled front garden extending along the street. The officer knocked firmly on the dark red door. No one responded until, after several knocks, a woman stuck her head over the parapet of the roof, where she was hanging laundry, and called down to us.

They exchanged words. I understood him to be saying something about *Americano . . . Inglese.* She pulled back and disappeared. We waited.

Minutes later the red door opened and the roof-woman stepped out. She was in her early twenties, dark haired, attractive, and very pregnant. She strode forward, extended her hand, and said, with a big smile, "Hi. My name's Christine, what's yours?"

I was startled. She spoke unaccented, American English.

Within minutes I had explained who I was and why I was there, been invited into their home, met Christine's family, been asked—indeed virtually commanded—to join them shortly for lunch, and begun to learn how my own father's history reflected the experiences of many in that area of Sicily.

Christine's given name was Crocetta. She had adopted the American version when she had moved with her family to Buffalo, New York. This detail was my second surprise. My father was born in Buffalo. His father, I understood, had emigrated to Buffalo from Montemaggiore as a young man.

Christine introduced me to her mother, Marianna Panzarella, who was busily preparing lunch in the kitchen. Her father, Angelo Pasquale, materialized from somewhere to join us. It became clear that he was retired; it was not clear what his occupation had been. Christine's younger brother, Vicenzo, came running in for lunch. When I was introduced to him, he too responded in excellent, colloquial American English.

At lunch, Christine explained her background. She had attended public schools in Buffalo from the middle grades through high school, worked as a clerk in an office during the school year, had American friends, and lived a typical American schoolkid's life. She had returned to Sicily with her family to spend each summer vacation in Montemaggiore. During those summer visits, Christine had fallen in love with and agreed to marry a young man her age.

Although Christine and her younger brother got along very well in Buffalo and were happy there, the same was not true of her parents. Her father found employment as a construction laborer; he disliked the work and was not successful in learning English. He determined to move back to Sicily. When Christine returned to get married during the summer after her high school graduation, her parents and brother accompanied her to Montemaggiore, moved back into the family house, and welcomed Christine's new husband into their home.

While lunch progressed through several courses, Christine translated to her parents my explanation of who I was and why I had come to Montemaggiore. As I related what I knew of my family's names, birthdates, and relationships, she and her parents became enthusiastic about my search, chiming in with suggestions of what we should do and whom I should meet. "He must meet Rose [Cicero]. She knows a lot. We'll talk to her father, Rosario. He's been back and forth to Buffalo."

Christine's husband, Antonino Manzella, returned from work as we finished lunch and were preparing to leave. They had explained to me that "Nino" worked for Telecom Italia; he usually returned from work by early afternoon. Meeting Nino, I was struck by his appearance. He was perhaps five feet eight inches tall, smiling and good looking, with a full head of very light blond hair and penetrating light blue eyes. My first reaction was that he did not look at all like a Sicilian. Then I realized that among the many different occupiers that have ruled Sicily over millennia, the Vikings and Norsemen were among the fiercest and most invasive. Apparently they left their mark. Blond, blue-eyed Sicilians—especially males—are still seen frequently many centuries later in all parts of Sicily.

Christine had explained that all the official records of births, marriages, and deaths were kept at the *municipio,* the city hall of the commune. A new municipio had very recently been completed, however, and she was not sure whether all papers and records had been moved into the new building. She and her father were enthusiastic about taking me there to search for information about my grandfather or his siblings.

Unfortunately, we could not begin the search immediately. The municipio was closed for the usual long lunch break until at least three PM, if not later. While awaiting the opening, we started a promenade around town to meet other people who Christine and her father thought might have information.

Our first visit was at the home of two families, the Panzarellas and the Dolces, who were Christine and Vince's cousins. It was not clear exactly how they were related to the Pasquales, although the Panzarella family obviously was connected on mother Marianna's side. These two families had emigrated to Buffalo with Christine's family. The children had also attended school, learned the language, returned in summers, and moved back to Montemaggiore about the same time as the Pasquale family.

I was met with immediate skepticism when I explained who my grandfather was and that he was born in 1854. One of Christine's aunts was adamant that if the person I named was really born in 1854, he could not have been my grandfather. She and others asserted that some of their families were in the fifth generation from ancestors born in the 1850s, rather than the third as I claimed to be.

They agreed, however, that they did not know any Ciceros still living in Montemaggiore who might be related to me. There were, however, some families named Cicero that had moved down valley to the nearby town of Aliminusa after World War II. They exchanged views about members of one of those families who they thought might be cousins of mine. One person, they explained, was an elderly priest. Another was a man who had been a math teacher in the Montemaggiore high school. Christine's father said he knew him; he suggested we drive to Aliminusa to see him.

We left the Panzarella/Dolces and visited two other homes on our way back to the municipio. Whenever we encountered friends, Christine introduced me and said I was visiting from America. More than once, the response to me was, "Oh, where in Buffalo do you live?" Clearly there had been a long and substantial migration from Montemaggiore to Buffalo, with many folks returning either temporarily in summers or, as in the case of the Pasquale and Panzarella families, to resume permanent residence in Sicily.

The experience at the municipio turned out to be interesting. The building was indeed new—in fact, it was so new that it smelled of plaster and had remnants everywhere of construction that had not yet been cleaned up. We climbed a set of stairs to the room that was to be the archives. It had a small anteroom with a desk and one chair and not much else. When my guides explained to the woman in charge of the archives what we were looking for, she rose from her desk, walked to the door, opened it, and beckoned us to follow her.

The room we entered was unusual for an archive. It was in a corner of the building. It had uncovered windows looking out in two directions. No shelves had yet been installed to hold the books, which were piled in stacks of varying heights all around the floor. It was immediately apparent that there was no organization by date or in any other manner.

The archivist left us to our search. The clothbound books were large and heavy. The records for each year had been assembled and sewn together. The original handwritten sheets were organized by subject; thus, there was first a section for births, then came marriages, and finally deaths. The records were arranged in chronological order within each subject. Entries were handwritten on both sides of a crinkly manuscript sheet. Index pages in the front listed in abbreviated form, again in chronological order, the names of the persons involved in the particular event being recorded. For example, a line item showed the name of the newborn infant and the names of the parents. Similarly, in the section for deaths an index summarized line by line the names of the deceased as well as the names of their parents.

No one supervised our examination. We handled as many volumes as we wanted. We moved them about as we needed. There was no table or chairs. When a volume was found with something of interest, we had to hold it up or rest it on a pile of books while we gathered around to examine it.

When I left later in the day, I wondered how long these old records would survive this type of handling, with visitors coming through and having free rein among the various original records. (When I next was in the archive more than a decade later, the books had all been arranged chronologically in cabinets with glass doors that pulled out from the top and hinged down in front of each shelf. All the glass covers were locked. No longer could the visitor touch the books. He or she had to look over the shoulders of the commune personnel as they handled the records.)

Soon I located the volume of records for the year 1854. It did not take much longer to find in it the original handwritten certification of the birth of my grandfather Giuseppe Cicero on December 11, 1854, in Montemaggiore. The certificate listed his father, Carmelo[1] Cicero, a farmer, age forty, and his mother, Angela Nicosia, no occupation specified, age thirty. The newborn's name was followed by the statement, "born 11 December 1854 0400." The certificate was signed by Domenico Pace, mayor, and Rosalia Chiabetta, midwife.

When I entered the room, I knew only my grandfather's name and year of birth. We already had accumulated additional information that I would seek to supplement in the coming years.

I suggested we search further to see if we could find records of the births of any siblings. Christine moved books until she found the volume of records for the year 1853; she reviewed it but found nothing of interest. I attacked another pile of volumes until I came upon the records for the year 1852. That volume revealed the birth of a brother, Rosario, born April 8, 1852, at ten o'clock PM. Father Carmelo and mother Angela were listed and described in the same way as on Grandfather Giuseppe's record. The names and signatures of the mayor and midwife were the same. The only thing that was different, curiously, was the parents' ages. In this record, they were listed as being ages twenty-eight and twenty-two, respectively, suggesting that they had aged twelve and eight years in the two years between the births of Rosario and my grandfather.

I had no idea whether grandfather had any other siblings, nor did I know what years they may have been born. We spent a short time looking through other volumes of nearby years but turned up nothing. Since it was already late in the afternoon, we decided to proceed to Aliminusa to try to find the Ciceros to whom we had been referred.

We walked out of the new municipio building onto the Piazza Roma and headed west several blocks, mostly downhill, to the Piazza Basilica, on which stands the town's mother church, the Basilica St. Agata. My hosts thought it likely my grandfather had been baptized there, although there were several other churches in Montemaggiore. We climbed the steep flight of steps and paused a few moments, admiring the splendid interior. St. Agata Church was erected in 1665 on a space adjacent to the ancient Church of the Oratorio, which still exists. St. Agata Church was raised to the rank of basilica in 1802. After several minutes in the church, we exited and made the long uphill walk to get my car, which was still parked in front of the gendarmerie, in order to drive the short distance down valley to Aliminusa.

Aliminusa is a much smaller town than Montemaggiore. As we drove, Christine explained that in the years after World War II many of the Ciceros who had lived in Montemaggiore had moved to Aliminusa. The reason was for this exodus was not clear to me. Although she was discreet, Christine implied that the Ciceros did not get along well with their community and decided to pick up and move to a town that might be more welcoming.

I noted when we entered Aliminusa that several streets were named for persons whose family name was Cicero. We drove first to the home of Mr. Cicero, the former high school math teacher. While Christine and I stood on the sidewalk beside the car, her father walked up the several steps and rang the doorbell. After a short time, a balding, middle-aged man pushed open the screen door partway and stepped onto the stoop to talk to Mr. Pasquale. He was dressed in a familiar manner: white undershirt, baggy cotton pants, sandals. Mr. Pasquale spoke to him, gestured toward me, spoke some more. Mr. Cicero glanced in our direction several times but kept shaking his head. Finally he shook his head again, nodded, stepped back into the doorway, and pulled the screen door shut behind him. Mr. Pasquale returned to us and explained that Mr. Cicero did not want to talk to me. Although Mr. Pasquale had explained who I was and what I wanted, Mr. Cicero did not want to become involved nor take the time.

We proceeded to our next potential source. I understood we were going to try to visit the elderly retired priest who was living with the family of a niece. He was, cousin Panzarella had said, related to my Cicero clan in some way I did not understand.

All three of us went to the door this time. When a woman answered our knock, Christine explained why I was in town and politely asked if they could introduce me to the priest. The woman said that it was not possible to meet him that afternoon. She explained that he was quite old (which we knew), that it was late in the afternoon (which we knew), that it was a hot day (which we also knew), that he had been napping and needed his rest, that she did not want to disturb him. Christine and her father both tried in gentle ways to persuade the woman that, since I had come all the way from America and had to leave for Palermo shortly, it would be a privilege for me to meet the old gentleman. Their pleas were unavailing.

Two strikes against us, we left. No one had any suggestion where to go to try for a third.

As we drove back to Montemaggiore, Christine and her father both tried to excuse what they considered discourtesies. They explained that Mr. Cicero, the high school teacher, was an irascible man who was difficult to get along with. I thought at the time that they were trying to console me. I since have heard from other Montemaggiore acquaintances who describe the teacher as a "totally crazy guy" or a crank who is always difficult in personal encounters. Whether he was being true to form or not, I did come away from the afternoon's experience in Aliminusa believing that there could be some truth to the legend Christine had related to me concerning the Ciceros being unpleasant folks who had been driven out of the town of Montemaggiore.

Late in the afternoon I said good-bye to my new friends and left for Palermo. Montemaggiore undoubtedly had been a remote and isolated place in the nineteenth century when my grandfather lived there before his departure for America in 1893. Now, however, as I drove north to the coast through Aliminusa and Cerda before turning west toward Palermo, in each town and along the highway in between there were signs marking the stops for public transit buses to Palermo. Residents of these ancient mountain towns had become commuters going to work in modern factories on the coast or in the city.

At the outskirts of Palermo, the traffic and congestion increased. By the time I entered the city, I was engulfed by a horn-honking, maneuvering mass of cars and trucks. I did not go into the center that afternoon. I had booked a room at the Grand Hotel Villa Igiea, a once elegant and now slightly down-at-the-elbows resort hotel. Its location on the sea, once one of its great attractions, was somewhat diminished by the presence next door of a large shipyard built during World War II. Tall cranes loomed over the hotel property. Nevertheless, although the ambience was impaired, it was a charming hotel. It was also most interesting to see the numerous photographs in corridors and bars of the English and European royalty that had frequented the hotel in the years between the two world wars.

I spent a day walking the downtown streets and port of Palermo, visiting the Norman Royal Chapel and Cathedral as well as older Arab houses of worship converted into Christian churches. The following morning I flew back to Naples to resume my work on the Amoco Cadiz lawsuit.

Two years later I again visited Montemaggiore. This visit came at the end of a three-week-long motor trip with my wife and two daughters, an occasion to celebrate the girls' graduations from junior high school and high school while giving us a comprehensive look at the Italian peninsula from north to south. Our itinerary began in the steep, cool mountain valleys of Piedmont in northwestern Italy, close against the French border, where we visited Balma, the small hamlet where my Balma grandparents had lived for eight years before departing for America. Stone walls without roofs and with only partial floors between the family home and the stables below were all that remained of the three or four stone huts.[2]

The next two weeks we visited many places in the beautiful and varied Italian peninsula. The night before taking the car ferry to cross the Straits of Messina into Sicily, we stayed in Pizzo Calabro, which I had visited with Captain Bardari three years earlier. We again had an enchanting late-evening dinner overlooking the sea.

The following morning, making the crossing by ferry to Sicily, we enjoyed the spectacular sight of Mount Etna drawing ever closer. We stopped in Taormina, staying as I had before at the San Domenico Palace Hotel. We passed two days visiting the ancient Greek and Roman ruins in Taormina, viewing more recent historic sites of later occupations, and enjoying the new tastes of Sicilian cuisine, its flavors derived from its Arab occupiers.

The next morning, we left to drive south on the autostrada past Catania and on to Siracusa and Agrigento. We soon had an experience I would never have expected—and that likely would be repeated in few places in the world.

About sixty miles from Taormina, as we approached the tollbooths outside Catania, we noticed several uniformed, machine gun–armed officers intently watching the oncoming vehicles. When one of them saw our car, he moved over quickly and waved for us to stop. We, of course, had no idea why we were being singled out.

The officer did not speak English very well. He leaned into the open window on the passenger side of the car, however, and conveyed his message clearly enough: "Call hotel. Very important."

He beckoned me to follow him in the car to the office, where he offered me the use of a telephone to call the hotel. When my call was put through to the front desk, the receptionist excitedly told me she was so pleased I had called because I had left my credit card at the desk when I checked out.

The hotel had apparently called ahead to autostrada authorities, giving a description of our car and asking them to warn us that we should return to the hotel for my credit card. We had not told anyone at the hotel where we were going. They knew our car, however, and there are only two principal routes by which tourists leave Taormina—either going south along the east coast of Sicily toward Catania and Siracusa or west along the north coast toward Palermo. They had obviously alerted authorities to cover both directions.

We drove the sixty miles back to Taormina and retrieved the card. We also marveled at the remarkable Sicilian courtesy we had experienced.

We left the San Domenico for the second time that morning and drove without incident to Siracusa. After several hours visiting the ancient Roman theater and other sights, we drove on to Agrigento to walk the row of temples. The following morning we drove north to Montemaggiore, as I had three years earlier. The road had been improved somewhat over my previous experience, and the Sicilian interior did not seem as alien to me as it had on my prior visit.

When we arrived in Montemaggiore, the Pasquale family was awaiting us. I had talked to Christine several times before our visit. Brother Vince was doing his military service in the navy at a base in the north of Italy, where he was one of the most capable English interpreters for top navy brass and foreign visitors. With notice of our coming, Vince had arranged a leave so he could be at home in Montemaggiore when we—and, I think, especially our daughters—arrived to visit.

We spent an interesting and memorable day, beginning with an elaborate lunch at the Pasquale home. We walked around town, seeing the principal piazzas and churches and again visiting the Panzarella and Dolce cousins. Later, we climbed a few blocks up the steep hillside street from the Pasquale house to the outskirts of town to see the agricultural properties owned and cultivated by the Pasquale and Manzerella families. We visited vegetable gardens, olive groves, orchards, and pastures. We saw their mules and farm equipment. We also saw similar farms and pastures that belonged to others.

Some of these lands have been in the same families for centuries. I learned very recently from the documents sent to me by a long-unknown cousin in Sicily that Grandfather Giuseppe had inherited upon his father's death a share in a vineyard outside Montemaggiore described for legal purposes, as properties were at that time, by reference to the adjoining landholders. The properties that abutted my grandfather's inheritance in 1873 belonged to an Antonino Manzella, the same name as Christine's husband, Nino. I have wondered whether any of the plots we visited with Christine and her family were contiguous to the one that a hundred years ago belonged to my family as well.

Toward the end of the day, as we were planning to leave for our hotel in Palermo, the Pasquale family invited us to join them on a typical Sunday evening excursion for a supper of pizza. We packed into two cars and drove the thirty miles to Cefalù, a beautiful and historic city on the north coast of Sicily. On the way, we passed through the main street of Aliminusa, where the Ciceros had been exiled from Montemaggiore, reminding me of my unsuccessful attempts to talk to potential relatives on my previous visit.

Cefalù is famous not only for its beautiful seaside location but in particular for the huge cathedral that dominates the town and can be seen at a great distance from the sea. This church, dating to the twelfth century, was the first major structure built by the Normans in Sicily. Many followed, as the Norman kings sought, in their short reign, to demonstrate their power, authority, and culture following the eviction of the Arabs who had controlled Sicily for eight hundred years.[3]

We visited the cathedral; we enjoyed magnificent views from points in the town, and then we went for dinner to one of the favorite places of the Pasquales and others who come down to Cefalù from the mountains. We were surprised by it. The very large pizzeria had a vast dining room that was crowded, hot, noisy, and full of families with children of all ages carousing, clamoring, crying. It was far from the quiet Sunday evening at a calm restaurant that we h ad anticipated. It was fun. I'm sure it was typical. And everyone remembers it.

We said good-bye to our friends in Cefalù and drove on to Palermo, the ancient capital of Sicily, nestled in a beautiful bay on the north coast in the shadow of Mount Pellegrino. This city, too, is historic with cathedrals, the Norman palace, and other magnificent structures erected by the Normans, or before them the Arabs, or before them the early Christians. It was also crowded, boisterous, and chaotic.

Years passed before I returned to Montemaggiore to renew acquaintances with the Pasquale family. In the meantime, I learned a great deal about my family's history in Montemaggiore and their way of life there.[4]

FAMILY LIFE

Montemaggiore Belsito is a centuries-old town forty-five miles southeast of the Sicilian capital, Palermo. As its name—"big mountain beautifully sited"—proclaims, it sits on a west-facing slope of the Madonie mountains looking across a broad river valley. It is a compact town, mainly comprising single family homes—often occupied by several generations of a family—and surrounded by fields, pastures, and orchards. For centuries its economy has been largely agricultural, with families owning small pastures, farmlands, and orchards outside the built-up town. Although in America we tend to think of farm families as living outside of the towns in small hamlets or on the land they worked, that was not generally the case in Italy. As one authority on Sicilian immigration observed, "The stereotypical yeoman farmer with his own self-sufficient homestead rarely appeared on the . . . rocky landscape. Peasants, whether they were smallholders, day laborers, sharecroppers, or tenants, resided in hill towns. Both owners and tenants daily walked long distances, sometimes five or more miles, to their scattered fields below. Day laborers seeking work wherever they could find it often experienced long separations from their village homes."[5]

Even after my initial visits to Montemaggiore, I knew very little of my ancestors' families or their way of life. With Christine's and her father's help, I had learned the names of my grandfather, his parents, and one of his brothers. I added a few other bits and pieces from family sources. In recent years, with the aid of research by one of my American cousins and, particularly, with information and the very interesting old records preserved by Carmelo (1973), a second cousin in Sicily whom I previously did not know existed, I learned much more.

My father's ancestors in Montemaggiore, like most others over the centuries, made their livelihood caring for animals and working the land. Thus, my great-grandfather, Carmelo, was a *mandriano,* a herdsman or raiser of cattle. Born in 1824 in Montemaggiore, in 1846 he married Marianna Angela Nicosia, age sixteen. Great-grandmother Angela (1830) gave birth to seven children over a span of twenty-one years, the last one when she was forty-one years old. While little is remembered in the family about Carmelo—who died in 1873, two years after the birth of their seventh child—Great-grandmother Angela is remembered as an imposing figure, forceful and vigorous. Reputedly blond, with direct, piercing blue eyes, she lived until age ninety, surviving her husband by forty-seven years. With her children, she farmed the family agricultural properties in the early years and was said to have been actively involved in managing the olive groves until well into her eighties.[6]

My grandfather Giuseppe Cicero was the fourth child of Carmelo and Angela. Born in 1854, he was a *pecoraio*, a shepherd and raiser of sheep. As a boy, Giuseppe helped with other chores in the farms and orchards and learned the skills of a butcher. According to family lore, when he was about eight years old, while tending sheep in the hills outside town, Giuseppe had his skull cracked by a rock in a robbery. This attack is said to have left him with a lifelong slow, deliberate way of speaking.

In September 1877, Giuseppe, age twenty-three, married Maria Castiglia, age nineteen. I have been able to learn almost nothing about her. Her family name remains a familiar one in Montemaggiore. The mayor, with whom Christine Pasquale and I visited in March 2008, was Stefano Castiglia. Our time with him was spent almost entirely listening to him talk about himself and the commune; I was unable to raise with him the subject of my grandfather's first wife with the same family name.

Giuseppe and Maria had five children together. The first, a son named Carmelo, died at birth in 1878 or shortly thereafter. The second and third children were daughters, Angela and Santa, born in 1880 and 1883. They were followed by two sons, the first again named Carmelo, born in 1886, and, two years later, Benedetto, born in 1888.

Although over the years I made several visits to Montemaggiore, I never was able to learn anything more specific about Giuseppe and Maria's or their ancestors' way of life. Remarkably, however, very recently I learned something of that subject as well as much more about my grandfather Giuseppe and the Cicero family. Unexpectedly, and by a momentous stroke of good luck, I learned that a line of descendants of one of Grandfather Giuseppe's brothers lives on in Sicily. The existence of relatives in Sicily was unknown to me or to any of my cousins in America.

At the very time I feared I was exhausting my search for information about family in Sicily, a young cousin in Sicily was lamenting the fact that his family knew of no relatives either in Sicily or in America. He was searching to find descendants in Chicago of my grandfather Giuseppe Cicero, his great-great uncle. Further, that line of the family, beginning with my grandfather's brother and continuing through three generations of cousins, had preserved a collection of original documents concerning Giuseppe and others in the family that go back almost 150 years, to the time of Giuseppe's marriage to Maria.

Among those ancient documents is a contract between Grandfather Giuseppe and his mother, Great-grandmother Angela Nicosia (1830), made on October 2, 1877, a month after Giuseppe's marriage to Maria Castiglia. The contract offers an interesting insight into my ancestors' lives and the varied ways they sustained themselves. The agreement related to the testamentary grants made to Giuseppe by his father, Carmelo. Carmelo's will and testament were published on September 5, 1873, a short time after his death. The 1877 contract was apparently intended to cash out the value of the grants in order to provide the newly married Giuseppe with money to establish his home and family. Giuseppe and his mother, Angela, with the assistance of a notary, executed an agreement itemizing and valuing the assets Giuseppe had been granted by his father's will—a value totaling 2527 Lira. The agreement stated that his mother would pay him the amount by bank draft.

The grants to Giuseppe included personal property for domestic use by him and his spouse, such as silver, lumber, cloth, raw wool, and similar goods, 413 liters of grain, thirty sheep, a quarter share of a five-year-old horse, and a half share of a cow. Giuseppe also received interests in several parcels of real property, including "a plot of agrarian land on country road Ficuzzi suitable for planting," a vineyard within the city limits of Montemaggiore—the site referred to earlier, described by reference to owners of contiguous properties, including Nino Manzella—and a one-fifth share of another plot of agrarian land "suitable for planting," with fruit-bearing trees and plants.

The grants to Giuseppe by his father did not include any share of the family house in Montemaggiore. The grants also may not have included other assets Carmelo had owned with his widow, Angela Nicosia.

Sometime after their marriage, Giuseppe and Maria bought a house of their own on Via del Collegio. The house was at the edge of town, very close to the fields and orchards surrounding Montemaggiore but also only a few hundred yards from the piazza and Basilica St. Agata, the mother church where Giuseppe had been baptized and the family worshipped.

For sixteen years, the family lived the typical lives of poor peasant farmer *(contadini)* families in Sicily. With parents, siblings, and cousins, all of whom lived in close proximity as members of an extended family, they raised, tended, and harvested the crops and animals, made many of their own clothes and household goods, and centered their social lives and activities around family and church. As youngsters, Giuseppe and Maria's four children helped with the crops, tended the animals, and lived at times out with the sheep as they grazed the nearby valleys. The girls learned the household chores and skills from their mother, aunts, and grandmother.

Despite their best efforts, it was difficult to support their family solely on subsistence agriculture. Paying work was not available. Accordingly, Giuseppe and Maria began to give serious consideration to emigrating to the United States. Many others they knew had done so to escape the rigors and poverty of their existence for an expected better way of life.

* * *

In the late 1880s, the tide of immigration to the United States from southern Italy and Sicily had begun to rise rapidly. Between 1890 and 1910, more than two million Italians entered the United States from the "South."[7]

While much is written about the amount of immigration from Italy into the United States, little generally is said concerning the large number of Italian immigrants who did not remain in America. In fact, more than 1.5 million Italians left the United States to return home in the first fifteen years of the twentieth century.[8]

Beginning in 1904, Italian officials began reluctantly to admit and to publish statistics showing that hundreds of thousands of Italy's workers had gone to the United States for what amounted to temporary employment while their families remained in Italy. Known as "birds of passage," many returned to Italy after relatively short periods in the United States. In the year 1904, almost 130,000 Italians returned to their home country after temporary residence in the United States. The number reached almost 250,000 in 1908, averaging in excess of 150,000 in the years 1904 to 1914.[9]

In April 1893, Giuseppe too left for the United States, leaving Maria and the children in Montemaggiore. On April 18, he departed from Palermo aboard the steamship *Initiziativa*. He was processed through Ellis Island on April 24, 1893, and immediately departed by train for Buffalo, New York, where many others from Montemaggiore had preceded him.

It is not clear whether Giuseppe and Maria intended to make a permanent move to America; whether he intended to work for a time, send home money, and eventually return to Italy; or whether he planned, as others did, to move back and forth, alternating periods of working in America and living in Sicily.

When Giuseppe departed for America, Maria and the children were left with the responsibility to care for their livestock and maintain their agricultural plots. They could count, of course, on the active involvement and assistance of their extended families. Giuseppe's mother and Maria's parents were close by in Montemaggiore, as were Giuseppe's sister Marina, her husband and family, as well as Giuseppe's brother, Salvatore Francesco. The long tradition of families helping each other continued in Giuseppe's absence.

Whatever his and Maria's original intentions, Giuseppe's family situation changed shortly after his arrival in Buffalo. On May 14, 1893, twenty days after Giuseppe passed through Ellis Island, Maria Castiglia, his wife of sixteen years, died at age thirty-five in Montemaggiore. She left behind their four children, ranging in age from five to thirteen years.

Following Maria's death, Giuseppe's younger sister, Marina, then age twenty-seven, her husband, Giuseppe Parisi, and their infant daughter moved into the Via del Collegio house with Giuseppe's four children. For the next six years, Marina and her husband cared for the family group that expanded to six children when she gave birth to a son in 1896. Also offering assistance was the children's grandmother Angela Nicosia, who maintained her own household nearby, one that included Giuseppe and Marina's youngest brother, Salvatore Francesco.[10]

In 1896, Giuseppe returned to Montemaggiore to see his loved ones and deal with family matters. He returned to Buffalo in November 1896 to resume his life alone.

6

Valledolmo

THE MORE I LEARNED ABOUT my family's origins on my father's side—through ancient records, travel to Montemaggiore, interviews of cousins, and other research—the more I realized how little information I had about Giuseppe's second wife, my grandmother Antonina. I'm not sure if I heard until very recently that her origins were in a town other than Montemaggiore. Even so, there was never clarity about the exact name or location of her hometown. Nor was there clarity about her name. I learned at some point that she was Antonina Panepinto. I learned also that she had been widowed from an earlier husband, but I did not know that Panepinto was not his name. The precision came later. Her husband's surname in fact was Scalia. Panepinto was Antonina's family name, which, in accordance with Italian custom, she continued to use after her marriage.

When I did learn that Valledolmo was the correct name of my grandmother's town of origin, it still did not resonate with me in the way that Montemaggiore Belsito did. My general impression was that Valledolmo was a remote backwater, in a more isolated valley than Montemaggiore, harder to get to, and of much less regional significance. It was a place I wanted to see someday because it was my grandmother's birthplace, but it was not a priority.

Thus, during my first trip to Sicily—when I drove there from Naples—Montemaggiore was my only destination. I spent a day there and in nearby Aliminusa. I never had any thought of going to Valledolmo. I'm not even sure I realized how close it is to Montemaggiore. My next trip, with my wife and two daughters, was the same. We drove to Montemaggiore after seeing the magnificent Greek temples in Agrigento, spent the day with Christine and family in Montemaggiore and Cefalù, and went on to Palermo.

Finally, when I knew more about the family origins, I was determined to learn about Antonina Panepinto and Valledolmo. I went there as soon as I could.

My first visit to Valledolmo left me with mixed impressions. I spent ten days in Sicily in May 2005. I wanted to see parts of the island that I had not previously visited, immerse myself in the Italian language, spend some time seeking information in Valledolmo concerning my grand-mother, and renew acquaintances in Montemaggiore. I hired a driver, a character named Benedetto d'Arrigo. My first day with him was Sunday, May 1, a national holiday and feast day of church processions and civic parades, large family dinners, and other events. We saw several parades and processions as we spent a most interesting day touring Palermo, Monreale, and nearby towns.

Benny picked me up at my hotel, the Grand Hotel Centrale Palace, at ten o'clock. It was the first time I had stayed in the center of Palermo, rather than on the outskirts at a resort on the coast. The previous after-noon and evening, after my arrival in Palermo, and from first light early that morning, I had very much enjoyed walking from the hotel at the Quattro Canti (The Four Corners), the ancient historic center of the city where the hotel is located, to the numerous beautiful, storied buildings, parks, port, and other interesting sights in old Palermo. Sunday morning, the day was still cool. The streets were quiet and mostly empty of traffic. Individuals or couples strolled leisurely, many walking dogs, along streets that would be jammed and turbulent at midday. Vendors, many accompa-nied by families, including small children, were setting up their stalls for the famous market at the Piazza Marina.

Later, when Benny and I left the hotel heading for the cathedral at Monreale, the holiday traffic in that direction and on other routes away from the city was heavy with vehicles filled with families on their way to a day of festivities. The beautiful Monreale Cathedral, founded by the Normans in 1172, with its magnificent gold mosaics depicting Old Testament scenes, is one of the most famous and highly regarded visi-tors' objectives in Sicily.[1] As always, Benny found a convenient parking place quickly, despite the number of other drivers on the same mission.

We walked up the hill past hawkers and other street vendors to the piazza in front of the portico and main entrance to the cathedral. In the bright sunshine, the piazza was a spectacular sight. Gaily decorated Sicilian carts, with their festooned mules and flower- or scenery-painted carriages, occupied much of the piazza. A large brass band played stridently from its half of the platform at one side of the piazza; the other half, lined with chairs, was being readied for the speeches and ceremonies to come. Happy families, trying to keep their small children in tow, threaded their way past the carts, the police, and other families moving in contrary directions.

After a quick coffee standing at a crowded bar at the edge of the piazza, we entered the front doors of the cathedral into the dark, relatively cool and quiet interior. A celebratory mass was under way. The seats were filled, as were the side aisles. Most of the sights to see in the interior are upward, on the high walls and roof supporting structure, all covered with mosaics. I stretched to view the splendid array of mosaics for a short time before Benny, grasping my elbow, led me to an empty side chapel, with glass doors separating it from the main sanctuary; there he could educate me with his practiced introductory oral history of the church, the Normans, and the successive civilizations that occupied Sicily. After another walk through the crowded cathedral, we left to work our way through the packed piazza to the car.

Benny had told me we would have a typical feast day dinner, midday, at La Montagnola, a favorite family restaurant in Borgetto, in the hills west of Palermo. The parking lot and restaurant were full when we arrived. A table had been saved for Benny. With only two places, it was by far the smallest in the restaurant and the only one not occupied by a multi-generational family. Most groups were well along in their dinners when we began ours. The atmosphere was festive, and the multicourse dinner chosen and served by the owning family—friends of Benny, of course—was excellent.

Our next stop was at a house in the country southwest of Palermo, where another friend of Benny's, Vicenzo Garifo, a noted Sicilian puppet master, was seated on the shady, grassy terrace surrounded by numerous family members who had finished their dinner and were enjoying their Sunday afternoon. We remained for well over an hour, chatting with the adults and playing with the children. I was introduced individually to each one: young, older, and old; sons and daughters and their spouses; aunts and uncles; grandchildren and their friends. I could not, of course, understand all the relationships, nor many of the names.

Late in the afternoon, accompanied by two family-filled cars, we drove to Partinico, a nearby town where, in a garage converted into a puppet theater and workshop, Vicenzo gave me a very interesting introductory course in the manufacture—all by hand—of Sicilian puppets: the dolls, weapons, and shields by Vicenzo; the clothes by his wife. Then we all enjoyed a short performance of one of the almost infinite number of chapters of the legendary sagas of Orlando, Charlemagne's knight, and the damsel Angelica.

We left the Garifos and their family just before dusk to drive to the Palermo airport to retrieve my luggage that had missed the close connection in Verona the previous afternoon. On the way, we passed through several small cities in the area of the airport that were of interest to me.[2] We ended a memorable day when Benny dropped me off at the New River Hotel in the quiet hills a few miles west of Palermo, where he had arranged for me to stay the first night of our tour.

Early Monday morning, Benny picked me up at the hotel, and we headed for Valledolmo. After an hour's drive through the beautiful, rugged, lush green hills south of Palermo, we reached the town of Alia, which climbed the mountain from a *bivio,* or fork in the road.[3] The left fork went up the road I had taken years before on my trips to Montemaggiore. We took the other, driving a few miles toward the east before we turned off and headed north up the Olmo River valley toward Valledolmo.

I began to feel again the sense of anticipation and curiosity I experience when I draw near a place I have long heard about and doubted I'd ever see. Shortly we topped a hill and Valledolmo lay before us, a few miles away. Stretching west to east along the crest of a ridge like many Italian towns, it seemed to spill gracefully and gently down the south-facing slope.

The impression of a gentle slope changed as soon as we entered the town on one of the east-west streets that ran along the side of the hill. Driving eastward, the cross streets were steep, uphill to our left and downhill to our right. All were narrow and lined with very old-looking gray stone houses. Some of the streets—or at least portions of them—were paved with embedded stone. Other sections were asphalt that may have once been smooth but was now broken and potholed. Most streets were simply stretches of loose gravel. On most blocks of houses, laundry hung out to dry on clotheslines stretched across the street between second-floor windows. Although I assumed this backdrop was due to the fact it was Monday morning, I saw the same scene on other days of the week when I visited Valledolmo on later occasions.

Few people were out on the streets. The immediate impression was of an old, not prosperous, almost empty town. One could easily imagine that it looked much the same 110 years ago when my grandmother Antonina still walked those streets, the only difference being the numerous cars now parked in front of houses in place of the mules and carts and manure that must have been there a century ago.

No signs gave us any guidance to find the municipio, the city hall of the commune. We continued looking, driving toward the east end of town. Suddenly and strikingly we entered a broad open plaza where we seemed to jump ahead more than a century in time and technology.

That weekend Valledolmo had hosted the Days of Agriculture, a three-day fair. The annual event features food concessions, booths promoting products for agricultural production, and the latest in farm machinery and implements. The fair had ended the previous night. Booths and displays were being taken down and equipment was being readied to move out. However, the plaza was still full of dozens of pieces of agricultural machinery. Many small, some huge, all brightly painted, they presented a striking sight in the sparkling Sicilian sun. They also represented a stark contrast to the seeming backwardness of the ancient town we had just traversed.

The market value of the equipment in that square was easily in excess of fifteen to twenty million dollars. Alongside, facing on to the plaza, a new convention center intended to draw commercial visitors for other events during the year was being tastefully created from old buildings. Later in the day we learned that thousands had attended the weekend's fair, some from distant places, and that there was a lively market in the area for such equipment.

Our few hours in Valledolmo that morning presented other contrasts, produced some useful information and left me with at least one puzzle. We learned little of any use at the commune office. On this Monday morning, the employees were not much interested in digging through the bound volumes of handwritten, barely legible birth, marriage, and death certificates from the middle of the nineteenth century. As we explained our mission, however, a number of people came into the office to greet friends on the staff. Indeed, it rapidly became difficult to tell who were commune employees and who were just passing through and involving themselves in the conversation.

The interest of passers-by in my search increased when they learned I was looking for an ancestor named Panepinto. Panepinto, I quickly learned, is perhaps the most common family name in Valledolmo. Each new person who stopped by was told by others of the search for a Panepinto. Animated discussion then ensued, with each regarding Panepintos he or she knew and names of parents, grandparents, and lines of descent. Brief conversation established that none was any kind of a relative of my grandmother.

Similarly, as I have traveled in Sicily, I have met other Panepintos whose origins were in Valledolmo. When I stayed at the Hotel Capo San Vito in the resort town of San Vito lo Capo later that same week, for example, the hotel manager, Calogero Panepinto, was a native of Valledolmo. We passed an interesting half hour in the outdoor seating area of the hotel bar one afternoon as he sketched out with pen on paper his Panepinto ancestors, going back several generations—far enough to establish that there was no direct relation between his line and my grandmother.

Two of the women of the municipio staff leafed through a few volumes of records. From family information, I believed that Antonina was born in 1862. In their quick review of the commune registry for 1862, however, they located only one Antonina Panepinto, born January 19, 1862, daughter of Calogero Panepinto and Agata La Tona. From other information I had, I knew that this person was not my grandmother.

The folks at the commune made clear they regarded any further effort to find the correct Antonina as an impossible task unless I could provide more specific information. They could do no more that day and suggested we visit the *chiesa madre,* the town's principal church, where we might be more successful in getting information.

At the parish offices of the Parrocchia Immacolata, the chiesa madre, the woman who managed the office was very courteous and helpful, despite the fact that we appeared just as she was locking the door to leave for lunch.[4] Remarkably, she asked us what we wanted, learned we were passing through, reopened the office, invited us in, and began a search of the church books. The registry was small and, as a result, records were more readily available than at the municipio. They provided new information concerning grandmother Antonina Panepinto and her first family.

Each volume of the registers was a tall bound book perhaps fourteen inches high, six inches wide, and two inches thick. The woman took several volumes from locked cabinets in a corner of the office, seated herself at her desk, and began to scan down the pages. The books, we learned, were all handwritten in Latin. When she found an item of interest, she read it aloud to us in Italian, translating from the Latin as she read. She soon found birth records that revealed that grandmother Antonina's husband, Antonio Scalia, was born June 1, 1859, the son of Stanislau Scalia and Calogera Iannè. An entry in the margin of the birth register recorded that he died on February 26, 1893. In other volumes, baptism records showed the names and birthdates of four children of Antonina Panepinto and Antonio Scalia. They were Stanislau Scalia, born March 4, 1883; Calogera Scalia, born January 24, 1885; Rosa Scalia, born April 20, 1887; and Concetta Scalia, born October 20, 1889. I already knew that Calogera and Concetta ("Jenny" in America) had emigrated from Valledolmo to Buffalo with their mother, Antonina. I did not know of the other two children, who apparently died in infancy.

Two pieces of information were quite puzzling, however. The church registry stated that Antonina Panepinto was born May 21, 1858, the daughter of Antonio Panepinto and Rosa Greco.[5] While details concerning my grandmother's date of birth had never been entirely clear within the family, the Thelen Genealogies said that Antonina's birth date was September 17, 1862, apparently based on my aunt Mary Thelen's recollection. The records of the 1910 and 1920 censuses, however, record her birth year as 1863. Mount Carmel cemetery records of her funeral have the year as 1866, apparently based on information supplied by my father, which also was the basis for the death certificate that bore the same date. Her tombstone, however, shows the year of birth as 1862. Nothing I had seen suggested a birth date for grandmother as early as 1858.

Secondly, there was no church record of any marriage of Antonio Scalia and Antonina Panepinto. Instead, with respect to their relationship, the Latin records state, as translated by the archivist into Italian, *L'unione non c'è* ("There is no union"). She explained that the entry was not uncommon, meaning Antonio and Antonina had never been married in a Catholic church ceremony but had appeared before church authorities for recognition of their union and for acknowledgement of their children. It is not clear when this request occurred. It may have been in connection with providing the necessary basis for their children's baptisms.

Unable to locate further information at that time, I left Valledolmo in May 2005 uncertain about key facts concerning Grandmother. Her date of birth was a puzzle and, of course, the church registry statement that there was no marriage presented a striking new fact.

By the time I returned to Valledolmo in March 2008, I had found no further information concerning Grandmother's birth date or marriage. I had, however, come to a greater appreciation of the town of Valledolmo, its role historically with respect to Italian immigration to America, and what life may have been like there and in other towns such as Montemaggiore.

Valledolmo played a significant part in Italian immigration to America, and emigration had a significant impact on Valledolmo. It all began in 1887, when, at age twenty-one, Francesco Barone left his home in that Sicilian agricultural town to travel to the United States. Valledolmo at that time was troubled, like many other towns, by underemployment and poor living standards. The town fathers sent abroad several respected young men like Barone to search for suitable settlements. Barone ultimately chose Buffalo, New York, established himself, and wrote back to Valledolmo encouraging others to come join him. Much of the town did so.[6] According to one writer, by 1910 "eight thousand of a total population of twelve thousand in the village of [Valledolmo], Sicily, lived together on the waterfront on Buffalo's lower West Side."[7]

The emigration to Buffalo from Valledolmo was echoed by other towns in Sicily and other southern provinces of Italy.[8] Buffalo was one of the major immigrant centers in the United States, attracting Italians and other immigrants with the demand for unskilled labor created by industrial growth, burgeoning commercial enterprises, and transport on the Erie Canal and Lake Erie. Buffalo's population more than doubled between 1880 and 1910, reaching almost one half million. Between 1900 and 1920, the Italian-born population increased almost threefold, from six thousand to sixteen thousand. The Italians were joined by immigrants from many other nations. In 1910, about three-quarters of Buffalo's residents were foreign-born immigrants and their children.[9]

Valledolmo today has a population of a little more than four thousand. It is situated at an elevation of 2,500 feet at the edge of the Madonie mountain range that extends east to Mount Etna and the eastern coast of Sicily.

I returned to Valledolmo in March 2008 to see the town at a leisurely pace and to search for more information concerning Grandmother Antonina. Christine and Vicenzo Pasquale drove with me from Montemaggiore, where I had been visiting with them. After some difficulty finding our destination—during which we drove around town and Vince, in particular, grumbled about how much he disliked Valledolmo—we parked on a steep hill in front of the commune offices and went in. These were the same offices I had visited in May 2005, accompanied then by driver Benny.

We arrived about 3:30 in the afternoon, shortly after the offices reopened from the three-hour lunchtime closure. As I recalled from my earlier visit, they are housed in several rooms, each of which has a large table in the center and files and shelves along the walls. If the walls have ever been painted, they don't show it. The appearance is of a bleak, old, gray building with unfinished plaster walls, high ceilings, and large windows.

Although at this time of year the weather in Sicily is normally warm and sunny, on this particular day a cold front was moving in. The afternoon grew colder, damper, and foggier as time progressed. The result was that the commune offices were even more bleak than usual. The room depends on windows for most of its light, which was lacking that afternoon. In addition, it was quickly apparent—in this office as well as in the commune offices in Montemaggiore—that the communes do not spend any money heating their facilities. All the staff were wearing coats or heavy sweaters against the cold, a practice we also followed during our two-hour stay.

No one was in the small reception area or the room behind the window of the reception counter. We walked farther into the offices to search out the staff. Several women sitting with others in a conference room greeted us warmly. When we told them we were looking for birth and other official records relating to my grandmother, whom I believed was born between 1858 and 1862, they took us into the adjacent room, where volumes of records of births, marriages, and deaths for each year were lined up on shelves. We began a search. All of the old records are handwritten in pen and ink and sewn chronologically into bound volumes. The volume for births in a particular year was perhaps an inch thick, comprised of many oversized pages of parchment that crinkled as they were turned.

We read of dozens of Panepintos births: there were as many as twelve births of infants named Panepinto in some of the annual volumes we examined. Birth, marriage, death, and other records in Italy provide useful clues for genealogical searches because they show the names of the parents of the principals involved in the particular certification. In searching for the birth of Grandmother Antonina Panepinto, we could not find a record with parents whose names matched what I understood to have been those of her parents. Three women staffers were looking through various volumes to see if they could find my grandmother's records. None was successful, and they concluded that there probably was no such record.

I suggested that we attempt to find a birth record for Antonina's husband, Antonio Scalia, whom I thought was born June 1, 1859. After searching each handwritten page of the volume of 1859 births, we succeeded in finding the certificate of Antonio's birth in Valledolmo on that date.

Now that we had confirmation of her husband Antonio's information, I suggested we try again to get to Antonina's birth date by attempting to find a record of his marriage to Antonina. A marriage certificate would show her parents' names, which might enable us to find her birth record. Additionally, however, I had in mind the church record I had seen three years earlier that said there was no marriage between Antonio and Antonina.

The search for a marriage record did not take long. From the church records I had seen, I recalled that Antonina's first child was born on March 4, 1883. When I shared this date with the others, a conversation ensued among the women concerning the probable marriage date of that child's parents. They quickly concluded that the child would not have been conceived before the wedding but likely would have been conceived promptly after. This assumption moved our attention to the book of 1882 marriages. A search of that volume soon turned up a record of the marriage between Antonino Scalia and Antonina Panepinto on November 12, 1882. That wedding date, three and one-half months before the birth of the first child, stimulated lively speculation as to whether he was born prematurely or whether, in fact, he had been conceived prior to the wedding date. During the course of that conversation, the clear implication was that it was not uncommon then or now for couples not to wait until after they were married.

The marriage certificate also furnished the names of Antonina's parents, Antonio Panepinto and Rosa Guzzetta. These details led back to a search of the indexes of the birth record volumes that had been reviewed earlier in the hope that knowledge of the parents' names would enable us to find Antonina's birth certificate—which proved to be the case. The office civil register showed that my grandmother Antonina Panepinto was born on February 9, 1862, in the commune of Valledolmo, Sicily.

The group's success in finding that information, about two hours after the search had commenced, prompted celebratory exclamations and the Sicilian version of high fives by the various staffers present.

Although the process of getting the attention of commune employees and finding the records was a slow one, obtaining official certifications of such records was quick. The woman who had emerged as the chief clerk went into the next room to retrieve the necessary forms and in a few minutes filled out, sealed, and stamped certified birth certificates for Antonino Scalia and Antonina Panepinto, as well as the certificate of their marriage.

We left the archives and crossed the street to the library, which houses the commune's public information services. I recognized one of the staff members from my visit three years earlier. She greeted us warmly, helped us gather a few brochures concerning the commune and the surrounding area, and asked us to sign the visitors' book before we left. Christine leafed through and exclaimed delightedly that she had found the entry from my previous visit expressing thanks and providing contact information. I was surprised at the emotions I felt on seeing my words and signature in such a remote place in the hills of Sicily.

As I left Valledolmo that cold, rainy afternoon, I was pleased to have confirmed significant information concerning my grandmother Antonina, information that, it seemed to me, was not known or shared among my father's family. We had established her birth date, that of her first husband, and the date of their marriage. We had also confirmed in the civil records the information I had received three years earlier at the chiesa madre concerning names and dates of the births of her four children. In addition, the birth certificates of Antonina and her husband had provided the occupations or means of livelihood of their parents: all four were described as *contadini*—peasants or farmers.[10]

Although I had found no reference to exactly where Antonina and her family had lived or what the patterns of their daily lives may have been, walking the streets of Valledolmo helped me visualize a bit of what Antonina may have experienced when she was a child, later as a twenty-year-old bride, and then as the mother of four children by the time she was twenty-seven. Young mothers stroll leisurely with children or other women, often pushing buggies or strollers. Others move briskly on a mission to or from somewhere. Little children walk the steep streets clinging to a parent's hand for support, often carrying a toy or doll or helping with bread or other packages. Small groups of older children laugh, yell, scurry about, and play games.

Children riding bicycles presented one of the most striking sights. Growing up in the Midwest, I and my friends, and doubtless millions of other American kids elsewhere, rode bikes fast on the relatively level streets. Moving slowly, teetering to keep balance was something we did only sporadically—usually in connection with a game. Pedaling a bicycle on the steep streets of Valledolmo is a completely different thing. I watched small children pedaling big bikes strongly but very slowly as they climbed hills, switched back at a cross street to climb farther, and then did it again and again, barely moving, just enough to maintain balance. Small wonder that Italians are consistently among the top climbers in the Giro d'Italia, Tour de France, Vela d'Espagne, and other classic European road races. The slow struggle up a mountain that Americans have learned about from televised races is something these Italian kids experience every day of their lives.

We do know also that Antonina's life with her husband and a small family did not last long. Two of her children, Stanislau and Rosa, died in infancy. And on February 26, 1893, at age thirty-two and after a little more than ten years of marriage, her husband Antonino died, leaving her a thirty-year-old widow with two young daughters.

PART III

BUFFALO

7

Two Grandparents;
Three Families

I NEVER KNEW MY PATERNAL GRANDPARENTS. Grandfather Giuseppe died in 1929, six years before I was born. Grandmother Antonina lived with us long enough to have pictures taken holding me in her arms; she died when I was fourteen months old.

I knew early on that my father was born in Buffalo—that is the kind of question a kid asks—and that he had moved to Chicago. At some point in my childhood I also became conscious of the fact that my father's mother and father were born in Italy and were immigrants to the United States.

From my early childhood, I remember aunts and uncles and cousins on my father's side of the family. There were many of them. Their ages overlapped; there were cousins older than aunts or uncles, something that in my limited experience did not seem the natural order of things.

There were my father's two brothers, uncles Carl (1886) and Benny (1888), who were several years older than he. I knew well my Uncle Benny and his wife, Aunt Jenny. They lived a block from us on the far west side of Chicago and were the relatives from that side of the family who were closest to our family. I do not remember my Uncle Carl, Uncle Benny, or Aunt Jenny having Italian accents. I do remember, however, the strong Italian accents of two aunts, Angela (1880) and Santa (1883), my father's two half-sisters on his father's side of the family. To my recollection, neither spoke English very well. I eventually learned why: both women were born in Sicily and came to America as teenagers. They did not go to school in the states; they lived as housewives and mothers. I also learned that on his mother's side, my father had two older half-sisters, Calogera (1885) and Jenny (Concetta, 1889).

Only as a young man did I began to understand the relationships which led to having aunts whom I could barely understand, uncles by marriage who spoke English with strong Italian accents, and cousins who were older than some of my aunts and uncles. I learned that both of my father's parents had been married and widowed before they met each other. Complicating the relationships further, I came to know that, after my father's parents had joined together in one family in Buffalo and their children from their first marriages had lived together for some thirteen years, Jenny, one of my father's half-sisters on his mother's side, married Benny, one of my father's half-brothers on his father's side

All of this seemed interesting to me, as well as a little confusing. It also seemed unusual.

It was some time before I fully comprehended the fact that my grandfather and grandmother each had lived full lives for years with other spouses and families in separate towns in Sicily before they were both widowed, emigrated to America, and met in Buffalo. Most of that understanding came years later when, as an older adult, I decided I wanted to know all that I could learn about the Cicero family background.

* * *

When Giuseppe Cicero and Antonina Panepinto emigrated separately to Buffalo in the 1890s, they had somewhat different motivations for leaving their ancestral homes. Their choice of Buffalo as a destination, however, was a logical one.

Buffalo at the turn of the century was one of the fastest growing and most dynamic cities in America. When the Erie Canal crossing New York State was completed in 1825, Buffalo, the western terminus, was a sleepy town of some 2,400 people. Canal boats and barges on the 524-mile waterway that started in New York City carried thousands of pioneers going to the western states. They debarked from their vessels at Buffalo and transferred to continue their westward journeys by rail or lake transport. Millions of tons of trade moved from and to Buffalo, heading westward by rail or by steamers on the Great Lakes or eastward by the canal to connecting transport along the Atlantic seaboard.

Population, commerce, and the economy grew rapidly from the time the Erie Canal opened, but never as much as in the last twenty years of the nineteenth century. Between 1880 and 1890, the population of Buffalo increased 64 percent—more than 100,000 people—and in the next ten years another 38 percent, the total population exceeding 350,000 persons by 1900 and making Buffalo the eighth-largest city in the country. Immigrants flocked in from Ireland, Italy, Germany, and Poland to work in the steel and grain mills and the port and harbor facilities that burgeoned due to the city's critical location at the junction of the Great Lakes and the Erie Canal.

Buffalo was a popular destination for Sicilian immigrants from Montemaggiore and neighboring communes in the province of Palermo, such as Aliminusa and Valledolmo. In Buffalo immigrants lived as they had in Sicily: couples had large families of their own and even larger extended families. Italian immigrants generally settled in neighborhoods populated by others who had come from the same geographical areas in Italy. Thus, the Sicilians congregated in their west side neighborhood. They were bordered immediately to the southeast by Italians from Calabria. Italians from other provinces, such as Campania, Campobasso, Abruzzi, and elsewhere, settled in neighborhoods farther away.

Even within their own provincial communities, the Sicilians maintained their identity and closeness to others from their same hometowns in Sicily. Thus, for decades in Buffalo, beginning in the late nineteenth century, there were a Montemaggiore Social Club and a Valledolmo Club, as well as numerous groups for Sicilians from other hometowns. The Montemaggiore Club was comprised only of men, who met regularly to play cards, exchange gossip, and reminisce. Women held their own meetings, less formal and regular, that also were devoted primarily to playing cards and gossip.[1]

As the decades passed, the clubs decreased in importance. Younger generations lost interest. Nevertheless, the clubs today maintain something of an identity and hold dinners on occasion to gather people of a common geographical origin. The St. Anthony Church schedule of events distributed the Sunday I attended Mass in July 2008 announced that the Valledolmo Reunion Annual Mass would be on a Sunday morning in August followed by dinner at the church.[2] I was told that a similar meeting of the Montemaggiore Club would be held later in the fall.

Although Giuseppe and Antonina undoubtedly had heard a great deal about Buffalo, they could not have been fully prepared for the life that awaited them. The contrasts with their prior lives, likely were much more than they could have imagined.

The bustling, crowded, congested, noisy, industrial city that was Buffalo in the 1890s contrasted sharply with Montemaggiore Belsito and Valledolmo, the small country towns my grandparents had left behind in Sicily. In addition, the climate, of course, was starkly different than in their home country, and likely much more harsh than they had imagined. Buffalo is one of the snow capitals of North America. Situated as it is at the east end of Lake Erie, the prevailing winds from the west during winter storms dump huge amounts of snow on the city. Extremely cold temperatures are frequent. Sicily, in contrast, has much milder winters characterized by cold rain, fog, occasionally snow or sleet, and temperatures that fall into the thirties and perhaps the twenties. Winters are short, however, and by late February the days are generally sunny and warm with temperatures in the sixties to seventies. By April, the weather becomes hot.

Giuseppe and Antonina also experienced unanticipated and perhaps painful contrasts in their church and religious life from that of their hometowns in Sicily. In Montemaggiore and Valledolmo, as in virtually every other Sicilian town, the chiesa madre, or mother church, is by far the grandest church and the largest building in the town. Moreover, there often are numerous other remarkable churches with beautifully appointed interiors of marble, stained glass, paintings, sculpture, and other embellishment. This description matches the Basilica St. Agata, the chiesa madre in Montemaggiore, Arcipretura Parrocchiale Immacolata, the chiesa madre in Valledolmo, and numerous other churches in those two towns.

In Buffalo, in contrast, the "Sicilian church," was and still is the Roman Catholic Church of St. Anthony of Padua, founded in 1891 in the heart of the area populated by immigrants from Sicily and other southern Italian provinces. St. Anthony was the only Italian Catholic church in western New York until 1905. It was the focal point for many of the social and cultural, as well as religious, activities of the newly arrived Sicilians.[3]

St. Anthony became the center of the religious and sacramental life of Giuseppe and Antonina. All four of their children who were born in

Buffalo were baptized at St. Anthony of Padua—my father, Francesco, in 1898, Antonio in 1900, Maria in 1901, and Rosario in 1903.[4]

The importance of St. Anthony to my grandparents' family could not have obscured the fact that it was a small, poor church that contrasted with the grandiosity of other nearby churches. St. Joseph Roman Catholic Cathedral, just two blocks away, dedicated in 1855, is an imposing edifice with a lofty and beautifully decorated interior. Similarly, St. Paul's Episcopal Church, two blocks farther away, erected in 1819, destroyed by fire, and rebuilt in 1890, is a grand, imposing stone structure that in those days dominated the area. St. Anthony of Padua, at the turn of the twentieth century, was a much smaller building with two low-ceiling floors—the upper church sanctuary and the lower school and meeting room floor—sandwiched into the vertical space now occupied by the sanctuary alone.[5]

St. Joseph Cathedral was located quite close to the buildings where Giuseppe and Antonina made their home. In the first few years of the 1900s, the family's residence at 296 Terrace Street North was almost directly across the street from the cathedral. During the next three years, at 166 Erie Street, they were only a block away. The cathedral was regarded as "the Irish church," however, and as such was avoided by the Sicilians, who lived quite close by, and by Italians from elsewhere in southern Italy, who lived in nearby neighborhoods.[6] Italian families to this day recite numerous stories of the hostility, including verbal and physical abuse, of the Irish toward the Italians, whom the Irish regarded as interlopers threatening their jobs.

The Sicilian neighborhoods on the near west side were adjacent to the downtown center of the city that was still, at that time, the location of many of the larger historic mansions of Buffalo's prominent citizens. The contrast between the poverty and overcrowded living conditions of the immigrants, on the one hand, and the "swells" of Buffalo society, on the other, was in the immigrants' faces every day. St. Anthony of Padua Church is a short block away from Niagara Square, for decades the center of Buffalo's grandest residential quarter. The home of Samuel Wilkeson, mayor, prominent citizen, the man credited with creation of Buffalo's harbor, and a principal promoter of the Erie Canal, was until 1915 directly across the street from the St. Anthony Church on the site that has been occupied since 1931 by Buffalo's imposing city hall. Giuseppe and Antonina, their children, and their neighbors walking up Court or Terrace Streets to St. Anthony Church had squarely before them the huge Wilkeson home. Also plainly visible from St. Anthony Church and the immigrant housing was the grandiose home of Millard Fillmore, president of the United States and prominent citizen of Buffalo; the Fillmore house faced Niagara Square next to the Wilkeson House.

* * *

Giuseppe Cicero was thirty-eight years old when he arrived in Buffalo in April 1893. Like thousands of other immigrants, he left behind his wife, Maria Castiglia, and their four children, traveling ahead to find employment and prepare the way for the family to follow.

Giuseppe's first living quarters in Buffalo were an upstairs room at 271 Court Street.[7] He may well have shared the room with other immigrants, a common practice, although there are no records to show the number of inhabitants at his residence. Although the lodging was undoubtedly confined, the location was only some two hundred yards from the Erie Canal at the end of Court Street and, just beyond the canal, the mouth of the Niagara River as it opens into Lake Erie. Looking to his right from the front door of his building, Giuseppe would have seen directly in front of him the barge and boat traffic on the Erie Canal, the docks crowded with cargo vessels, and the open reaches of Lake Erie beyond, a perspective that faced directly into the icy gales and snow off the lake in winter.

If the cranes, piers, grain elevators, storage towers, factories, and warehouses at the docks were a constant backdrop to life in the neighborhood, they were also a principal source of employment for large numbers of Italian immigrants. Work was available and close by, but, like construction and railroad and similar occupations, it was outdoor work and therefore largely seasonal, which, in Buffalo's long, hard winters, meant chronic unemployment

Within days after his arrival in Buffalo, however, Giuseppe received news that Maria had died. He was now alone in Buffalo without the hope of being joined by the wife with whom he had talked often about making a new life in the new world.

Giuseppe found work as a laborer, probably at the nearby docks. In Montemaggiore, for more than twenty years of his adult life, Giuseppe earned his livelihood raising sheep and other livestock, maintaining gardens for family use, and working as a butcher. In Buffalo, he never was employed other than as a laborer. He was a hard worker, however, saving money to send home to support his family and to collect the means to bring his children to America.

Giuseppe worked three years before making his first trip back to Montemaggiore in 1896. He returned alone to Buffalo in late November 1896 to resume his working life.

Giuseppe soon met the woman who would become my grandmother. Antonina Panepinto's hometown of Valledolmo is only about ten miles southeast of Montemaggiore Belsito. Although the two communes are contiguous, they occupy different river valleys with a tortuous mountain passage directly between them. Even today, the only easily traveled roadway between the two communes is more than thirty miles long, down one valley through Alia and up another to Valledolmo.

Antonina had emigrated to the United States in 1897, four years after her husband's death in February 1893. She was accompanied on the long journey by her two daughters, Calogera, then twelve, and eight-year-old Concetta. They had traveled by train from Valledolmo through Messina, Sicily, on a ferry across the Straits of Messina to Calabria, and on to Naples, where they boarded the steamship *Victoria* for the arduous trip across the Atlantic. After arriving at Ellis Island on April 28, 1897, they transferred by ferry to the Battery in Manhattan and then by train to Buffalo.

It is easy to understand why Antonina was motivated to leave Valledolmo for America with her two young daughters at the precise time that she did. She had lost two infants and her husband in the space of ten years. In the four years before her husband's death, three of his younger siblings had departed for Buffalo.[8] Moreover, one of them, Antonina's brother-in-law Leonardo was married to Antonina's older sister, Theresa Panepinto. When Leonardo left for America in 1891, Theresa had stayed behind in Valledolmo with their three children. She was there with Antonina when Antonino Scalia died in February 1893. Three months later, however, in May 1893, Theresa also departed for Buffalo with her three young children, ages three, nine, and eleven.[9] Antonina not only lost her older sister, her two daughters lost their three close-in-age cousins.

Other relatives and friends also undoubtedly had gone to Buffalo among the several hundred Valledolmesi who emigrated there each year. Left a widow with two young daughters who overlapped in age with cousins and friends who had emigrated, it was a logical and natural thing for Antonina to do as well.

I do not know how Grandfather Giuseppe and Grandmother Antonina met. Romantic family lore says that Giuseppe was a courier who traveled between Buffalo and Montemaggiore, taking money back to families in Sicily and escorting family members across the ocean to Buffalo. Deriving from that tale is the further supposition that Giuseppe and Antonina met on a voyage from Sicily to New York, either because he was retained to escort her to the states or simply because they happened to be on the same vessel.

Evidence to support these scenarios does not exist. Giuseppe did make one trip back to Sicily in 1896. His return trip from Naples aboard the steamship *Italia* reached New York on November 23, 1896, five months before Antonina and her daughters made their voyage on the *Victoria* and were processed through Ellis Island on their way to Buffalo.[10]

From all we know, Giuseppe and Antonina met in Buffalo in late 1897, within a short time after her arrival in Buffalo in May. Widower, age forty-two, and widow, age thirty-five, they may well have been introduced by friends in the close-knit Sicilian community or met at St. Anthony of Padua Church, located squarely in the middle of the neighborhood where the Sicilians from Montemaggiore and Valledolmo resided.

However they met, Giuseppe and Antonina formed a bond that resulted in five children born to Antonina when she was thirty-six to forty-three years of age; that endured the turbulent life of a household combining three families with eleven children ranging in ages by more than twenty years, as well as spouses of children and, soon, grandchildren; that moved the large family to Chicago and established a new life there; and that ended only with Giuseppe's death two days before Christmas 1929.

When Antonina and Giuseppe first began their relationship, there were the two of them and her two daughters. A little over a year after her arrival in Buffalo, the family she and Giuseppe had formed took a new direction. Antonina was pregnant. On November 25, 1898, my father Francesco (later Frank) was born. The family thus was comprised at that time of Giuseppe and Antonina, a newborn son, and two older sisters, ages thirteen and nine.

Six months later, the size and dynamics of the family changed again with the arrival in Buffalo of three of the four children Giuseppe had left behind in Montemaggiore. On May 29, 1899, Santa, then age sixteen, and her younger brothers, Carmelo, age thirteen, and Benedetto, age eleven, arrived at Ellis Island from Naples. They had crossed the Atlantic on the same steamship, *Victoria,* on which Antonina and her two daughters had traveled two years earlier. With their arrival, the family grew to eight people, with six children ranging in age from sixteen years to six months.

By this time Antonina and Giuseppe had moved into a rented tenement apartment at 326 Erie Street. This larger space remained their home for several years as the family continued to enlarge. The same tenement building was also the home of Antonina's brother-in-law Leonardo Scalia, his wife, and four children, who ranged in age from six to nineteen years at the time of the 1900 census.[11] The Scalia children thus overlapped in age with their Scalia cousins, Antonina's daughters, as well as Giuseppe's children.

The Erie Street tenement was only a block and a half behind St. Anthony of Padua Church, which quickly became the center of religious life for Antonina, Giuseppe, and their family. My father was baptized there on December 3, 1898, a week after his birth. In the next four years, three more infants would be baptized at St. Anthony as they were born to Giuseppe and Antonina. Thus, in June 1900, Antonio Cicero joined the family. He was followed in October 1901 by a sister, Maria. On New Year's Day 1903, Rosario, another son, was added to the family.[12]

Thus far, despite diligent searches, I have uncovered no evidence of a marriage between Giuseppe and Antonina. St. Anthony of Padua Church, where their four children born in Buffalo were baptized, has no record of a marriage. Nor does St. Joseph Cathedral, which is located close by the Terrace Street apartment. Several resources have been unable to locate any civil records reflecting such a union.

The family continued to grow in age and size with the arrival of Giuseppe's older daughter, Angela (1880) (later Angeline), who emigrated to Buffalo in April 1903 with her husband, Philip Leone, whom she had married in 1897 in Montemaggiore. They brought with them two infant children and soon had a third child in Buffalo. Joining the household was Santa's new husband, Calogero Pace, also from Montemaggiore.

Thus, by early 1904, Giuseppe and Antonina's family in Buffalo had grown to seventeen people: the two of them; their four infants ranging in age from five to one; Antonina's two daughters, Calogera and Concetta, ages nineteen and fourteen; Giuseppe's younger daughter, Santa, then twenty-one, and her husband; Giuseppe's two sons, Carmelo, age eighteen, and Benny, age sixteen; and Angela's family of five.

Angela's brood eventually grew to include five children. The first three, born in 1899, 1902, and 1904, were close in ages to Giuseppe and Antonina's children. They all lived together in Buffalo and for a while after they all moved to Chicago. Indeed, Angela was said to have been in many ways a second mother to my father and his siblings.

We know few details about the Ciceros' time in Buffalo. Life was undoubtedly busy and turbulent for such a large family. By 1904, Giuseppe had lived in Buffalo for eleven years. Although he had experience as a butcher in Montemaggiore, he is recorded in the 1900 census working as a laborer in Buffalo, which continued as his employment throughout his time there. By 1904, Giuseppe's sons, Carl (Carmelo) and Benny, aged eighteen and sixteen, respectively, added to the family income by working when they could. Angela's husband, Phil Leone, had first arrived in Buffalo from Montemaggiore in November 1892, six months before Giuseppe. For several years he traveled back and forth between Buffalo and Montemaggiore, where he courted and then married Angela in 1897 and fathered two children before the family moved to Buffalo in 1903. Phil, an experienced foundry worker, was employed in Buffalo and helped support the extended family. Antonina's older daughters, Calogera and Concetta, had important roles rearing their much younger siblings and maintaining the household.

8

Witnesses to History

IT WOULD BE INTERESTING TO KNOW what the Cicero family heard, and how they and their immigrant community reacted, to two historic events that occurred in Buffalo in the early 1900s. The first was the Pan-American Exposition, a world's fair held in Buffalo from May 1 through November 2, 1901. Plans for the exposition, to herald the coming of a new century and technological progress, particularly with respect to electricity, began in the late 1890s. Buffalo was chosen for the fair over the city of Niagara Falls because of its size and its railroad and other travel connections. Additionally, its twenty-five-mile distance from the power-generating source at the falls enabled the fair's promoters to turn the exposition into a living demonstration of the newly invented alternating current system of power's ability to transmit electricity over distances.

The fair was organized at a newly developed park and grounds in the northern part of the city, about six miles from the old center where the Italians and other immigrants lived. For two years before its opening, the entire area was a huge construction project, employing hundreds of laborers, skilled craftspeople, and others in the usual rush to complete the fairgrounds in time to open the exposition. As had been the case with the Columbian Exposition of 1893 in Chicago, all of the buildings except one were temporary structures, designed to be torn down as soon as the fair ended.

The crowning feature of the fair was the Electric Tower, an elaborate building featuring a four-hundred-foot tower. Buffalo was probably the most electrified city in the country at the turn of the century, and the Electric Tower and many other light displays at the exposition were designed to celebrate the power of electricity. Every evening, the tower became a huge display as thousands of light bulbs were illuminated along its silhouette and other architectural features. The exteriors of many other buildings at the fair were also covered with thousands of light bulbs. Altogether, the evening light show was spectacular.

It is interesting to speculate about the Sicilians' knowledge of this grand exposition and its effect on the community. Within the family, I never heard anything referring to this event, perhaps not surprising in that my father was only three years old at the time and, if it was ever discussed, the details were not significant enough to pass along. The huge construction projects may have been a source of work for laborers and craftsmen from the Italian communities. The fair itself may have provided amusement to the immigrant community, if any of its members had the means to attend.

It was said that the thousands of eight-watt light bulbs covering the Electric Tower could be seen more than twenty miles away. If such was the case, the northern glow in the evenings undoubtedly would have been noticed in the Italian community.

The fair was a huge tourist attraction, drawing more than six million visitors from all over the world. Although overall attendance was very large during its six-month duration, enthusiasm for the event and attendance fell off sharply as a result of the second historic occurrence late that summer.

On September 6, 1901, President William McKinley was mortally wounded at the fairgrounds on the second of two days of speeches and other public events. Leon Czolgosz, a self-described anarchist, approached McKinley, who was shaking hands with the crowd as he departed from the Temple of Music. Holding a revolver concealed by a handkerchief, Czolgosz shot the president twice.

McKinley died eight days later, after initially appearing to be recovering from his wounds. Upon his death on September 14, 1901, he was succeeded by Vice President Theodore Roosevelt.

The Buffalo papers gave extensive coverage to McKinley's shooting and to the vigil that followed. Vice President Roosevelt hurried to Buffalo and was a conspicuous presence throughout the week that McKinley lived.

After McKinley's death Roosevelt took the oath of office in Buffalo, one of the few American presidents to be sworn in outside of Washington.

Prayer vigils and, later, memorial services were held at churches and other public places throughout Buffalo. Some took place on Niagara Square, one block from St. Anthony of Padua Church and only two blocks from the Terrace Street tenement where the Cicero family was then living. We can only wonder what their involvement was, what their thoughts were about the civility of political life in their new country, and whether they feared a reaction by elements of the public against "foreigners" like themselves.

9

Troubles in Buffalo

I HAVE NO MEMORY OF EVER HEARING anything from my father or his family concerning the Cicero family's life in Buffalo. How poor or prosperous the family was, how healthy they were, how pleasant or unpleasant their lives were, I do not know, except for the happy fact that my grandmother Antonina gave birth to four babies—all of whom were healthy and lived to old ages—between November 1898 and January 1903. Likewise, in 1904 her stepdaughter, Angela, gave birth in Buffalo to a healthy child, her third.

We do know that something occurred—apparently rather suddenly—to cause Giuseppe and Antonina to uproot their sizeable family and move to Chicago. Referred to in the family only as "troubles," whatever happened has always been murky. The hazy account that has seeped down over time came from my father's sister, Mary—who was only two years old at the time of the move to Chicago—to her sons decades later. Those few "facts" dimmed, or perhaps embellished, by the passage of time suggest that grandmother Antonina's daughter, Calogera—nineteen years old in 1904—had some kind of an encounter with children of another family in the neighborhood during which she was "stabbed" in the head with a scissors. Although no one has ever suggested a direct tie, the fact that Calogera later either was mentally impaired or suffered from seizures has been linked to this incident by implication. Her condition grew so grave later in Chicago so that she was confined to the Dunning Mental Hospital, where she lived out her life.

Family lore also suggests that the incident involving Calogera was aggravated in some way after Angela, Giuseppe's older daughter from his first marriage, came to the United States with her young family in 1903, at age twenty-three. According to the murky family legend, after her arrival in Buffalo, Angela and her husband, Philip Leone, were involved in another confrontation—this time an attempt at extortion of money from Philip that was accompanied by a Black Hand notice. The term *Black Hand* referred to extortion attempts by loose gangs or small criminal organizations among South Italian immigrants in the United States that involved a letter decorated with threatening symbols and signed with a hand imprinted in black ink. The letter was delivered either by painting it on or leaving it at a home. It typically warned that, unless a ransom was paid, serious harm, including death, would occur to a member of a family. Whether in fact money was paid in response to such threats, or reprisals imposed if it was not, was always left very unclear.

Whatever the background facts, as the story goes, Giuseppe took the matter seriously. He is said generally to have had a righteous and separatist attitude about mixing in Buffalo with people from the old country. After Calogera was stabbed with the scissors, he tried to restrict sharply the family's contacts with other Sicilians in Buffalo. When the second incident occurred, Giuseppe's reaction was to take steps to separate entirely from the community. He told Angela he was going to see people to resolve the matter. He returned home to announce to the family, "It's all settled. We're moving to Chicago.

PART IV

CHICAGO

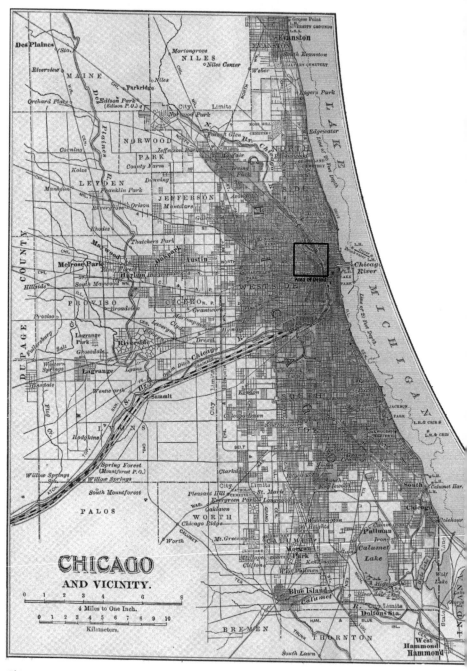

Chicago 1900. Reprinted with permission from Encyclopedia Britannica,
©2010 by Encyclopedia Britannica, Inc.

10

The Fastest-growing City Ever

CHICAGO IN 1904 was a huge, crowded, noisy, bustling, smoke- and dust-filled commercial and industrial metropolis. The city had grown in less than a century from a frontier fort to one of the world's great industrial centers. When incorporated in 1833, it had a population of 350; there were Potawatomi Indian settlements nearby. Chicago was blessed, however, by geography that made it the best portage between the Great Lakes and the Mississippi River system and by the simultaneous arrival at midcentury of industrial, agricultural, communications, and transportation revolutions. Before the completion in 1848 of its first canal, railroad, and telegraph line, Chicago was little more than a booming but isolated port in a remote corner of the Great Lakes. The canal and railroads extended the city's reach inland more than one thousand miles.[1]

By 1900, Chicago was perhaps the fastest-growing city ever. It expanded from some 300,000 residents at the time of the Chicago fire in 1871 to the second-largest metropolis in the country, with a population of just under 1.7 million in 1900. Huge numbers of new residents flocked in from rural communities, as did tens of thousands of immigrants from Europe. That inflow would be augmented starting in 1910 by thousands of African Americans migrating from the South.

Chicago's population growth was matched by an increase in manufacturing and commerce. The Union Stock Yards was preeminent in the nation's packing trade. The city was the world's largest rail hub and one of its busiest ports.

Chicago's growth was accelerated by the World Columbian Exposition of 1893, held in the Windy City to celebrate the four hundredth anniversary of Columbus's voyage to the New World. The exposition was a spectacular display of industrial and technological might and also of the wonders of the wide-open West. Its scale and grandeur surpassed other world fairs. More than twenty-seven million people, equivalent to half the U.S. population, attended the exposition during its six-month run.

The rapid growth of commerce and industry—and the population that sustained it—created overcrowding and difficult living conditions in many parts of the city. The neighborhood in the southeast corner of Chicago's densely occupied seventeenth ward, into which my two pairs of grandparents moved in 1904, was among the most crowded and miserable.

The seventeenth was a great manufacturing ward, with numerous factories and shops churning out a wide variety of products from bottles and brooms to pianos and shoes. Like other river wards, the noise, dirt, and smoke of industry made the seventeenth an unpleasant and unhealthy place to live. Because of the low cost of housing and the proximity of streetcars, rail lines, factories, and other employers, it was inhabited by recent immigrants. The Irish were the first to settle this district. Following the Great Fire of 1871, Norwegians and Germans flooded in, and by 1890 they were the ward's predominant element.[2] They in turn were rapidly displaced by incoming Italians in the 1890s and 1900s.

The Irish, Germans, and Norwegians resisted the arrival of the Italians. The Irish and the Norwegians, in particular, became involved in confrontations with the newcomers, but they were unsuccessful in stemming the tide. The third-largest Italian settlement in Chicago grew there in the late 1800s in the area along Grand Avenue west of Halsted Street, bounded on the south by railroad tracks and freight yards and on the north roughly by Chicago Avenue.

As the ethnic character of the neighborhood changed, its agencies and institutions passed from the hands of the old settlers to the new arrivals. Norwegian, German, and Irish legends on the windows of stores, saloons, and shops were removed, and new inscriptions in Italian appeared. The Norwegian Turner Lodge became the headquarters of the Unione Siciliana.

One writer describes the sale of the Norwegian church at Peoria Street and Grand Avenue to the Italians in 1899 as "the most conclusive evidence of the new ethnic order."[3] The church was rededicated as the Church of

Santa Maria Addolorata, which my Cicero grandparents immediately adopted as their home parish when they moved into a house next door on Peoria Street.

Although Italian immigration to the United States in the 1890s and first years of the 1900s was more than a five-to-one ratio from southern as compared to northern Italy, the population of the northwest side Little Italy in Chicago where my grandparents settled was much more diverse. Thus, Rudolph Vecoli, himself an immigrant as a child who became a leading scholar of immigration history, observes,

> The Grand Avenue colony reflected within its bounds the full spectrum of Italian immigration to a greater extent than any of the other settlements in Chicago. There were substantial groups of immigrants from the northern as well as southern regions of the peninsula, including Piedmontese, Lombards, Venetians, Emilians, Tuscans, Marchesans, Romans, Abruzzese, Apulians, Neapolitans, Potenzanese, Calabrians, and Sicilians. With representatives from almost every region of Italy, the settlement in the seventeenth ward was less a true colony than a cluster of regional colonies among which relations were at best tenuous and sometimes hostile.[4]

Walking around these neighborhoods today, it is difficult to visualize conditions at the beginning of the twentieth century.[5] Principal arteries were paved, but most residential streets, such as Peoria and others in the neighborhood, were not. Children played in streets that alternately were either dusty or muddy. Dirt and smoke were the area's predominant characteristics, creating a climate precarious for health.[6]

The ward contained some of the worst housing in the city. The problem of overcrowding was compounded by the presence of two buildings, and sometimes three, on a single lot. The structures in front facing the street were generally three but sometimes four or five stories high; many were of brick but most were of frame construction. The lowest floor was often below street level; the "basement" dwellings were usually damp and dark. Buildings were unsoundly constructed, inadequately lighted, poorly ventilated, and dangerously overcrowded. Toilets, often located under the sidewalks, were ill-smelling and out of order. Each floor generally contained two apartments of four rooms each, although there were also many one- and two-room apartments. Each unit in turn housed one or more families, and often boarders or lodgers as well, who shared kitchen and bedroom facilities. The rear tenement typically was a one- or two-story frame structure; often it was an old cottage that had been moved from the front to the rear of the lot.[7]

By 1904, there were some sixty thousand persons living within one square mile in that area, the highest population density in the city. It is not hard to understand why the neighborhood was especially susceptible to epidemics of infectious diseases like diphtheria. The area's mortality rate was one of the city's highest. Indeed, these conditions contributed directly to the deaths of the Balmas' two infant girls and threatened the life of my mother, Mary, the first Balma child to survive to adulthood.[8]

Despite the poor living conditions, the area was attractive to new immigrants because of the low cost of housing and the proximity of public transportation and numerous employers. One of the draws of this district for the Italians, in particular, was that it offered easy access to the railroad yards for laborers and to the produce markets for peddlers. Indeed, the produce markets became the principal source of income for my father and his brothers for their entire lives.

Conditions did not quickly improve. During the depression year of 1907, for example, the Sicilian families had the lowest incomes among the various immigrant groups: 60 percent of families earned under $500, 25 percent under $300.[9]

Rudolph Vecoli viewed the plight of the Italian immigrants with a sympathetic eye: "How can anything different be expected from these poor people, crowded as they are into miserable habitations in districts where the smoke hangs a large part of the time like a pall over gray, broken-down houses, and unkempt streets; where constantly recurring unemployment makes it impossible for them to obtain the barest necessities of life; where ignorance is unenlightened and despair seizes on many a heart."[10]

Both the Balma family, directly from Italy, and the Cicero family, from Buffalo, moved into that area, only a block and a half apart, in 1904. Their homes were only a few steps west of Halsted Street, a major north-south commercial thoroughfare heavily traveled with horse and wagon, truck, street railway, and other vehicles. Cutting through diagonally was Milwaukee Avenue, a similar high-traffic commercial street that ran northwest from downtown Chicago. As they stepped from their homes, less than a mile northwest across the Chicago River from the city's down-town retail and commercial center, there was no direction they could turn without being confronted by the bustling congestion that so characterized the city.

Chicago Near NW Side

A - First Italian Presbyterian Church, 1891–1913

B - Balma family residence, 1904–1912

C - Santa Maria Addolorata RC Church, 1899–1931

D - Cicero family residence, 1904–1917

E - Cicero family residence, 1917–1922

F - First Italian Presbyterian Church, 1913–1927

G - Balma family residence, 1912–1924

H - Erie Chapel Presbyterian Church

11

First Days in Chicago

VERY EARLY TUESDAY MORNING, April 26, 1904, James Balma arrived by train in Chicago, the city where he would pass the rest of his life. His friend who preceded him from Italy, Francis Peyrot, met him at Dearborn Station. It was a very rainy day. James's first impression upon leaving the depot—an impression he never forgot—was that the streets paved in red brick were shining and clean from the rain. They rode by horse and wagon to his new home at 71 West Ohio Street, a rented basement room he would share with three other men.[1] The quarters were close. The beds, which were pulled out at night, had to be put aside in the daytime in order to use the table and chairs.[2]

Despite the long trip, James was in a hurry to begin to make his living. The afternoon he arrived he went with friends to buy a bed and the shovel he was required to provide for his work with the City Department of Streets and Sanitation.

Early the next morning, James started out for his first day on the job. Walking half a mile west to reach the street railway at Ogden Avenue, he rode the streetcar some eight miles to Twenty-second and Cicero—at that time on Chicago's far southwest side—where he transferred to travel several more miles southwest to the day's work site. After a long day of manual labor, the trip was reversed in the evening.

The work was hard, and within a short time, as James described it later, he was "so disgusted with America" that one evening as soon as he had accumulated enough money, he bought a ticket to return to Italy.[3] It is unclear whether he was disheartened by each day's hard labor, whether the long daily commute was too discouraging, whether he was depressed by the desolate living conditions, or whether he was lonely and longed for the isolated beauty and quiet life in the mountains of Italy. In any event, his friends persuaded him to stay for a time. In due course he became accustomed to the work and never left. He worked "pick and shovel" until he was sixty-three years old.[4]

Although work was necessary, most important to James were his church and his religion. Shortly after he began the job, James learned he was expected to report the following Sunday. He promptly told his friend Francis Peyrot, who had secured the position for him, that he would not work on Sunday and that he intended to inform the foreman before the weekend. As grandfather related it to me many years later, Peyrot was terrified that James would be fired and, further, that he, who had recommended James, would also be dismissed. He tried to persuade James not to take such a step. James, of course, persisted. When he told the foreman he would not work on Sundays, the response was, "You don't work Sundays, you don't get paid for Sundays. We'll see you on Monday." Grandfather recalled this event as a sign of the Lord's intervention and protection to keep him in America.[5]

My grandmother Marguerite Balma and her daughter Elena reached Dearborn Station in Chicago from New York on October 18, 1904. Their arrival, as my grandfather later described it, was also an adventure:

> The funniest thing about it: she sent a telegram to me when she was in New York but the telegram never reached me. She had no address to send it except to our church at 807 [*sic*] Ohio Street. That was our mail post office and everything else in there. They got to the Dearborn Station at 11:00 or 1:00 in the morning down there. In those days there was no automobile. They had a blind horse and a few Greeks down there with rickety wagons. They put them all in the wagon. They went about three or four blocks away and the wheel fell off of that wagon and they had to wait until the police found another wagon to send them home. When they reached home down there at the address they looked for Balma, Balma, Balma, but they could not find me. Finally they go to the third floor and there was a man that know me, so he said, "yes, I know him, I can bring you over there." We were just living about half a block away.[6]

Marguerite joined James in the cramped basement quarters at 71 West Ohio Street, where he was then living in, to her, unexpectedly crowded conditions: "My poor wife, she was thinking that I was living in a great big apartment, but I was living down in the basement. She was kind of surprised. Finally she say, well, I guess it is a little better here than where we come from."[7]

On Christmas Eve 1904, they moved from the dark, cramped basement space to a first-floor room, which Grandpa later described as light and luxurious, although it had no heat except the stove and was barely lighted by kerosene lamps. Shortly thereafter the cold caused them to move in with a friend; they remained there until the summer, when they were able to rent an apartment of their own: "Every day in cold weather we had frozen water. Finally we moved in with a friend whose wife was going to the old country. We moved in with them. The wife was supposed to be the cook and take care of darning the socks. We stayed there until the Fourth of July. Then we started to rent a flat for my own."[8]

In early July 1905, James and Marguerite Balma and their one-year-old daughter, Elena, moved into a rented apartment at 814 West Ohio Street, just one short block east and one block north of the Cicero household where my father, then six years old, lived with his family on Peoria Street at Grand Avenue. The Balmas would remain in that home for almost eight years.

12

The First Italian Presbyterian Church

HIS FIRST SUNDAY IN CHICAGO, James attended church services. He did not have to travel far. The First Italian Presbyterian Church of Chicago met in the same structure he lived in at 71 West Ohio Street. With small apartments and rooms for residents and a meeting space for the church, the building was a focal point for Waldensian immigrants from the same remote Piedmont valleys as James.

That first week in Chicago, Grandpa Balma began a relationship with "the Waldensian Church" that would be his and his family's most important spiritual affiliation for more than three decades. As a child and on into adulthood, I never paid much attention to references to that church. By the time I reached junior high school, my grandfather, my mother, and the rest of her family were all active members and faithful participants in nondenominational Bible churches. They valued their conservative faith and their independence from mainstream Protestant denominations and churches.

Neither my modest grandfather nor any of the family ever said anything about the significant part he played in the life of "the Waldensian Church." Nor was there ever any hint that the church was part of a mainstream denomination—in fact, I would replicate his role unknowingly decades later in the same denomination. Similarly, nothing ever indicated the significance of "the Waldensian Church" and others it sponsored to the maintenance and spread of Protestant beliefs among Italians in Chicago.

When I began my research into the family and religious history of my ancestors, I had no idea that it would lead into a Presbyterian church. The references that I heard my mother make about Sunday school, summer vacation Bible school, and church camp were about "Erie Chapel." I never had a clear idea what Erie Chapel was, however, inferring that back in the "old neighborhood" there was some type of independent, small, perhaps quaint little chapel catering to like-minded Waldensian families.

Accordingly, I explored the Chicago Historical Society looking for information about Waldensian churches and Erie Chapel. In examining the archives of Erie Chapel, I saw occasional references to joint activities of Erie groups with "the Italian church at Noble and Ohio," two blocks away from Erie. That detail piqued my interest: I knew of no such church. Searching further, I saw other references to an "Italian church" at the corner that, to my surprise, was a Presbyterian church. The name, I learned, was the First Italian Presbyterian Church.

The church no longer existed. The offices of the Presbytery of Chicago informed me, however, that books and records of defunct Presbyterian churches are preserved in the archives at the Presbyterian Historical Society in Philadelphia. More specifically, records of the First Italian Church of Chicago had been transferred there. The presbytery offices furnished me a letter of introduction to examine original records of the First Italian Church of Chicago in those archives.

My visit to the Philadelphia archives proved to be an exciting experience. In the Presbyterian denomination, a register is kept by every church. The register is a prebound, preprinted book containing instructions on how to keep minutes and other details in a standard form. It is the official record of the particular local Presbyterian church, listing baptisms, marriages, deaths, minutes of session meetings, a roster of pastors who have served the church, a list of the elders, and other official information.[1]

The Presbyterian Historical Society archives hold the two original volumes of the register of the First Italian Presbyterian Church of Chicago. Volume I covers the years 1891 to 1913. It is handwritten in ink in Italian. The pages reflect the input of several different pens and writers, including the minister and others. They also evidence other events with coffee stains, pages that were dried, hard, and crinkled from having been wet, ink spills, and other markings. It is easy to imagine the entries being laboriously written at the kitchen table or elsewhere in crowded family quarters.

The First Italian Presbyterian Church was formed on December 31, 1891. The initial Sunday worship service was held on January 3, 1892, at 71 West Ohio Street, the same place my grandfather attended his first service in April 1904. Worship services and other meetings were held in Italian.

Forty-five Italians comprised the original members and first communicants. The founding minister was the Reverend Filippo Grilli, who had been ordained by the Waldensian Church in Italy. After coming to Chicago, Reverend Grilli had been admitted to the rolls of the Presbyterian ministry by the Presbyterian Synod of Chicago. The original members, all Waldensians, had comfortably changed their denominational status to Presbyterian. For these immigrants, the doctrine, forms of worship, and organization of the Presbyterian denomination were familiar, the closest to their Waldensian churches in Italy.[2]

The first minutes, dated December 31, 1891, record the desire of Italians "to gather together those who were converts and who had recently come from Italy for the purpose of forming a religious congregation and gathering together at the table of the Savior."

Recording baptisms, marriages, and deaths, the church register tersely recites the most significant events in the lives of these immigrant families. The entries give only the briefest insights into the dramas that played out in these families. They were of particular interest to me, of course, for the illumination—and, at times, the puzzles—relating to my family.

The register recites, for example, that on Christmas Day 1904, my grandmother Marguerite Balma, who had arrived in Chicago two months earlier, was admitted as a new communicant (member) of the church. It was not until a year and a half later that my grandfather James Balma was admitted as a member, although he had arrived in Chicago and begun attending the church six months before his wife. Why she joined immediately, why he did not sign on sooner, and whether anything had occurred that made the sequence of events in any way significant, I do not know.

While it was interesting to see the original register entries relating to family milestones including baptisms and deaths, the most unexpected revelation concerned my grandfather's role and status in the church. The office of elder is the highest a layperson can hold in a Presbyterian church. An elder is a member of the session, the governing board of the local church. Although elders serve specific terms as session members, they are ordained for life to serve the church whether during a formal term of board service or not. I was an elder of the first Presbyterian church in our hometown of Evanston, Illinois, and had served several terms as a member of its session. I was astounded to see in the First Italian Church of Chicago register that my grandfather James Balma also was a Presbyterian elder. Beginning in 1912, he served the church as an active elder for twenty-five years. During much of the time, James functioned as a member of the session; he was also treasurer of the session.

I never knew that my grandfather was a Presbyterian, let alone that he served for many years as an ordained elder. I also learned that James was a significant and reliable supporter of the church in material ways. The register reports several occasions of extraordinary needs for repair of church structures, including a new roof, and for expenses of coal to heat a nearby church mission on Superior Street. Although James was a "pick and shovel" laborer, he stepped up at critical times with plentiful financial support. The register reports that on one occasion the funds needed for substantial repairs to the church structure were "borrowed from brother Giacomo Balma, the church not having the money to buy the new material." On other occasions as well, the needed financial support apparently was contributed by James.[3]

The nucleus of the First Italian Presbyterian Church was a close-knit community of Italian immigrants who were all Waldensians from the Piedmont valleys. The names of elders, pastors, and communicants recorded in the register for almost three decades are familiar from my grandparents' commune in Italy or from others nearby. Among the most common names are Balma, Grill or variations such as Grilli and Grille, Peyrot, Garrou, Pons, and Tron. In Chicago they lived in close proximity to each other and generally maintained their connections as they relocated.

In 1912 James Balma and his close friend Pasquale Servi bought a two-story, four-apartment building at 1420 West Ohio Street. Others of the Waldensian community lived nearby. In June of the next year, the board of the Presbyterian Synod of Chicago agreed to purchase for the Italian church a run-down building at the corner of the same block on the condition that the congregation support the expenses to repair it. Grandfather and other members agreed to do so. In November 1913, the church began to meet in its new home at 1400 West Ohio Street, on the corner of Ohio and Noble streets.

The small church group maintained contact with Waldensian communities elsewhere. Church records report exchanges of information with the Waldensian churches in New York City and Valdese, North Carolina, and with church headquarters back in Piedmont, Italy. There were occasional visits to the Chicago church by members of these other communities and vice versa.

As was true in Piedmont, the Italian Waldensians generally spoke at least three languages. My grandparents, for example, could read and write both French and Italian. At home, the family spoke the local patois of their home area in the Val Germanasca in Piedmont. Their fellow immigrants shared this facility with language, varying by the several patois spoken in different Piedmont valleys.[4] At the outset, Italian was the language of the Italian Presbyterian church in Chicago. By the time my mother and her siblings attended the church in the second decade of the 1900s, English was spoken in the children's Sunday school, while Italian continued to be the language of the worship services. As noted before, the large Waldensian Presbyterian church in Valdese, North Carolina—its members from the same valleys—used French in their services.

The Chicago History Museum archives contain a curious memoir by a retired German Lutheran minister who visited the Chicago Waldensian community in 1910. The memoir is handwritten by the Reverend Franz L. Braun in a spiral-bound notebook. Braun had served for years as a Lutheran missionary to Waldensians in the alpine valleys of Italy. Retired at the time of his visit, he does not make clear his motives for coming to Chicago and whether he traveled on a church or a self-appointed mission. It appears his purpose, however, was to "form in Chicago the first French Lutheran mission in all the U.S."[5]

Braun marveled at what he found in a one-mile stretch of West Ohio Street—where the Balmas lived at the time—"When in May 1910 the reporter of this sketch, a retired Lutheran pastor Rev. Franz L. Braun, a graduate of Leipzig University was sent . . . into the polyglot West Ohio Street from #745-1575, he found there Italians, Greeks, Polish, Slovaks, Hungarians and a few Germans, Norwegians, and Swedes."[6]

It seems he expected to find French Waldensians in Chicago. He sought out James Balma's good friend, whose name Braun had in French as Francois Peyrot. Peyrot and his family lived in the rear house at 814 West Ohio Street, on the floor above the Balma family. Reverend Braun found Peyrot's wife with a babe in her arms "in the rear house . . . on the top floor after climbing a rickety stairway." He addressed her in French, which she spoke fluently. She told him, however, that she was Italian. That puzzled Braun because, "I supposed her to be a Roman Catholic like all inhabitants in that Italian settlement but saw no holy picture on the wall as I was wont to find in the poorest homes." When he asked her the reason, she told him she was a Protestant, a Waldensian, and further, "She told me there is no French Waldensian church in Chicago, but an Italian at #810 W. Ohio Str. whose service she attends and whose pastor, Rev Grilli, her special countryman from the alpine glens and Waldensian church brother is now a member of the Presbyterian church synod."[7]

Reverend Braun promised to return another day to read her a Lutheran sermon in French. Five months later, on a Sunday afternoon in October 1910, he again visited the Peyrot home. Braun confirmed that the woman's name was "Mrs. Suzanne Peyrot nee Grille" and read her a French-language sermon by Martin Luther. He concluded, "Afterwards I asked her if she had fully understood it and she gave such a clear, lucid answer about it as I never had heard."[8]

Reverend Braun, who apparently spoke no Italian, seems never to have quite been able to comprehend that Waldensian immigrants from Italy were truly Italian, that Italian was their mother tongue, and that they may have voluntarily and willingly affiliated with an Italian-language Presbyterian church. Referring to the Ohio Street congregation, he states, "The French Waldensians of Italy about 8 families of 50 souls and quite a number of singles are not supplied at all with services in their French mother tongue, but are compelled by Presbyterian church law to attend the Italian service (Waldensian Presbyterian, as their countryman pastor has joined the Presbyterian Church synod)." He concluded, "By a clerical ruse the Waldensians have become in facto Presbyterians."[9]

* * *

The First Italian Presbyterian Church was never very large. By 1906, the church had 134 members, with 120 attending Sunday school. Beginning early, First Italian Presbyterian, following the evangelistic impulses of the Waldensians through the ages, had fostered efforts to extend its reach to other Italian Protestants. Transport in Chicago was difficult and time consuming. To nurture Protestant faithful, First Church and others sponsored missions or missionary efforts in other neighborhoods where Italians had settled.

In the 1890s, during the church's first decade, members of First Italian Church, on Chicago's near northwest side, underwrote support for a mission at Grand and Western avenues on Chicago's west side and another on Taylor Street on Chicago's near southwest side. The Taylor Street Little Italy was the largest in Chicago; at its peak it contained some twenty-five thousand Italian immigrants and families, a third of the city's Italian population. The mission started in the 500 block on West Taylor Street. In 1914, Reverend Pasquale R. De Carlo began work there. Shortly thereafter, the mission moved west to 1206 Taylor Street, where it became the Garibaldi Institute, an important Presbyterian neighborhood house. In 1930, Reverend De Carlo and a founding group of parishioners from the Garibaldi Institute formed St. John Presbyterian Church. For more than twenty-five years, St. John's was the largest Protestant church in the city serving Italian-speaking immigrants and their families.[10] Five years after its founding, St. John's and Reverend De Carlo also would play a significant role in the lives of Frank Cicero and Mary Balma: they were married there when others would not perform the service.

13

Family Life in Chicago

THE BALMAS ON OHIO STREET

Life was undoubtedly hard and infant mortality high in the remote mountains of northwestern Italy. Long, harsh winters, insufficient diet, poor sanitation, disease, lack of medical care—all took their toll. It was little better in Chicago in the early years of James and Marguerite's life there. Neighborhoods were cramped and crowded. Sanitation conditions were bad. Cold, smoke, and foul air all had an impact.

Elena, the baby girl born in November 1903, five months before Grandpa's emigration, had been sickly most of the time in Italy. She improved upon arrival in Chicago and, sixteen months later, in February 1906 was joined by a baby sister, Emma. Once again, James and Marguerite had two young children in their household. And once again, the situation was not to last. Elena, three years old, died in February 1907, two days after Emma's first birthday. And just seven months later, in September 1907, Emma also died, at age nineteen months. For the second time in their lives, James and Marguerite had buried two babies within one year. And again, at ages thirty-six and thirty-two respectively, after twelve years of marriage and after watching five infants die, James and Marguerite were left childless.

The joy and sorrow of the births and early deaths of Marguerite and James's babies are reflected poignantly in the First Italian Presbyterian Church register. Thus the session minutes note the baptism of Emma Balma in November 1906. While it is curious that her baptism is recorded as taking place nine months after her birth on February 8, one can still visualize the family's joy as she joined her two-and-a-half-year-old sister,

Elena. Tragically, only four months after the happy occasion of Emma's baptism, the session minutes record the "departure for her Heavenly Home" of Elena on February 6, 1907. Too soon again, the death seven months later, on September 6, 1907, of one-and-a-half-year-old Emma is also observed in the session minutes.

Elena, in February, and Emma, in September, were buried in Mount Olive Cemetery on Chicago's far west side.[1] This area of the city was at the time undeveloped; nearby were some homes but also extensive prairies and an open-pit clay quarry and brick-making factory. Eighteen years later, the Balmas would make their final move as a family to 3422 North Narragansett Avenue, just a few blocks south of Mount Olive's arched ironwork gate. Decades later, Marguerite in 1942 and James in 1959 would also join their daughters in Mount Olive Cemetery.

As noted before, with the death of Emma, James and Marguerite were childless for the third time in their marriage. The situation did not last long. My mother, Maria Margherita, was born on July 25, 1908, ten months after Emma's death. Mary was followed by three siblings: Caterina Emma, born two years later, on July 15, 1910, another daughter, Elena Louisa, on June 27, 1912, and, finally, a son, Giovanni, on September 10, 1915.

The births and baptisms of Mary and Elena were recorded in volume I of the Italian Presbyterian Church register in the Italian language used in that volume. Curiously, the birth and baptism of baby Caterina were not recorded in the register, although she and her siblings agree that she was indeed baptized at the Italian Presbyterian Church. When the last child, Giovanni—the third son to be given that name—was born, his birth and then his baptism a year later, on September 3, 1916, were recorded in the register, volume II, in English as John Balma.

There can be no doubt that the trauma of watching two daughters die in America after burying three sons in Italy had a severe impact on Marguerite and James. Still, their appearance in a formal family photograph taken perhaps two years later, with their next infant, my mother, Maria Margherita Balma, is—to me, at least—astonishing for their apparent confidence, dignity, youthful appearance, and purposeful directness. In the photograph James is seated, holding Mary on his knee, with Marguerite standing proudly alongside. Mary is perhaps eighteen months old. Marguerite is not obviously pregnant with Catherine, her next born. At age thirty-four, after six pregnancies and births, she is poised and youthful.

Except for the image of young Giacomo in his army uniform, I know of no photographs in Italy of Margherita or Giacomo or their four infants born there. I know of very few photographs of the early life of the Balma family in America. The three earliest are formal photographs taken in Chicago in which Marguerite and James documented their growing family. The photo described above of the proud parents with their daughter Mary is the earliest; it may have been taken toward Christmastime in 1909. The next is a formal photograph of Mary with her younger sister, Catherine. In the third photograph, the two older daughters are joined by Helen.

There are undoubtedly millions of such photos of proud young immigrant couples and their American children. I find these images notable for the calm confidence in the expressions of the parents in the first photo, and also for the fact that this couple, who as far as is known had no photographs or physical mementoes of five passed infants, seized the occasions to document their growing family. The parents' pride as they watched the photo sessions of the girls can easily be visualized.

* * *

The Balma family lived at 814 West Ohio Street for seven years, from July 1905 until early in 1912. Six families comprising thirty-one people occupied the three separate dwellings at that address. The 1910 census, apparently taken early in the year before Catherine's birth, lists James as head of one family household with his wife Margherita, daughter Maria, and a border named Elvira Pellegrini. Another family household at the same address was headed by Frank Grill, with his wife, daughter, son, and two boarders, one of whom was named Philip Berger. More than twenty years later, Grill and Berger family members owned a produce business at Randolph Street market; they hired Mary to work in their office, leading to her meeting my father, Frank.[2]

Typical of the communities in which the immigrants lived, the houses were small, poorly maintained, and poorly ventilated. Coal and wood smoke filled the icy air in winter. Dust and heat, poor sanitation, still-common horse traffic, close quarters, and congestion made life miserable in the summer.

James worked hard six days a week as a laborer with the City Department of Streets and Sanitation—the "Water Department." The days were long. He traveled by streetcar to and from the department yard where he was assigned or, at times, directly to the work site. The intense physical labor left him tired much of the time.

Their house, like those of their neighbors, was filled with small children, noise, cries, and turbulence. Their lives consisted of maintaining their homes and families in difficult conditions. Their support was drawn from the old country friends who lived all around them, shared the same burdens of supporting and raising families, and enjoyed the same spiritual lives based in the same church. Although closely circumscribed, their lives were fulfilled by friendships, their ancient religion, and their common purpose in sharing the two.

My mother and aunts, of course, were too young to have any recollection of life at that house. Grandfather James remembered that he worked hard, paid the rent, and managed to save money—"a hundred dollars or something" from time to time.[3] Indeed, he was successful all his life in saving from his meager wages to invest in his family's and church's needs. It was at the 810 West Ohio church location in 1910—five years after his arrival as a penniless immigrant—that he loaned and later gave to the church monies to make needed repairs.[4]

During seven years in the rented house, James also saved enough to buy a better house in a better neighborhood with a close friend, Pasquale Servi. James years later described that first home purchase: "Between a friend of mine and I we decided to buy a house. We went out looking around. We find a house and we buy it. We pay that house $7,200 cash money. That was the first time I ever see a thousand dollar bill, but that day I handed seven one thousand dollar bills to the man who sold the house."[5]

The "house" was in fact two buildings at 1420 West Ohio Street; each structure had apartments on the first and second floors. The Balmas and Servis moved into the two houses in 1912. The Servis occupied the second-floor apartment in the front building. The Balmas moved into the four-room apartment on the second floor of the rear house. The other two flats were rented. A yard paved with brick between the two houses became one of the children's primary playgrounds.

In September 1912, James and Marguerite saw their first child off to public school. My mother, Mary, followed by her two sisters and brother, attended James Otis Grammar School at 1500 West Grand Avenue, one block from their home. As with countless other children of immigrants, public school was the first—and perhaps most significant—step away from the linguistic and cultural confines of their parents' families and backgrounds and toward being "Americans."

In 1992, at age eighty, Aunt Helen, my mother's younger sister, wrote out her detailed memories of life at 1420 West Ohio Street. The kitchen was rather large. A huge wood-burning cookstove was also used for heating. An old oak table and chairs took a lot of room but also provided the family's work and play space. On Mondays, wash day, mother Marguerite placed a large tub in the center of the kitchen floor. The smell of hot water, soap, and soup simmering on the stove filled the kitchen.[6]

One of the two bedrooms belonged to James and Marguerite. The other was shared by the three girls. All three slept in a full-size bed; Helen recalls that she stretched across the foot. In early years, after they were tucked in, James placed a large board across the front so they would not fall out. Another bed in the living room was used by younger brother John.

One room was singled out for special comment by Helen: "The bathroom consisted of a long, dark room with only a commode that had a pull chain. [There was] a make-shift closet along one side to conceal a long trunk. This trunk had carried Dad's belongings when he came from Italy. We kids thought the trunk looked like a coffin, and we always felt spooked when we had to use the room."[7]

Several years later, the Balma family moved to the first floor of the front house, below the Servis' apartment. The new flat was more spacious, with a dining room and a full bathroom.

Nineteen thirteen was a momentous year for the Balma family. First, James and Marguerite became U.S. citizens. On July 18, 1913, James was admitted to citizenship by the Superior Court of Cook County, Illinois. The Certificate of Naturalization describes him as forty-two years old, five feet, eight inches tall, and white with dark skin, blue eyes, and black hair. His wife, Marguerite, thirty-seven years of age, is recorded as living with him at 1420 West Ohio Street along with their daughters Mary, five, Catherine, three, and Ellen, one.[8] Under U.S. law at that time, Marguerite became a citizen upon her husband's naturalization. The girls, of course, were citizens by virtue of their birth in the United States.[9]

* * *

My mother, aunts, and uncle describe their family life as happy but also strict and rigorous. Father James was a sober man, a hard worker, stern and demanding; the phrase I heard in later years was that for him it was "my way or else." Mother Marguerite wore neat, clean, and plain cotton dresses and tucked her hair into a bun. She had a hearty laugh and could see something funny in most circumstances. She constantly reminded the children that "cleanliness is next to Godliness." She was also a patient and able teacher, instructing the girls in skills such as sewing clothes, knitting, and crocheting.

The family spoke the patois of the Piedmont valleys at home. Mother Marguerite spoke little English. She did listen to the radio; a particular favorite was baseball games, and she reported the scores to the children. As they grew older, the sisters agreed that they would continue to speak patois among themselves in order to maintain the language. They did so into their adult years. I recall as a child hearing my mother's end of telephone conversations with her sisters and conversations at home with Grandpa in patois. (One of the ironies—and one of my regrets—of course, is that in raising their own family, my mother and father—he spoke the Sicilian dialect and also Italian—wanted me and my siblings to be "American." The native languages of their parents, in which they were fluent, were not taught to us.)

The parents were strict about religion and their faith. James and Marguerite were prayerful, and they spoke to the children about Jesus Christ, personal faith, and serving God. The family read the Bible together and were dutiful in attending church services and observing Sunday as a rest day. Their dress and manners were conservative. The girls were not allowed to cut their hair, which was thick and curly and became heavy as it grew longer. In the summertime, Marguerite would raise up the top layer in back and cut from underneath to lessen the weight. As before and since with millions of children, when they returned from playing outside with others, an inspection for head lice was mandatory.

The Balma children found many things of interest in the neighborhood. The butcher shop across the street from the house was fascinating, its floor covered with a thick layer of sawdust. There was always the sound of cackling hens coming from the cages of live poultry both inside and outside the shop. The owner, Mr. Lapatina, was a friendly man whom the kids particularly liked because he would cut slices of bologna for them as a treat while they waited their turns.

They had a little wagon used for many things, most memorably for the run to the bakery. Mother Marguerite prepared the dough at home for several loaves of bread; the girls put them in a pan and pulled them in the wagon to the baker on Grand Avenue. Hours later they returned to pick up the warm loaves; the aroma of freshly baked bread accompanied them on the walk home. The wagon was also used to pick up unfinished pillowcases and yards of embroidered edging from the textile factory several blocks down the street. Marguerite trimmed the pillows, which the girls returned to the factory the next day, thus earning a few dollars to help with household expenses.

There was the grocery shop next to the Italian church, with large glass jars of much-coveted cookies. A block away on Erie Street, in addition to the popular Erie Chapel, was the pharmacy—which in those days sold nothing but medicine—its large glass vials filled with red, green, gold, and purple water to attract customers. Also on Erie Street was a bakery that was the source of special treats on Saturday-morning walks to buy a dozen sweet rolls. And not far away was Eckart Park, the destination for Sunday-afternoon walks that ended with the simple pleasure of a half box of Cracker Jack to each child.

As may always be true of childhood memories, the children recall particularly heavy snowfalls in the winter. They measured the piles of shoveled snow by how high they came up the necks of the wagon-pulling horses that made the daily milk deliveries—and in the summer the deliveries of ice.

The First Italian Presbyterian Church, which had moved in the summer of 1913 to 1400 West Ohio Street, on the corner of the block where the Balma and Servi families lived, remained the center of the family's spiritual life during their thirteen years there. James continued to serve as an elder, as the session's treasurer, and as a dependable supporter of the church. The entire family attended weekly Sunday school and Sunday worship services, and James, at least, participated in numerous other church meetings.

Another milestone in the Balmas' church and family life is reflected in volume II of the Italian church register. On June 4, 1922, shortly before her fourteenth birthday, my mother, Mary Balma, was admitted as a communicant of the church on confession of faith. While always an occasion celebrated by church and family, it undoubtedly had special meaning for James and Marguerite. After the loss of so many infants and the dangerous health crises survived by Mary, the oldest child of the family had now passed a milestone of their faith. Two years later, she was followed into church membership by her sister Kay. Helen and John also eventually became communicants of the Presbyterian Church.

* * *

In 1912, when the family moved from 814 to 1420 West Ohio Street, James and Marguerite also were introduced to Erie Chapel and Neighborhood House. Erie Chapel was located at 1347 West Erie Street, one block north and one-half block east of the Balmas' new home. The institution would have an important place in the lives of my mother, her sisters, and my grandmother.

Although the First Italian Presbyterian Church was the spiritual home base of my grandparents for twenty-five years from their first days in Chicago and was also the home church of my mother and her siblings through their childhoods and teen years, I do not recall ever hearing my mother refer to the Italian Presbyterian Church. I did hear a great deal, however, about Erie Chapel, of which my mother spoke fondly all her life. Whenever she reminisced about going to Sunday school or church as a child or about summer camp or vacation Bible school, as far as I can remember it was about Erie Chapel.

My mother's cherished experiences at Erie Chapel began when she was a small child and continued into adulthood. Shortly after the family moved to the neighboring block on Ohio Street, Grandma Balma began to attend ladies meetings at Erie. There were cooking classes, language classes, citizenship classes, classes on homemaking, health, and sanitation, and others. My mother and her younger siblings, as they came along, were enrolled in preschool at Erie while their mother attended her meetings. When the girls grew older, they joined after-school clubs on Monday and Wednesday afternoons. Activities included art and crafts, various types of handwork such as sewing, housework, and cooking, and more. Every Friday was movie night at Erie, which the children happily attended.[10]

The Balma children joined in for Sunday school at Erie Chapel on Sunday afternoons—after attending Sunday school and worship services at the First Italian Presbyterian Church earlier in the day. Summer camp was an important and much-coveted experience for the Balmas and other children at Erie. Erie itself did not own a camp but regularly sent children to Camp Gray in Saugatuck, Michigan, owned by the Presbyterian church extension board. My mother spoke often of her happy memories of time spent there, even as a young woman. While it is not clear how early she started to attend Camp Gray, the years spanned to young adulthood, to as late as 1934 when, unknown to her family, she and my father were courting and he visited her at the camp.[11]

Although I heard about Erie Chapel in general terms from my mother, I never learned much about it. I never saw it. Erie Chapel, from what I could tell, was one of those places that used to be in the "old neighborhood" and no longer mattered.

Then, as an adult in the 1970s, I learned that Erie Chapel still existed. I was elected a deacon of our family's church, First Presbyterian of Evanston. One of our responsibilities was to support the Presbyterian-affiliated neighborhood houses in Chicago. When it came time to choose which one to work with, Erie Neighborhood House was on the list. Although I may have heard of Erie Neighborhood House, it was a revelation to discover it was the present incarnation of the Erie Chapel I had heard so much about for so many years—and that the Erie Chapel my mother so loved was part of a Presbyterian institution. I had never known that.

I signed on to be one of the deacons working with Erie. Shortly after, I visited Erie for the first time. My childhood visions of a quaint chapel were far from the mark. I found instead a busy, crowded, sprawling neighborhood house with meeting rooms, kitchens, gymnasium, auditoriums, and other facilities. There was indeed a chapel in the buildings. Exploring it, I discovered French-language hymnals and learned that Presbyterian worship services in French and Italian had been conducted there regularly until the early 1970s.

Over the next three years, I participated in activities at Erie on a number of occasions. These included workdays painting and assisting in meal service at events connected to religious services. Aside from some commemorative plaques and photos on walls, however, I learned little about Erie's history. After my service as a deacon ended and I moved on to other responsibilities at our Evanston church, I seldom thought much about Erie.

However, when I began my research concerning the history of Protestant Italian families in Chicago. I took a closer look at Erie Chapel. Visiting Erie, I discovered that much of the staff and virtually all participants now were Hispanic. I also found that all old records concerning Erie were no longer there; whatever existed had been turned over to the Chicago Historical Society. In those archives, I learned much about Erie's history, a history that reflects the changing patterns of immigration in Chicago.

The institution that became Erie Chapel was started in 1870 as a small Dutch Presbyterian church located at Erie and Noble streets. At that time, the neighborhood was fairly well to do, comprised largely of Norwegian, Dutch, and German families.[12] In 1882, responsibility for the church was assumed by the Third Presbyterian Church of Chicago, several miles away at Monroe and Ogden Avenue on the city's near west side. Third Presbyterian renamed the church the Noble Street Mission and supported it as a mission responsibility.

By 1886, the Noble Street Mission had far outgrown its quarters. Memoranda in the files state that at that time "there was a Sunday School of some fifteen hundred, and it was known throughout the city for the crowds that attended." A new two-room "barnlike" building was constructed to house the mission's work.[13] In 1909, the Erie mission was reorganized as a separate church, the Erie Chapel Presbyterian Church.[14] At that time, the Sunday school had a regular attendance of more than eighteen hundred and the weekly preaching services reached more than six hundred adults every Sunday.

Those attending Erie were still primarily Protestants of Dutch, Scandinavian, and German descent. In the next several years, however, about the time the Balma family moved close by in 1913, the neighborhood changed rapidly. Protestant parishioners moved out to the west and north, and Catholic families—mostly Polish and Italian—moved in. Several Protestant churches closed their doors or moved to other neighborhoods. Roman Catholic churches and schools appeared.

As the population of the area became predominantly Catholic and worship and Sunday school attendance steadily decreased, Erie developed a neighborhood ministry with a wide range of institutional services, including English classes, citizenship classes, sewing and cooking groups, and other clubs and interest gatherings. A large preschool and kindergarten was established for children of mothers who were working or attending Erie events. Tiers of seats in one of the large meeting rooms were torn out to make a gymnasium.[15]

Many of the activities at Erie were conducted for decades in Italian as well as in Polish. Records are fragmentary, but reports in the archives show that in January 1918 an average of 104 persons attended Italian-language Sunday services at Erie. In February, the number had increased to 165, and in March an average of 149 attended. In addition to the Italian-language services, in the year from April 1917 through March 1918, Erie held a Polish-language Sunday service that claimed an average attendance of fifty persons and also an English-language service specifically for Poles that averaged thirty.[16]

Italian immigrants and their families continued to be the largest ethnic group at Erie Chapel Presbyterian Church for decades. As late as 1933 there were several mothers' clubs, the largest called "Buoni Amici [*sic*] ('good friends') for the old country Italian mothers."[17] Mothers' clubs were comprised of almost four hundred women, 75 percent of whom were reported to be Italian. Continuing through the 1930s, there were Italian-language Sunday morning worship services and afternoon Sunday school classes. Church membership was reported to be 446 persons, the predominant number of whom were Italian.

By the 1920s, Erie had outgrown the old building. In 1933, it was demolished and new facilities were constructed on the same site, at 1347 West Erie. In March 1936, the new building was dedicated as

Erie Neighborhood House. At that time, the population served was about 60 percent Italian, 20 percent Polish, and the balance sixteen other nationalities.

Participation in Erie Chapel activities, including Sunday school, vacation Bible school, and Camp Gray was an important socializing as well as spiritual experience for my mother and her sisters. They shared these experiences and growth with girlfriends from backgrounds other than the strict, conservative Waldensian heritage of the First Italian Presbyterian Church.

Waldensians in Piedmont were strongly anti-Catholic—and even more strongly anti-papist. The attitudes of isolation and of being a beleaguered people were deeply felt and did not abate when the Waldensians established themselves and their churches in the Americas. On the contrary, Waldensian immigrants regarded themselves as different. They kept much to themselves, largely restricting friendships and social contacts to their own people.

In these attitudes, the Piedmont Waldensians did not differ greatly from other Italian immigrant groups. Many commentators have observed that Italian immigrants in Chicago, as elsewhere, tended strongly to cluster with others from their same areas in Italy—even from their same villages.[18] The Waldensians added a religious overlay to that practice. In the immediate neighborhood where the Balmas lived, for example, many of the Catholic churches celebrated feast days commemorating one or another saint. These patron saint feast days were observed with decorations, banners, flags, illuminations, food stands, rides, games, at least one long street procession, often led by a statue of the saint carried from the sanctuary of the church, and, especially, the flying angels. A street festival was held almost every weekend.[19]

My Cicero cousins remember well the patron saint celebrations from their neighborhoods. As children, they particularly remember the "flying angels." Men tied heavy ropes between third-story windows across one of the main streets. During the festival, as a statue of the patron saint was carried in procession, two young girls wearing harnesses and dressed in flowing white dresses were pulled across the ropes on pulleys. They met in the middle and sprinkled rose petals on the crowd and procession below.

The Balma daughters did not venture from the confines of their Waldensian community to attend the Catholic patron saint festivals, which sometimes took place only a few blocks from their home. Although John remembers being a distant spectator to some of these celebrations when he was a young boy, there was little if any social involvement with Catholic families in their neighborhood.

Erie Chapel provided a broader social setting. The amalgam of the strict cultural and home experience of the Balma girls with the different backgrounds of their friends in a shared environment is well illustrated by a group photograph of my mother and her sister Catherine with others who were all apparently very happy participants in a club activity or class, perhaps at Erie. Because the Balma girls, adhering to old country custom, were not permitted to cut their hair, they are easy to pick out in the photo, as they undoubtedly were also easily identified at school or on the playground.

The strong anti-Catholic background of the Waldensians is reflected in the register of the Italian Presbyterian Church regarding a meeting of the session on January 5, 1915. The entry offers a hint at a doctrinal issue in the church on which James Balma appears to have been urging a stricter attitude toward Catholics. The minutes of the session meeting of that date state, "Mr. Balma made a motion about the 'padrine' at baptism asking that more attention be given in accepting Catholics."[20]

Padrine are godparents. This cryptic entry suggests James cautioned the session to be more careful about accepting Catholics as godparents in baptisms at the Italian Presbyterian Church. The register nowhere else notes any discussion or action on this motion.

In the confines of the family, the centuries-long anti-papist attitudes of the Waldensians did not disappear. My aunt Cleo recalls an occasion before her marriage in October 1942 to my uncle John, the youngest of my mother's siblings. Cleo proudly wore a new dress of a deep red or maroon shade to the Balma home. When Grandmother Marguerite saw it, she observed, "That's the Pope's color"—far from a compliment. Cleo did not wear the dress again in sight of Grandmother.

As they reached school age, all three Balma girls attended James Otis Grammar School, one block west of their home. Mary graduated after eighth grade in 1922. Kay graduated early, in January 1923 at age twelve and a half: because of overcrowding, the Chicago public schools eased the space problem by moving certain bright students ahead. The family moved to Narragansett Avenue during Helen's eighth-grade year; she graduated from O. A. Thorpe grammar school in 1925. John attended grades one through four at James Otis; he graduated from O. A. Thorpe in 1928. Kay, enrolled at McKinley High School when the family moved to Narragansett Avenue in March 1924, traveled back to the old neighborhood in order to finish her studies there. She graduated at age sixteen and a half in January 1927. Helen and John graduated from Carl Shurz High School.

My mother and aunts always spoke happily about the time they lived at 1420 West Ohio, attended the Otis school, and enjoyed the year-long variety of activities at Erie Chapel. Nonetheless, conditions at that location, as earlier at 814 Ohio Street, were in many ways harsh and unhealthy. Housing was crowded. Air quality was terrible. Streets were unpaved and dusty. Smoke, dust, cold, heat in summer, poor sanitation, close quarters, and congestion made life difficult and precarious.

My mother, Mary, was a sickly child. Her condition at times was so poor that it raised fears for her life among her parents and exposed the emotional toll the earlier deaths of five infants had taken on my grandmother. One occasion in particular remained vivid in the memory of my aunt Helen, four years younger than Mary. Helen recalled, even into her nineties, an event when she was very young. Mary was quite sick, with an extremely high fever. She was losing her hair. Grandma, bathing her in an ice-filled bathtub, was weeping hysterically, saying over and over that she was about to lose another child.[21]

Little Mary did not die on that occasion, of course. There were no more infant deaths. Mary lived until a week before her eighty-fifth birthday. Helen died at age ninety-six. Catherine and John live on in their nineties.

Mary did continue to suffer from health conditions that the family doctor warned were aggravated by life in the central city. As James later related, "And we had a very sickly old daughter that always had a headache and many visits to the doctor. The doctor was an old Norwegian, a good friend of ours, Dr. Hansen. Whenever he came to visit Mary he would always say [mimicking the doctor's Norwegian accent], 'Mr. Balma, why don't you move from along here? This is not a place to raise your family. You have to move out from along here. Find a place outside.'"[22]

Finally, they did move to a place outside. In early 1924 James sold his half of the Ohio Street property to Pasquale Servi and moved the family to the far west side of Chicago. The house was five blocks beyond the end of the streetcar line. The area consisted of city blocks that were mostly prairie with a few scattered houses. The streets were not paved. The large clay quarry and brick kilns were in full operation at Diversey and Narragansett avenues, a few blocks south of their house. James described the move:

> So finally I agree with Dr. Hansen, and we sell the place to my partner down there. I guess we make about a thousand dollar profit on the cash down there. With the cash money that I have we move to the sticks. Out here at 3422 [North] Narragansett Avenue. In those days it was the sticks. There were no streets paved. We have five blocks to walk to go to the first streetcar. I was working way down at Twenty-second and Ashland, so you see that I had to raise pretty early to go down there to be on time because my motive was to reach on time wherever I had to go, even to church I always tried to be on time.[23]

James and Marguerite purchased the house at 3422 North Narragansett Avenue on March 26, 1924, from the contractor who had built it and lived next door. A year later, James also bought an adjacent vacant lot from the same seller. Uncle John remembers the total price being $5,200.[24]

The girls were fifteen, thirteen, and eleven and John was eight when the family moved to Narragansett Avenue. Living conditions were much improved. Life at 3422 North Narragansett in a real sense was life in the country. The well-remembered pleasures of urban life with its many nearby attractions were gone, but so were the crowded, congested city conditions.

The house was comfortable, especially after the living room was enlarged by enclosing the front porch. There was a dining room, large kitchen, and two bedrooms on the first floor and a large bedroom that filled most of the second floor. I remember the house well; it had a steep, narrow stair to the attic areas around the second-floor bedroom that was a great attraction for me and my cousins. It also had a vacant side yard, with a lawn and a garden, and a rear yard between the house and garage that was furnished with a cherry tree, its large low branches perfect for climbing.

But my memories were made much later. The Balma children recall that it was the first time they had their own home and yard, and it had a telephone—a coin phone on a kitchen wall; Grandmother Marguerite was the keeper of the nickel trove. Payments for the mortgage were made once a year. To be ready, Marguerite regularly stored cash in a metal garbage can hidden in the basement.

James made wine in the basement each year for the family's use. The grapes were delivered in crates; John saved the wood in order to make various things. At least one barrel was set aside, not to be used until a year or more later.

In addition to the expansive play areas surrounding the house, the Johnson family across the street filled their large yard with an ice skating pond in the winter. Riis Park was several blocks away, but shortcuts across vacant lots and neighbors' yards shortened the trip.

There was no shortening the trip, however, to the many parts of their lives that took place in the central city. James lamented the long daily walk to the Irving Park streetcar, which he made very early to reach his job on the southwest side of the city and repeated later to return home in the evening. The girls lamented the same walk—especially in the winter—and the fact that the trips they each made to events in the city regularly took at least an hour. The situation changed, and travel became much easier, when bus service began on Narragansett Avenue.

For almost twenty years at three addresses on Ohio Street, the Balmas had lived in close proximity to many friends from families familiar to them from the Piedmont. They lived together, worked together, raised their children together, attended and supported the church together, and shared the joys, hardships, and sorrows of their lives. Like the Balma family, as the children grew, attended public schools, spoke English, became "American" and as family members maneuvered into better jobs and prospered, they moved away from the area. In time, they joined other English-speaking churches in different neighborhoods.[25]

By the mid-1920s, many fewer of the longtime members of the First Italian Presbyterian Church still lived in the old neighborhood. In October 1923, thirty of them were among the founding members of a new church, Samaritan Presbyterian at 2506 West Superior Street. At year-end 1926, the remaining parishioners at the First Italian Presbyterian Church on Ohio Street decided to combine their church with Samaritan. A new church, the Waldensian Presbyterian Church, was formed in April 1927 out of the merger.

The new church's initial board meeting was held on April 18, 1927. The first business was the treasurer's report by James Balma, who had announced he was retiring from office at the conclusion of the meeting.[26] Following almost twenty years of service, James Balma did not again hold an office in the church.[27]

From the time of their move in 1925 to the house on Narragansett Avenue, the Balma family had returned regularly to attend Sunday school, worship services, and other activities at the First Italian Church on their old 1400 block of Ohio Street. For several years, they continued to attend the new Waldensian Presbyterian Church. My uncle, John Balma, became a member of the church in 1927 after completing catechism classes. The Balma sisters taught in the Sunday school for years into the early 1930s.[28] Uncle John remembers that the sermon and other portions of the services were generally in Italian. In fact, Waldensian Presbyterian continued into the 1950s to be the only church in the Presbytery of Chicago ministering to Italian-speaking people.[29]

In the 1930s, Balma family members became dissatisfied with Waldensian Presbyterian Church and began to attend Moody Church at LaSalle Street and North Avenue in Chicago. By that time, Moody for more than fifty years had been the largest and most storied Protestant church in Chicago and one of the most famous evangelical churches in the world. The church traces its founding to the year 1858, when Dwight L. Moody, a traveling shoe salesman from Massachusetts, began a Sunday school mission for underprivileged children in an abandoned Chicago saloon. By 1860 the school had changed its location to larger halls as it attracted more than one thousand regular students. The children's parents had begun to attend, leading to additional services for them. That year, at age twenty-four, Moody retired as a shoe salesman to devote his full attention to the Sunday school and church missions. By the late 1860s he had become famous in the United States and Europe as a crowd-drawing evangelist. After outgrowing several other buildings, a new church that could hold ten thousand people, along with related structures, was built in 1876 at Chicago Avenue and LaSalle Street. In the last two decades of the nineteenth century, church attendance exploded as a result of Moody's evangelistic campaigns, consistently filling the auditorium to capacity, leaving overflow crowds to stand outside. After Moody's death in 1899, the church continued to prosper under others' leadership. In 1925 it moved to a newly constructed building at North Avenue and LaSalle Street, where it continues its ministries to this day.[30]

When the Balmas began to attend Moody Church in the 1930s, the auditorium that seats four thousand people was regularly filled. The church attracted worshipers from all over the city, including hundreds of young people who joined the many youth groups and relished the opportunities to meet new friends.

Aunt Helen remembered that the migration of family members to Moody Church began after she was "kicked out" of the Waldensian church by the pastor, Ernesto Merlanti. Helen had enrolled in evening classes at Moody Bible Institute after work. Reverend Merlanti gave her an ultimatum: she could not pursue studies at that school and continue as a Sunday school teacher at the Waldensian church. She left Waldensian Presbyterian, continued to take night classes at Moody Bible Institute, and was the first of the family to attend Moody Church.[31] John also remembers that the family left Waldensian because they were dissatisfied with Merlanti, who they thought was a "modernist" drifting away from the faith.[32]

Moody became the Balma's church home. The trip to the church was a long one, requiring a mile walk south on Narragansett to take the streetcar seven miles downtown. Later, gas and eventually electric buses replaced the streetcars. Every Sunday, James and the children made the trip to attend the Sunday school and morning services. They returned home for dinner. In late afternoon, the young people journeyed back to the city for youth groups and the evening service.

The family was accustomed to public transportation. For thirty years, James, Marguerite, and later the children rode streetcars and buses—and walked—everywhere. Life changed significantly in 1934. John, a favorite to many people at Moody Church because he often sang at services, was provided by an older friend there with the opportunity to buy a new 1934 Ford four-door sedan for $600. He persuaded his two working sisters, Mary and Kay, to join him in contributing $200 each to the purchase.

Black and shiny, it was a grand car that could carry the entire family and shift their reliance on public transportation.[33]

As young adults, the Balma siblings regularly attended the Christian Companionship Club at Moody Church. The "C.C. Club" was a fellowship that drew young people from all over the city. Helen Balma met Henry Molter, her future husband, there. John Balma met his future wife, Cleo Ellis, there. My wife's parents, James Pickett and Adelyn Anderson, met there. It was frequently said, "Everybody met there."

My mother became friends with Jim Pickett and Adelyn Anderson at the C.C. Club before they were married. Years later, she and Jim and Adelyn Pickett, joined by my father, would attend my marriage to the Picketts' daughter, Jan.

The oldest child in a strict Italian family in a new world, Mary engaged with her parents in an ongoing process of accommodation between the conservative, sheltering instincts of their traditional culture and the new culture and mores of a thriving American city in the 1920s and '30s. Leaving home to start public school in itself was a big step, even if the James Otis Grammar School was only one block from their home. At her graduation in 1922, Mary was the age, fourteen, when girls in Italian families traditionally were expected to assume much of the responsibility for the care of the house and younger children.[34]

Going off to high school was beyond what Mary's parents considered necessary at that time. High school not only involved traveling greater distances but also meant more time away from family and expected work at home. Mary did not start high school. Instead, she helped with the house and family and continued activities at Erie Chapel and the Italian church while considering what kind of work she could do.

Like many other young women, Mary, along with her parents, concluded that business school was the best option. It took two years. It was not far from home. It offered the concrete prospect of a steady and respectable job.

In the mid-1920s when she turned sixteen, Mary began full-time studies at Columbia Business College. Columbia was a well-known school offering courses at two locations, both not far from the Balma home. Over the next two years, Mary took some 2,300 hours of classes in bookkeeping, business administration, English, shorthand, typewriting, and general secretarial studies. She became a proficient operator of Underwood Bookkeeping Machines and mastered other bookkeeping, arithmetic, and calculating skills that she enjoyed using all her life. In her later years, after the disability and later death of my father, Mary easily found full-time work as long as she lived in the Chicago area. Following her move to a retirement community at Shell Point Village in Fort Myers, Florida, she continued full-time employment as an office worker for some years and, after retirement, helped support herself by handling bookkeeping and accounting for other residents of Shell Point.

In April 1929, Mary went to work as a bookkeeper for General Laundry Machinery Corporation at 822 West Washington Boulevard, taking charge of the company's accounts receivable records. Her employment terminated sixteen months later, on August 23, 1930, when the organization underwent significant change. The reference letter from the company at its closing describes Mary as "an experienced operator on the Underwood Booking machine" and states that "her work was always performed in a very satisfactory manner." The letter concludes, "It is with regret that we are compelled to dispense with her services due to the fact that we are disposing of our Laundry Machinery business and moving our General Offices to the East."[35]

The depression year of 1930 was not a good time to seek employment. Nevertheless, the skills Mary had learned in business school and sharpened in the workplace, combined in particular with the friends and families network among Italian Waldensians, enabled her to obtain work at the wholesale produce markets—a common workplace for Italian immigrant men but much less so for women. The move to the markets would change her life. There she would meet my father.

THE CICEROS OF GRAND AVENUE

Although Giuseppe's decision to leave Buffalo for Chicago may have appeared to be a precipitate and headstrong action, he and Antonina—with their older children—likely had spoken about making the move. Chicago was a logical and frequent destination for Italian immigrants in Buffalo. It was the magical and storied city at the other end of the Great Lakes.

Lake freighters that were loaded in Buffalo with raw materials and manufactured goods coming off the Erie Canal transferred their cargoes in Chicago to rail and canal transport headed for the great lands and cities of the West. The ships returned across the lakes to Buffalo with agricultural goods destined for the eastern seaboard by way of the Erie Canal. Chicago was prosperous; jobs were said to be plentiful.

For Sicilians whose lives centered on St. Anthony of Padua Church in Buffalo, there was an emotional tie to Chicago as well. St. Anthony had been organized by the Scalabrini Fathers in 1891. The order had been founded four years earlier in Milan by Bishop Giovanni Battista Scalabrini specifically to minister to the needs of immigrants. The Reverend Joseph Quigley, a Buffalo native who had served in that city as rector of St. Joseph Cathedral and later as bishop, had moved to Chicago as archbishop. In Buffalo, Father Quigley had been instrumental in organizing St. Anthony. He had been impressed thereafter by the work of the Scalabrini Fathers there. In 1903, in Chicago, Archbishop Quigley purchased the building at Grand and Peoria that had housed the Trinity Norwegian Lutheran Church, a historic structure built of brick in 1865 that had escaped destruction in the Chicago fire of 1871. Archbishop Quigley bought the building in order to serve Italians who had settled within the boundaries of the heavily Irish St. Stephen Church, dedicated it as Santa Maria Addolorata, and invited the Scalabrini Order to come to Chicago and take over the newly formed church.[36]

Undoubtedly, the parishioners at St. Anthony in Buffalo knew of and perhaps celebrated recognition of the fathers' work and expansion of it to the Chicago church. Additionally, the migration of Bishop Quigley to Chicago followed by the Scalabrini Fathers may well have inspired or at least given comfort to parishioners in Buffalo considering such a move.

In any event, Giuseppe and Antonina transferred their seventeen-member family to Chicago in the latter part of 1904. When they arrived in Chicago, the family settled in a basement apartment at 466 North Peoria Street, next door to the Santa Maria Addolorata Church. Most of the homes on Peoria and many in the neighborhood were tall, peak-roofed structures with three residence floors that virtually filled their twenty-five-foot lots, separated from each other only by narrow sidewalks. Most lots had another multistory house at the alley to the rear. The structure at 466

Peoria into which the Ciceros moved, however, was a much larger building on a wider lot, with four stories plus a sunken basement floor. Built to the lot line adjacent to the Addolorata Church, it is plainly visible in photos of the church. Another large multistory tenement building was behind it on the same lot at the alley. The two structures housed numerous families in several apartments.[37] The Ciceros' basement lodging had no outside entry door: the family had to enter and leave through a tall window.

The Ciceros' new home and church on Peoria Street at Grand Avenue, where they would live for thirteen years until 1917, were only a block and a half from the First Italian Presbyterian Church at 810 Ohio Street and the tenement at 814 Ohio into which James and Marguerite Balma had moved a few months earlier. The two homes were in the same Grand Avenue Italian colony in the densely occupied seventeenth ward.

Just as James and Marguerite Balma began to attend the Italian Presbyterian Church immediately upon their arrival on Ohio Street, Giuseppe and Antonina sought out the Santa Maria Addolorata Church. Antonina in particular was a habitual and devoted parishioner. She regularly went next door for confession. She particularly liked the fact that the church was staffed by Italian priests, some of whom spoke the Sicilian dialect. Although Giuseppe learned to speak some English, as did Antonina, apparently their English was never very good and Antonina felt much more comfortable conversing in Sicilian.

The place of religion in the lives of Sicilian immigrant families has been a subject of much discussion. While some writers and certainly many Italians emphasize the importance of church and religious life, for many in Sicily and southern Italy Christianity was only a thin veneer. Various types of magic rather than religion permeated their everyday lives. Rituals, symbols, charms, and other superstitions were extremely important. Many festivals celebrated patron saints, but their religious significance was often lost in the carnival atmosphere. Some writers assert that American priests serving in the immigrant communities were shocked by the Italians' indifference to the church. Antonina in particular but also others in the family were not indifferent to the church.

Indeed, with respect to Grandfather Giuseppe, I received a most memorable artifact from the trove of documents inherited by my newly discovered Sicilian cousin, Carmelo (1973), when I visited him in Sicily in March 2008: a prayer book that once belonged to Giuseppe. The book appears to be quite old, battered, undoubtedly secondhand when he acquired it, with some loose pages and many insertions of prayer cards. Bound in leather, the book is designated on the title page as selected prayers of the Catholic Church, translated from a sixth German edition by a Catholic priest and published by a Swiss company.

The book is remarkable to me because of a handwritten Italian inscription in the back:

> *Libro Riscattato Dalla Chiesa Dolorata Chicago Ill; 50 soldi 1905 Cicero Giuseppe fu Carmelo Da Montemaggiore Belsito provincia Palermo Italia*
>
> Book ransomed [*sic*] from the Dolorata Church Chicago Ill 50 cents 1905. Giuseppe Cicero son of the deceased Carmelo of Montemaggiore Belsito province of Palermo Italy.[38]

Apparently shortly after his arrival in Chicago, Grandfather Giuseppe purchased this little prayer book at the Santa Maria Addolorata Church.

Another handwritten inscription written sideways in the margin on the same page, again in Italian, reads, "From my brother Giuseppe 24 December 1939 Chicago, Illinois USA. Salvatore Cicero."

The date appears to be a mistaken reference to Giuseppe's death on December 23, 1929. Giuseppe's brother, Salvatore Francesco, who remained in Sicily, visited Buffalo and Chicago during the fall and winter of 1929–30 after his retirement from the Italian National railroad. He was with his son in Buffalo at the time of Giuseppe's death but was apparently designated by Giuseppe himself to receive the book. Salvatore Francesco, who for many years kept a meticulous diary that is now in the possession of cousin Carmelo in Ispica, apparently added the notation some years later and erred about the date.

Grandfather Giuseppe's prayer book is a significant memento of the grandfather I never knew, among other reasons for what it indicates about his attention to his church in his first months in Chicago.

Two years after Giuseppe and Antonina and their large family moved in next door to the Addolorata Church, the church was front-page news in the *Chicago Daily Tribune*. On Monday morning, February 25, 1907, the paper featured a story that headlined,

TRAMPLE THIRTY IN CHURCH PANIC;
Cry of Fire during Children's Mass Stampedes
Worshippers in Catholic Edifice on West Side

The cries of fire, the fire alarms, and the subsequent panic were a reaction to a cloud of steam that was mistaken for smoke when it was released from radiators by "three mischievous boys." The crush to escape downstairs from the second floor auditorium resulted in a "twenty person deep" pileup on a stair landing and many serious injuries.[39]

Ironically, the Santa Maria Addolorata Church that, as noted before, had survived the Great Chicago Fire, was destroyed in 1931 in a 4-11 alarm fire that left only the brick walls standing.[40] By that time the Ciceros were living three miles west on Central Park Avenue. The diocese purchased another Norwegian Lutheran church and reopened Santa Maria Addolorata a few blocks west of the old site. That church was razed in 1952 for the construction of the Northwest (now John F. Kennedy) Expressway, as were the former site of the church at Grand and Peoria and the tenement building at 466 North Peoria in which the Ciceros had lived. Curiously, the rebuilt Santa Maria Addolorata Church stands today at the corner of Ohio and Ada Streets, one block from the Ohio and Noble site of the First Italian Presbyterian Church that the Balma family attended for many years.

Although many records of the Addolorata Church were destroyed in the 1931 fire, some of the originals are preserved at the offices of the Chicago Archdiocese. They record significant Chicago milestones in Giuseppe and Antonina's family, as did St. Anthony Church in Buffalo. Thus, the register records the baptism on January 11, 1906, of my father's youngest brother, Stanislau Joseph, who was born December 27, 1905. The extant records also show the baptism on February 14, 1915, of my cousin Maria Angela Cicero, born January 26, 1915.[41] Mary was the daughter of Uncle Benny and Aunt Jenny.

The age span between the children of Giuseppe's and Antonina's first marriages and the children they had together was significant. The older children had very different lives from the younger ones. Giuseppe's sons, Carl and Ben, were eighteen and sixteen when the family moved to Chicago in 1904. Antonina's daughters, Calogera and Concetta (Jenny), were nineteen and thirteen. The children Giuseppe and Antonina had together ranged in age from my father, who was six, to Ross, who was one year old when the family moved to Chicago. The next year, 1905, the youngest child, Stanislau, called Joe, was born in Chicago.[42]

Part of the family also was Giuseppe's older daughter, Angela. Now called Angeline in America, she was twenty-four when the family moved to Chicago. She and her husband, Philip Leone, had three small children, ages five, three, and one. Giuseppe thus had grandchildren the same ages as his children with Antonina, and my father and his younger siblings lived with nieces and nephews their same ages.

In most respects life in Chicago for Giuseppe and Antonina and their family was typical of other Italian immigrants, especially those from southern Italy. All the older women maintained the household and assisted with raising the children; my father and his siblings remember that their half-sister, Giuseppe's daughter Angeline, was in effect a second mother to them. Although Giuseppe had lived off the land in Sicily, he worked as a laborer on the docks in Buffalo and in a mattress factory in Chicago. The older sons also worked from an early age to help support the family.

Carl (Carmelo), Giuseppe's oldest son, became established in business in Chicago very early on. The 1910 Chicago *City Directory* shows Carmelo in business with Anthony Arrigo manufacturing wagons. The 1917 directory lists his business as a company called Cicero and Arrigo at 2901 North Halsted; he lived a few blocks away at 1456 Addison. Giuseppe's younger son, Benny, worked as a laborer for several years until he secured a position as a buyer and farmers' contact at LaMantia Bros. Arrigo Co. at the Randolph Street wholesale produce market. Philip Leone, Angeline's husband, a foundry worker in Sicily, went into the foundry business with a man named Catalano under the firm name of Catalano and Leone.[43]

As they became established, Carl, first, and then Phil and Angeline Leone moved out of the family home on Peoria Street. Philip and Angeline, Carl, and others in the family were good examples of a common enterprising spirit among Sicilian immigrants. Although Giuseppe and Antonina apparently were renters all their lives, the others, like my grandparents on my mother's side, saved their money and as soon as possible bought real estate in which they could live.

As they came of age, the younger children began to attend school. Although Santa Maria Addolorata operated a parochial school on the lower floors of the church building, the Cicero children attended a public school. Montefiore School was located on Grand Avenue just across the alley west of the Addolorata Church; the public playground behind the school was only a few steps away from the rear of the lot at 466 Peoria, with the school immediately adjacent.

My father attended school through the fourth grade. His three younger brothers and his sister, Mary, all attended Montefiore School. Ross, Mary, and Joe completed school through the eighth grade. Tony may not have attended as long. Mary was the first to pursue education beyond elementary school. When she was completing eighth grade, the Montefiore principal arranged for a scholarship for Mary to attend high school. She enrolled in Holy Name High School for one year, traveling to and from school on the streetcar. Her brothers escorted her to the street-car in the morning and met her when she returned in the afternoon. After the single year of high school, she went to work.

My father always said he had to begin taking odd jobs at an early age. As a teenager he worked as a laborer and for a time in the same mattress factory as Giuseppe. He lived with his parents and the siblings who remained at home in the apartments on Peoria, Curtis, and Central Park Avenue.

The family dynamic was continually changing. In 1912, while the family lived on Peoria Street, Giuseppe's son Benny—who, of course, was my father's half-brother—married Jenny (Concetta) Scalia, Antonina's younger daughter—who, likewise, was my father's half-sister. They had lived as part of the same large family from the time Giuseppe's children, Benny, Carl, and Santa, arrived in Buffalo from Sicily in 1899 to join the group that included Antonina and her two daughters. After their marriage, Ben and Jenny continued to live with the family in the Peoria and Curtis Street apartments. Their first two children, Mary in 1915 and Joseph in 1917, were added to the family while they lived on Peoria Street. Later, when the Cicero families moved to Central Park Avenue, Ben and Jenny and their family settled into the first-floor flat beneath the apartment of Giuseppe and Antonina and their five children.

In 1917 Philip and Angeline Leone bought an apartment building at 529 North Curtis Street, on the corner with Ohio. That location was only four blocks west and a block north of the Peoria Street address; it was still in the heart of the old Sicilian neighborhood. (Curtis Street later was renamed Aberdeen. Both the Peoria and Curtis buildings were eventually torn down to build the Kennedy Expressway.) The same year Giuseppe and Antonina and the rest of the family that were still living in the basement apartment on Peoria Street moved to the Curtis Street building owned by Angeline and Philip.

The children remember that the Curtis Street building was grand. A six-flat apartment building, with three units on each side of a central entry and staircase, it had a semicircular corner with windows. Six separate families, totaling thirty persons, shared the building. Giuseppe and Antonina and their family lived on the second floor on the south side; they considered the apartment a luxury because it had a full bathroom and electricity throughout. Angeline and Philip Leone lived in another unit.[44]

The Curtis Street building, like the house on Peoria Street, was in the center of a traditional Italian neighborhood. The numerous festivals honoring patron saints, with their processions and flying angels, were celebrated each year. Many of the residents were peddlers. They kept their horses and carts in a barn a block away from the Curtis Street building.

A number of other Ciceros lived in the Curtis neighborhood. Most were peddlers of various types and people in the produce business at the markets. They were not relatives but descended from Ciceros that came from Cefalù and Cerda, Sicily, towns just to the north of Montemaggiore in the province of Palermo.

Social and community organizations, including in particular so-called settlement houses, played an important role for the Cicero family, as they did among immigrant populations generally. The Cicero children and young people participated in activities at the Chicago Commons. The Commons, at Morgan and Grand, was two blocks west of their home on Peoria Street and, later, two blocks east of their next home on Curtis.

Settlement houses were important reform institutions in the late nineteenth and early twentieth centuries. While Chicago's Hull House, founded in 1889, was the best-known settlement in the United States, Chicago Commons was one of the oldest. The Commons was founded in the early 1890s at the same time as the Northwestern University Settlement a few blocks north at Noble and Augusta and the University of Chicago Settlement near the stockyards on the near southwest side.

Commons founder Graham Taylor had come to teach at Chicago Theological Seminary. Following the pattern that gave settlement houses their name, he with his wife and four children moved into a large house—that is, *settled*—in the heart of the near northwest side immigrant area. With other "settlers" residing in the house, they shared their education, knowledge, and culture with impoverished, illiterate, or poorly educated neighbors, few of whom spoke English.[45]

Taylor and the other settlers started a kindergarten, clubs and classes, and a civic forum for discussion of current events. In 1901, Chicago Commons constructed a five-story building at Grand Avenue and Morgan with a gymnasium, auditorium, activities rooms, and living quarters for a dozen residents. In contrast to the smaller Erie Chapel and Neighborhood House four blocks away, which started as a mission outpost of the Third Presbyterian Church of Chicago and broadened into a settlement house in the early 1900s but continued as a Presbyterian institution, Chicago Commons and most other settlement houses founded in that period avoided any religious orientation.[46]

Several of the Cicero young people attended activities at Chicago Commons; some were more active than others and for a longer time. The youngest brother, Joe, met his future wife, Helen Schroeder, at Chicago Commons. Sara Pagliaro, whom Joe married after Helen's death, also became a close friend of the Cicero family at the Chicago Commons.

Other institutions provided educational activities as well. When she was in grades six through eight, my father's younger sister, Mary, attended cooking classes at the Washington School at Carpenter and Grand, three blocks west of their home. Along one wall of a basement room were long rows of gas burners. Children learned how to make full family meals in a program that stressed good dietary practices and hygiene. Following the afternoon session, they took home their "lessons" for consumption by the family, all in identical gray enameled pots.

By the time of the 1920 census, most members of the Cicero and Leone families who were living at 529 Curtis reported to the census taker that they were working outside the home. Giuseppe and Antonina's five children all remained at home. Giuseppe, my father Frank, then age twenty-two, and Ross, age seventeen, were all recorded as working at a mattress factory, Giuseppe and Frank as "helpers" and Ross as a machine operator.

Tony, age twenty, was doing clerical work at a fruit market, and daughter Mary, eighteen, clerical work at an auto factory. Fourteen-year-old Joe was simply recorded as living at home. At the same address, the 1920 census reports Phil Leone as a foundry worker and his two sons, age eighteen and sixteen, working for an electrical company and a mail-order house.

By 1920, Giuseppe's oldest son, Carl, had been established in business for years with members of the Arrigo family, a long-lasting relationship that would also prove beneficial to several other members of the Cicero family. Thus, in the early 1920s, Carl's connection to the Arrigo family led to employment for Tony Cicero, my father's next-younger brother, as a clerk at LaMantia Bros. Arrigo Co., a wholesale produce seller at the Randolph Street market. Tony was soon followed there by brothers Ben, Frank, Ross, and Joe. Ben's primary role was in "field work," traveling to contract with the farmers or making the purchases when the farmers brought their produce to market. My father was a salesman working the "floor" at the market, haggling throughout the day with buyers who ranged from small store and restaurant owners to buyers for some of the largest retail chains. Joe was employed as a dispatcher. Ross left LaMantia shortly after his marriage in 1924. The other four Cicero brothers worked at the firm into the 1950s, first at Randolph Street and later, when the market moved, at South Water.

As noted, at the time of the 1920 census, all five of Giuseppe and Antonina's children were living at home. By 1930, three of the five had married and moved into homes of their own. Mary, the only girl, was the first to marry. She was also the first of Giuseppe's eleven children to choose a non-Italian. Her courtship with a young man of German descent was apparently watched with considerable interest by her brothers and—although he feigned ignorance or disinterest—by her father.

Mary had worked as a clerk in a millinery store for a short time after her year in high school and later in a clerical job in an automobile factory. By her early twenties, she was a telephone operator and receptionist at the Fairbanks-Morse Company. There she met her future husband, John Thelen, when he made a business call. Fearing Giuseppe would be displeased that she was dating a man of German descent, John would bring her home early but try to avoid being seen. Mary's mother and her brothers all knew John, thought well of him, and were trying to figure out with Mary how to tell Giuseppe. The matter was resolved one cold winter evening, as Mary and John were outside saying good-night. Giuseppe spoke up loudly to Antonina in the living room, saying, "It's cold outside; why doesn't she invite him in?" Giuseppe did decree that when Mary and John went on dates a brother should accompany them, but he would have insisted on this rule regardless of her suitor's nationality. It was also an issue easily handled as she and John began regularly to double-date with at least one of her brothers. Later, Mary's two younger brothers, Ross and Joe, both also married non-Italians.

The Leones sold the six-apartment building on Curtis Street in 1922. At that time, the two Cicero families—Giuseppe and Antonina and their five grown children, and Ben and Jenny and their three young children—moved into a newly built two-flat apartment building at 1108 North Central Park Avenue, significantly farther west and north of the old, close-knit Italian community. Phil and Angeline Leone and their four children moved even farther west, to a house in the adjacent suburb of Oak Park.

Giuseppe and Antonina's household soon began to empty. Mary and John Thelen were married in June 1923. The next year Ross married Marge Nelson, who lived next door on Central Park Avenue and was the daughter of the contractor who had built the Ciceros' apartment building. (At the urging of his entrepreneurial father-in-law, Ross left LaMantia shortly after his marriage to enter a young, new industry. He became a movie projectionist, working his adult life in various theaters around Chicago.) In January 1925, Tony and Della Baldasso married and he moved from the family apartment. Thus Frank, their oldest child, and Joe, their youngest, were the only children living at home with Giuseppe and Antonina after 1925.

Grandfather Giuseppe Cicero died on December 23, 1929, six years before I was born. For most of my life, that was all I knew. I did not know where or how he had died. I did not know whether he had relatives or family in America, other than the uncles, aunts, and cousins who were direct descendants. I knew nothing about my grandparents' life in Buffalo and never heard anything suggesting that they or my parents had any contact with relatives there. I also believed—wrongly, as I learned—that Giuseppe had long been the lone member of his generation, severed from any ties or contact with the old country, and died with only relatively few descendants to know or care.

My understanding of my grandfather's life and connections all began to change very recently after I learned of the existence in Sicily of my second cousin, Salvatore Francesco Cicero (1931), and his son, Carmelo (1973). By very lucky happenstance, I received by an indirect route a copy of a letter Carmelo had mailed to every Cicero for whom he could find an address in Chicago. The letter included a family tree he had prepared and a note that he was looking for descendants of "Giuseppe Cicero, who died at 1108 Central Park Avenue on December 23, 1929." I did not personally receive a letter from him because I did not have a mailing address in Chicago. One letter, however, was opened by a woman named Susan Cicero, an administrator at a large law firm in the city. Although we had never met, she knew my name in legal circles. After checking with her father and learning that Giuseppe and the writer were not related to their line of Ciceros, she forwarded the letter to me in the event it might be pertinent to my family.[47]

Astounded upon reading the letter, I immediately sent Carmelo an e-mail message introducing myself and asking for information about him and his family. He wrote back promptly, explaining his family relationship and revealing that he had numerous documents concerning Cicero relatives in Chicago and Buffalo—letters, telegrams, legal documents, and other records—dating back to the nineteenth century. He sent me some samples.

One of the documents Carmelo forwarded to me provided the first evidence I ever saw of a tie in the twentieth century between relatives in Sicily and the United States. Carmelo's great-grandfather, Salvatore Francesco Cicero (1871)—a younger brother of my grandfather Giuseppe—had never emigrated from Sicily. But in 1929 he had made a lengthy trip to the United States to visit a son in Buffalo. Salvatore Francesco had been employed by the Italian National Railroad all his working life. Several years after his retirement, he had filed for and received a U.S. Immigration Service permit to remain in the United States for seven months, from August 5, 1929, through March 15, 1930. The application stated that the name and address of the son whom he intended to visit was Salvatore Cicero, who lived at 1471 Jefferson Avenue in Buffalo.[48]

There it was. My father's uncle, brother of my grandfather, had come from Sicily to the states to stay at the home of my father's cousin in Buffalo—this when my father was thirty-one years old and living in an apartment with his parents in Chicago. I had never heard of such a thing!

I subsequently learned from other documents that Salvatore Francesco—who came to be known as Uncle Frank to nieces and nephews in the United States—first had visited his son, Salvatore ("Sam"), in Buffalo in 1929. Sam had emigrated there from Sicily in 1920. Salvatore Francesco went on to visit his brother, Giuseppe, and other relatives in Chicago in the fall of 1929 before returning to spend more time in Buffalo prior to departing for Sicily.[49]

Further revelations came in two more of the many remarkable documents Carmelo provided. Also dated in 1929, they related to the death of Grandfather Giuseppe. The first was a Christmas card from my father's sister, my Aunt Mary Thelen, to Uncle Frank from Sicily, in care of his son Sam in Buffalo. A handwritten note on the card, dated December 22, 1929, informed Uncle Frank that his brother, Giuseppe, had "taken a turn for the worse."

Dear Uncle Frank,

Father is sick in bed doctor told him to stay there or that when he sits up he should put a chair under his legs. Has heart trouble, kidney trouble, and dropsy. Saw him today and he told me to wish you all a Merry Christmas and a Happy New Year. How are you all. John and I send our love to all of you. Sorry I couldn't be there when you left. I remain as ever.

Your neice [sic],
Mary Cicero Thelen[50]

The second document was a telegram from my uncle Benny sent the day after Aunt Mary's letter. The telegram, dated 9:04 PM, December 23, 1929, was addressed to Salvatore Francesco in care of his son in Buffalo. The telegram informed Salvatore Francesco that his brother, Giuseppe, had passed away that evening. It stated simply, "FATHER PASSED AWAY EIGHT OCLOCK THIS EVENING. BEN CICERO."[51]

These two communications were striking to me. They were the first elaboration I ever received on the timing and circumstances of my grandfather's death. Even more, they were the first evidence I had of direct communications from a member of my family in Chicago to a Sicilian relative. In addition, they revealed that a relative had visited Chicago and was in Buffalo at the time of my grandfather's death with another relative who, at least in 1929, resided in Buffalo.

There were more. My grandmother Antonina had sent handwritten letters to Salvatore Francesco in 1930 at the address in Buffalo after Giuseppe's death. One of them referred to Salvatore Francesco having made a visit to Chicago in the fall of 1929 and later having been hurt in a fall on the ice in Buffalo, an injury that delayed his return to Sicily.[52]

The Christmas card from my aunt Mary and telegram from my uncle Ben to Giuseppe's brother about Grandfather's final illness and death revived memories on the part of my cousin Elaine, Ben and Jenny's younger daughter, who was eight years old at the time. Their family lived in the first-floor apartment on Central Park Avenue below the grandparents' flat. Elaine recalled that Giuseppe was very ill, suffering from "dropsy" (edema) and other ailments. She had been upstairs at her grandparents' apartment while the family was decorating Giuseppe and Antonina's Christmas tree but had returned with her mother to the first floor. They heard a loud bump from upstairs. Jenny ran to the upper flat and learned that her stepfather, Giuseppe, who had been up and moving around, had suddenly collapsed and fallen to the floor. He died within hours.

Giuseppe on his deathbed asked to see a valued photo of his mother, Angela Nicosia (1830). This account, which had been passed down from Giuseppe's brother, Salvatore Francesco, to his son Carmelo (1899) and his grandson Salvatore Francesco (1931), was passed along to me by his son, Carmelo (1973), in one of his early letters. To my knowledge, I had never seen a photograph of my great-grandmother Angela Nicosia. Carmelo soon sent me a wallet-sized photograph that had been handed down in his family. The image was a close-cropped picture of her head only; it appeared to have been cut from a larger photograph.

With Carmelo's photo in hand, my sister Nancy began another search of her collection of photos accumulated by our mother, which Nancy had possessed since Mother's death. Among them she found what appears to be the photo from which the small head-only image was cut. It is a portrait photograph of Great-grandmother Angela Nicosia with two of her grandchildren mounted on a cardboard backing with an embossed frame. The reverse bore stamped imprints showing it had originally been taken by an itinerant photographer from a studio in Palermo and had been copied by a photo studio in Buffalo. The reverse also bore an inscription to my grandfather Giuseppe showing that it had been sent to him by someone in Buffalo.

The photograph is plainly the one that was at Grandfather Giuseppe's side when he died. It was among his widow Antonina's possessions when she passed away at our home in February 1937.

When Nancy and I originally saw this photo years ago in one of our mother's keepsake boxes after her death, we had no idea who the people were. The excised portion sent by Carmelo had identified the woman for us. The photograph is now a valued keepsake of ours, the only image our grandfather had of his mother, Angela Nicosia.[53]

Antonina's home that once was full of family was now reduced to herself, her oldest son, Frank, and her youngest son, Joe. Close by, of course, she still had her other children, stepchildren, and numerous grandchildren.

Frank, Joe, and Ben continued to work at the market, employment that required six twelve-hour or longer workdays each week beginning hours before dawn. Life was changing as the working men were able to buy automobiles, shortening their travel time to and from work and increasing the families' mobility to accomplish necessary errands and enjoy a wider range of activities in whatever leisure time they had.

Joe, in his twenties, was courting Helen Schroeder, whom he met at Chicago Commons. They married and Joe moved from the Central Park apartment in July 1934. As for my father, I do not recall ever hearing anything from him or other family members of church or social organization activities. Small wonder, I suppose, that he met the woman who would become his wife while he was at work.

14

Bridging the Divide

THE LARGEST WHOLESALE produce market in Chicago in the early decades of the twentieth century occupied the area along Randolph, Fulton, and South Water Streets, from the Chicago River west to several blocks past Halsted Street. The market was squarely in the northwest side Little Italy described earlier. Mary went to work for the Grill and Berger wholesale produce house at Randolph and Green streets, five blocks south of her birthplace at 814 West Ohio Street. "Grill" and "Berger" were Messrs Grilli and Bergere, both Italian Waldensians from the same area in Piedmont as the Balmas.

The Grill and Berger firm was not large. As was common at the markets, it shared storefront space with another small firm. It also struggled to succeed and pay its workforce. After two years, Mary moved to a better-paying office position in a nearby wholesale produce house. LaMantia Bros. Arrigo Co. was one of the largest firms at the market, occupying two full storefronts on Randolph Street and employing several times as many people as Grill and Berger. Among the staff were four Cicero brothers. One of them, Frank, would become my father.

The produce market was a turbulent place. The salesmen, buyers, shippers, truck drivers and laborers who worked on the three floors of the wholesale houses among high stacks of crates and bushels of fruit and vegetables were loud, tough, and profane. A sale and purchase transaction was often a shouted negotiation; a salesman might be dealing with several different buyers on the telephone and in person at one time. In the office where Mary worked, the noise level was lower, with little of the shouted invective common on the sales floors. Activity was constant, however:

salesmen and others came in and out of the office continually throughout the day.

Mary met Frank as soon as she started at LaMantia. Frank's younger brother, Tony, worked alongside Mary in the office, but no one could ever recall whether he introduced them or exactly how they met.

Although the men on the sales floors were often profane in dealing with each other, my mother said that all were gentlemen and treated her as a lady. Nevertheless, walking the floors at LaMantia and the streets of the market was undoubtedly a very different experience from the Waldensian society in which she had grown up.

Mary and Frank began dating in 1933. By early 1934, Frank, who owned an automobile, was driving her home every day after work. By summer their relationship had passed beyond dating to serious courtship, accompanied by valentines, notes, and letters expressing their love and, when Mary was away at Camp Gray, how much they missed each other.

Mary spent her summer vacation in 1934 at Camp Gray in Saugatuck, Michigan, the camp she had first begun to attend as a young girl at Erie Chapel. By this time she was twenty-six years old. It had been nine years since the Balma family had moved from 1420 Ohio, around the corner from Erie Chapel, to "the sticks" on Narragansett Avenue. Mary was one of several close friends who had maintained contact with Erie and continued to participate in activities there. They had gone to Camp Gray as children; as young adults they returned each summer to the wooded dunes on the shore of Lake Michigan.

I do not know when Frank first met any member of Mary's family. I do know that the family did not regard her friendship with him well. The fact that he was Catholic was a very serious matter, likely aggravated by the fact that he was Sicilian.

When Frank and Mary first began to date, James and Marguerite were concerned. Reflecting the centuries-long attitudes of Waldensians in their valleys, they did not think a Waldensian girl should be in a romance with a Catholic boy. As the relationship grew more serious, James and Marguerite made more explicit their opposition to Mary seeing Frank. Mary's next-younger sister, Catherine (Kay), however, was more than simply unhappy: she strongly and outspokenly opposed their relationship. When Mary made clear that she and Frank were planning to marry, Kay argued against the family doing anything to recognize or celebrate the marriage; she convinced her parents there should be no wedding party of any kind.

Mary and Kay were very close in age. They shared the same circle of friends. According to my mother, Kay succeeded in preventing their friends from holding a wedding shower or other party for Mary. Kay also sought to persuade their friends to boycott the wedding ceremony and tried to make them promise to shun Mary if she went ahead and married Frank.

The pressure on Mary can readily be imagined. Raised in the centuries-old anti-Catholic reformed faith and in a close-knit circle of family and church-centered friends, she was pursuing a course against all that she had been taught. Many of her friends turned against her. She knew that no minister at Moody Church would bless a marriage with a Catholic, particularly in the face of her family's staunch opposition. She could not go back to Reverend Merlanti at Waldensian Presbyterian; his reaction might well be harsher than all the others, and in any event she and her family had parted company with him and his church.

Mary and Frank had discussed the issues raised by their different faiths. The Roman Catholic Church imposed on its member of an interfaith marriage the obligation to raise any children in the Catholic faith. The Waldensian Church held the same belief just as strongly as a matter of expression of the true faith. Mary also firmly believed that any children should be raised as Protestants. Frank agreed. Although he was not prepared to convert from Catholicism, he was willing to make that concession.

I always heard that my parents "ran away" to get married. I never cross-examined my mother for details but always assumed that they were married at the county clerk's office or, perhaps, by some other civil official.

In a fashion, they did run away. It was Saturday morning, February 2, 1935. Mary and her two sisters shared the upstairs bedroom in the Narragansett Street house. Helen recalls, "I awoke in the middle of the night. Mary was getting ready and left early in the morning before others were up. Mary motioned to keep quiet and left." Helen did not know why Mary was leaving but said nothing to anyone. Helen remembers the specific date: she was looking forward to her "first real date" with her future husband, Henry Molter; that afternoon they were going to see the Ice

Capades at the Chicago Stadium. When Helen returned home from the stadium, she learned that Mary and Frank had come to the house earlier and told the family that they had married.[1]

The wedding plan was not a secret to everyone. In researching the family history, I came upon an old cardboard stationery box of my mother's. After her death in 1993—a week before her eighty-fifth birthday and fifty-eight years after her marriage—the box was among the things I took when my brother, sister, and I cleared out her apartment. I had never focused on it before.

Inside were a small number of old documents, well-worn and often-folded letters, cards, and telegrams, yellowed newspaper clippings, baptismal and birth certificates for her and my father, and other keepsakes. Among them, carefully stored in a special slide-in envelope, was a five-by-eight-inch white bound booklet, the *Marriage Service from the Book of Common Worship,* published by the Presbyterian Church. At the front is a certificate attesting to the marriage of Frank Cicero and Mary M. Balma on the second of February, 1935. The service was performed by the Reverend Pasquale R. De Carlo; he signed the church marriage certificate and also the civil marriage license and certification.[2]

I was stunned. I realized for the first time that my parents in fact were married in a church. Indeed, in 1935 it was the largest Presbyterian church in the Chicago area ministering to Italian immigrant families, St. John Presbyterian

The minister at St. John's, Reverend Pasquale Ricciardi De Carlo, was a storied figure among the Italian immigrant population in Chicago and the ministers and priests serving that community. An immigrant himself, born in Italy in 1863, he came to the United States in 1888 at age twenty-five to establish himself in business. He did so successfully. By his own story, De Carlo converted from Catholicism after receiving a Bible from a former priest who urged him to read it. De Carlo became zealous to spread the gospel of Jesus Christ. He began by spending his time and a large part of his money establishing missions in Providence, Rhode Island, Springfield, Massachusetts, several cities in Connecticut, and Detroit, Michigan.[3]

De Carlo felt called to Chicago in 1914. He began his work at the mission at 567 Taylor Street, founded in the 1890s by the First Italian

Presbyterian Church. First Italian had operated it for many years and in 1908 had sponsored its separation into a stand-alone entity.[4] De Carlo initially renamed the mission the Italian Christian Institute. In 1919, De Carlo moved the institute west to 1206 Taylor Street and renamed it the Garibaldi Institute. The Garibaldi Institute remained an active Presbyterian neighborhood house for decades.

In 1930, a group of Italian men and women organized St. John Presbyterian Church out of the Garibaldi Institute with Reverend De Carlo as its minister. With the aid of the church extension board of the Chicago Presbytery, St. John's church purchased a large building at Harrison and Hoyne.[5] A sizeable Italian congregation soon was attending weekly worship services and Sunday school at St. John's as well as a summer vacation Bible school that attracted hundreds of Italian children.

My grandfather, James Balma, and Reverend De Carlo knew each other from their work together in the Chicago Presbytery. De Carlo was also known to Mary and others in the Balma family. Entrepreneurial, open-minded in attitude, practical, outreaching, and also a converted Catholic, De Carlo was someone Mary apparently felt she could ask to perform the wedding, and De Carlo was willing to do so. It is interesting to wonder whether Grandpa James played any role in Mary's arrangement with De Carlo.

In any event, the Reverend Pasquale De Carlo united Frank Cicero and Mary Balma on Saturday morning, February 2, 1935, at St. John Presbyterian Church. The two witnesses to the marriage, and the only people at the wedding other than the bride, groom, and minister, were Nida Richard, Mary's very close friend—who was also a good friend of Mary's sisters, Catherine and Helen—and John Balma, Mary's nineteen-year-old brother. Mary had asked John, with whom she was very close, to be a witness at the wedding. He and Nida drove to the church that morning in the 1934 Ford.

At a later time, five others added their congratulations below Nida's and James's signatures in the marriage book. They were Nida's sisters, Sue and Evelyn Richard, and Grace and Mary Cultan—all four close friends of the Balma sisters. Later, Mary's sister Helen also signed the marriage book. Catherine never did.

Following the service, John returned home. He had kept Mary's secret and had not told anyone about the wedding. He believes, however, that his parents knew or strongly suspected where he was going that morning. Mary and Frank also drove to the Balma home after the ceremony to tell the family about their marriage.

In addition to the obvious forewarning to Nida Richard and John Balma, the upcoming wedding was publicized at the market where both Mary and Frank worked. A small news article appeared days before the wedding among the columns of produce price quotations in Chicago's daily market newspaper. It read,

What A Man!!

Well let the bells ring out—who cares. Let freedom reign again for the moment, but 'tis rumored that one Frank Cicero, of the LaMantia Bros. Arrigo Co., takes his marriage vows Saturday. The young lady is none other than Mary Balma. If this be the truth, good luck to the newlyweds and please Frank your good wishers want you to know that running a boss in the home is a heck of a lot different than selling vegetables.[6]

When Mary and Frank returned to the Balma home after the wedding, mother Marguerite insisted that they stay for dinner with the family. The newlyweds then went to the Palmer House, one of Chicago's grandest hotels, where they spent their combined wedding night and one-night honeymoon. The bill totaled $9.40: $7.00 for the room and $2.40 for breakfast at the restaurant.[7]

Sunday, February 3, 1935, Mary moved into the second-floor apartment at 1108 Central Park Avenue where Frank lived with his mother, Antonina. Monday, Frank went to work at the market. Mary did not return to work after their marriage.

Mary soon was pregnant. On November 30, 1935, I was born at St. Elizabeth's Hospital in Chicago. I was named Frank Jr. after my father, with no middle name or initial because he had none and it was important to him that I be a "Junior."

From anything I ever heard, my parents' life with his mother during the two years following their marriage was a harmonious one. Mary and her mother-in-law liked each other and got along well. Mary also liked

Ben and Jenny, her brother- and sister-in-law who lived downstairs in the first-floor apartment, and their family; indeed, Mary and Jenny were quite close until Jenny's death in 1942.

Culturally, there may have been some friction, although I never heard of specific issues. My mother continued to attend Protestant churches after her marriage. I do not know where she worshipped during the year she lived in the apartment on Central Park Avenue. Nor do I know whether I was ever baptized as an infant or, if so, where. After our family moved to Neva Avenue at the far western boundary of Chicago, my mother, brother, and I attended Sunday school and worship services at the Judson Baptist Church on Austin Avenue in Oak Park.

I did hear often from my mother as well as from my Balma aunts and uncles that Mary learned to "cook Sicilian" while she was living with her mother-in-law. The dish most often cited as an example was ravioli, a detail I find ironic since, while my mother did prepare it for special occasions, she always complained about the labor involved in hand making each piece. She also cooked many other dishes with red sauce, which historically was not a part of the Piedmont tradition. Whether red sauce had been used in the Balma home, I do not know, but it definitely became part of her cuisine after her marriage.

In 1936 my father and Uncle Benny moved their families into two new houses they had built on Neva Avenue, the last street before the far west side city limits of Chicago. The houses were identical, except that the plan was flipped so that both, though built on opposite sides of the street, could have a screened porch off the dining room on the sunny south side. The screened porch was without doubt the single-most important element of the house to my father, perhaps due to the crowded, dark basement quarters in which he had lived until he was seventeen.[8]

The porch at 1709 North Neva was a prototype for my father. He elaborated and "improved" it at the two other homes he later owned. Each porch, on the next house in Westchester and the last house in Western Springs, was larger than the previous one, with a much more intricate system of awnings and pulleys.

Grandmother Antonina moved into the Neva house with us. In less than a year, she died at age seventy-five on February 24, 1937. She was buried in Mount Carmel Cemetery alongside Giuseppe. My younger brother, James Joseph, was born a year later, on March 10, 1938. He received two names, those of our grandfathers.

Five years later, on January 21, 1942, my other grandmother died. Marguerite Balma had been suffering from asthma for a long while—probably a result of the same poor air quality conditions that had caused such peril for her daughter, Mary. The illness became much worse each year, eventually weakening her heart. She was buried in Mount Olive Cemetery on Narragansett Avenue, two blocks north of the family home, where her two infant daughters, Elena and Emma, had been interred thirty-five years earlier in February and September 1907. Doctor Porter of Moody Church conducted the services at the funeral home; he had been a friendly visitor to the Balma family home a number of times. Marguerite particularly liked him and appreciated his visits. Her poor understanding of English made it difficult for her to enjoy the services on the infrequent occasions she attended church.

Shortly after Marguerite's death, James Balma received a gracious letter from the Reverend Pierre Griglio on the letterhead of the First Waldensian Church of New York. After condolences and warm praise for Marguerite's personal qualities, Reverend Griglio described her as "one of our earliest immigrants to this City" and referred to her having "faithfully carried out her tasks here." The letter is of interest because it indicates that there was ongoing communication between Waldensian communities in New York and Chicago and because it refers to Marguerite's immigration through New York thirty-eight years earlier.[9]

* * *

Life on Neva Avenue was life in the country for children. Our house was one of only three on the entire block. All the rest was "prairie," as Chicagoans called any vacant lot overgrown with wild grasses. We could run, play, dig foxholes, hide treasures in vast open spaces. The same was true of the next block south, on which Uncle Ben's house was located. His place had an added attraction, however: behind it on the west half of the block was a ball field enclosed by a high wood fence with the entrance on Harlem Avenue, the western boundary of the city of Chicago. On summer evenings it was the site of softball or soccer games played in one of the leagues of tavern or local business-sponsored teams. I would join my favorite and idolized cousin, Benny and Jenny's youngest son, Anthony, and some of his friends—they were very mature, all being ten years older than I—in climbing out a rear attic window to sit on the adjacent garage roof looking over the fence and watching the games played under the lights. A special treat was on promotional nights, which drew a capacity paying crowd to watch the donkey softball games, contests of particular skill by players riding donkeys, which they could dismount only to pick up a ball from the ground, after which they had to re-mount before making their next move.

We lived in the Neva house until two weeks after my tenth birthday. I played in the prairies, ran with neighbor kids, attended the Sayre School two blocks from our house from kindergarten through the middle of the fourth grade, and generally lived the carefree life of a young boy.

Several things stand out in memory from the years we lived there. First, because Uncle Benny's house was only a block away, I saw much of the Cicero cousins who were part of Benny's large family, as well as other Cicero cousins, aunts, and uncles who visited there often. They were all ages. Some of the older aunts—in particular my father's two half-sisters on his father's side of the family—spoke English with very heavy accents; one, I recall, I could hardly understand. They had arrived in America at ages sixteen and twenty-three and never attended school, spending their time at home among family, maintaining households and caring for children. I do not remember the uncles, who had all gone to public schools in Chicago and worked outside the home, as having such strong accents or, indeed, any accent at all. Whether that was the case or whether I interacted with them in a different way, I do not know.

Apart from the fascinating excitement and confusion of this vibrant family, I remember most the fact that cousins exposed me to mysteries of their Catholic faith. They did not eat meat on Friday. They attended something called *mass* that, as they described what occurred there, sounded spooky and strange. The boys also groused especially about having to be there early to serve as something called an *altar boy.* They complained about having to go to confession on Saturday mornings and to something called *catechism,* also a very strange word to me. There were wedding masses on Saturday morning—my child's impression was that they fasted before mass, but I don't know if that was true—followed by celebratory lunches. I heard about and occasionally saw rosary beads, but I had no idea what they were for. There were crucifixes hanging in almost every adult bedroom, always, it seemed, over the bed, something that gave each room a haunted feeling. I never had a conversation about what any of these things was or meant. They were just part of the background noise of what their families were and ours wasn't.

World War II was, of course, the second thing that was life in those years. I was present at the beginning. I remember my mother—I think after receiving a phone call—hurrying into the living room, where I was playing on the floor, in order to turn on the radio because something important had occurred. An elaborate wooden floor model perhaps three feet tall, the radio was the dominant piece of furniture in the center of one wall. I lay on my stomach, my head propped on my elbows a few inches from the wood-framed fabric cover of the speaker, listening to news bulletins and the recorded words of President Franklin Roosevelt describing the day that would live in infamy. The memory of that Sunday afternoon, December 7, 1941, is the earliest I can place in time. I recall no other that was earlier.

Compared to millions of others, our family was little affected by the war. My father, who had celebrated his forty-third birthday on November 25, 1941, five days before my sixth, was never called to serve in the military, although my mother worried much throughout the war that he would be. I do not know why he was not drafted. I remember hushed conversations about the matter, but I never knew what was being said. My father continued to be employed at LaMantia Bros. and to bring home every Friday the crate of assorted vegetables that was a welcomed perquisite of his job. We had a fine automobile. Dad, who liked substantial new cars—and apparently had courted my mother in one—had bought a 1941 Buick in the summer just before the war broke out. We had rationing, of course: food and gasoline stamps and perhaps others. We worked on paper and scrap metal drives and other activities to support the war effort, but our family life was not disrupted.

I was hugely fascinated by the war. I followed with great interest the amphibious invasions of the Pacific Islands, starting with Guadalcanal and proceeding up the line toward Japan until the finale at Okinawa. I had my own longest days in the print and radio news after the Normandy invasion in June 1944. I knew all the big battles and the names of the generals who led the conquering Allied forces. I made aircraft models and could identify all the Allied and Axis planes. I took action myself: with my younger brother and my buddy Bob Gonnella of the family that owned the largest Italian bakery in Chicago, we dug sod-roofed foxholes in the prairies beside our house and fought off the "Jap" and Nazi invaders.

By the later years of the war, as I grew older and more aware, I heard my father complain frequently about his work for LaMantia Bros. He thought he was treated badly and that his contribution to the business was not recognized by owners "J.V" LaMantia and his son, "P.J." Uncle Benny, Dad's older brother, shared that view. In the early spring of 1945, Dad and Benny decided to go into business themselves. I remember weekend planning meetings of Benny, my dad, and my mother around our dining room table. Mother was gathering purchase orders, sales receipts, invoices, and other business forms—all imprinted with a new "Cicero Brothers" logo—and other supplies that she knew were necessary for the business. Benny was responsible for the contacts with farmers and shippers to arrange for the produce to sell. Dad was handling the arrangements with prospective customers. They obtained shared space at another wholesale house at South Water market, where the old Randolph and Fulton markets had relocated.

After weeks of planning and work, early on a Monday morning they opened for business. The company lasted three long, pressure-filled, and—they said—very successful days. Toward the end of the second day, the Cicero brothers were visited by J.V. and P.J. LaMantia. Although there were implications that I—a nine-year-old—thought I heard of men in overcoats with pulled-up collars making implied threats, my parents maintained that they were bought out by the LaMantias in a friendly transaction. Benny and Dad closed shop and returned to LaMantia on Thursday.[10]

The Cicero brothers' abortive business venture, as well as the triumphant end of World War II shortly thereafter with V-E Day in May and V-J Day in August, were overshadowed by an event that changed forever our family life. During the early morning hours of a Sunday in July 1945, my brother and I were wakened by a commotion in the hallway our room shared with our parents' bedroom. Sitting up in bed, I watched as uniformed men wheeled our father out on a gurney to a waiting ambulance. Dad had suffered a heart attack so severe that Dr. Lavieri, our longtime family doctor, told Mother he was unlikely to live out the day.

After early critical days—initiated by a clamorous arrival at the hospital, where my father was placed in a room to share with a heavy smoker, causing my mother, the doctor, and some intimidated attendants to move the smoker's bed out of the room and push it down the hall away from Dad—and weeks of hospitalization, my father returned home to a drastically altered lifestyle. He was disabled from working the remainder of the year and did not return to the market until the spring of 1946. The heavy smoking and drinking, the overeating and extra pounds were curbed.

With my father unable to work, my parents sold the Neva Avenue house to save their capital and move into less expensive rental housing. Shortly before Christmas in December 1945, we set up in an old house at 523 North Catherine Avenue in La Grange Park. The new location was a significant change for children of immigrants who had known nothing but Chicago city life. La Grange Park was an old, leafy suburb with broad streets, huge elms, old homes, and the feel of a country village. At the corner of our block was a family-run grocery store that carried almost everything a household needed—except meat, which was supplied by the butcher shop next door.

The house was an adventurous playground for my brother and me and our cousins when they visited. Probably built early in the century, the three-story frame structure had a broad front porch and a large bay in the living room. The kitchen was original, with an ice-box refrigerator for which an iceman made semiweekly deliveries and a gas stove that must have been one of the oldest in town. A wide two-landing staircase connected the first and second floors and had a banister perfect for sliding. The second-floor bedrooms—there were several—had closets that were long and narrow and turned corners with niches and recesses ideal for hide-and-seek games. The third floor, at the top of a narrow staircase, had a couple of storage rooms and a big attic that was only partially floored and had no insulation beneath the roof.

The basement was the most interesting new experience. Down a narrow stair from the kitchen, dark, enclosed by a stone foundation, it was dominated by a coal-burning furnace fed by a coal-devouring stoker that was supplied from a large coal "bin" that was one of the larger rooms in the basement. As soon as we moved in, my brother and I learned that it was our job at least once and sometimes twice daily to fill the stoker by shoveling coal from the bin and to clean out the ashes and "slag" from the roaring furnace. We also learned early that jumping into and burying ourselves in the peaked coal pile formed by the coal-truck deliveries—from which we emerged coated with black coal dust—was not an accepted form of play. That lesson was also grasped by some cousins when they visited and we "forgot" to warn them against such fun.

I loved the house, the neighborhood, Ogden School a mile away to which we bicycled every day, rain or shine, pomegranates from the corner grocery store that stained our hands and clothes, the ramshackle dirt-floored garage that provided a wonderful gym in bad weather, and the Oak Junior High School playground across the street. But we did not stay long. About the time that there was no longer a need to shovel coal, in April 1946, my parents bought a house in Westchester and we moved there.

Also a suburb of Chicago, Westchester was very different from La Grange Park. It was closer to the city, adjacent to communities that were more working class, but almost entirely undeveloped. Westchester had been on the cusp of a boom in the late 1920s when the Depression hit. An "El"—the Chicago electric transit railroad line—had been extended to end there in the middle of broad blocks of open prairie. A residential housing developer had started a community of single-family homes and abandoned them as brick-walled shells with roofs and varying degrees of interior framing. Almost two decades later, at the beginning of the post-war boom, new contractors finished the old structures.

Like many others, my parents had the home-owning ethic. They did not like renting, and my mother intensely disliked the ancient kitchen in the La Grange Park house. When my father went back to work at the market in the early spring of 1946 and they found the comparatively less expensive Westchester house and community, they seized the opportunity to buy one of the small, newly finished Depression-era bungalows. At spring break, my brother and I left the grand old two-story yellow brick Ogden school in La Grange, with its spacious large-windowed classrooms and wide halls, and finished our third and fifth grade years at a public school annex in the basement of a Lutheran church, where two grades shared each cramped classroom.

Two things stand out in my memory of Westchester. The first was important. In July 1946, a few months after we moved into the house on Manchester Street, my sister, Nancy Joan, was born. I never knew where those two names came from. I did learn soon that—eight and ten years younger than my brother and me, and a girl, besides—she added a whole new dimension to life in our family.

The second was much more trivial in the broad scheme of things but at the time much more fun. For a dime we could board the El in Westchester, ride it all the way to downtown Chicago, change trains at the large, elevated station outside Marshall Field's in the Loop, and ride to Wrigley Field, the home of the Chicago Cubs, on the North Side. (We also could have taken it south to Comiskey Park to watch the White Sox, but the thought never occurred to us.) We would show up early, well before batting practice, as the Cubs players were arriving at the ballpark. We would stay all day, roaming from one end of the upper deck to the other, watching batting practice, chasing foul balls, paying attention to at least some of the game, and remaining afterward in a quest for autographs as the players left the park. Then we would reverse the trip for another dime, sometimes arriving home after dark.

With my father back at work, our lives returned to the new normal, with a baby girl as part of the mix. Our years were filled with school, lessons, model-making, family vacations at lakes in Michigan or Minnesota. For these, beginning in 1948, we had a new car, a 1948 DeSoto. My father always announced his intention to buy a car by just showing up with it one day after work. I do not recall any discussion about buying a new car, and certainly my opinion on the matter was never sought. The purchase of the DeSoto was a double surprise—it was a new car, but it was not a General Motors brand, a huge shift from Dad's oft-expressed beliefs about what cars were best. I never understood the reason for this departure, but the disloyalty was cured with his next purchase—a 1952 Oldsmobile 88. He did not stray again: his final automobile was a 1955 Oldsmobile Super 88.

Our lives also were filled with church activities. When we moved to La Grange Park in 1945, my mother, brother, and I began to attend the La Grange Bible Church. Uncle John Balma, Aunt Cleo, and their family had been members of that church for several years. We continued to attend La Grange Bible Church during the time we lived in Westchester. After we moved again, we became very active at the Western Springs Baptist Church, which remained the home church for me and my siblings until, as adults living elsewhere, we affiliated with other churches.

We moved to Western Springs a few days before Christmas 1948, during my eighth-grade year. Western Springs was in the same high school district as La Grange and La Grange Park. Our parents had been looking for some time for a home in that area so we could attend the very highly regarded Lyons Township High School and live in a prettier, leafier suburb than Westchester, which was in the Proviso Township High School district.

I did very well in high school. From the beginning of my freshman year, I intended to continue on to college. That impulse was first planted in me and thereafter strongly encouraged by my freshman social studies teacher, Mr. John Davis, who was also the boys' guidance counselor for our class of 1953. Over the course of four years, he was a great influence on my life.

In the first weeks of my freshman year, Mr. Davis arranged for me to attend a meeting with representatives of Princeton University, who were at the school primarily to interview juniors and seniors. Following up on that beginning, each year thereafter he arranged for me to see college representatives visiting our school in order to gain experience interviewing and also to feel comfortable with the idea of aiming high as I thought about college. Very early in my high school career, Mr. Davis encouraged me to meet the debate coach, Ivan Rehn, who soon became another valued teacher and adviser. That introduction initiated for me a four-year run of Illinois State Debate Championships and trophies in other oratory and writing competitions.

During all four years of high school, and especially as I began to consider where I would go to college, Mr. Davis's office was always open and he was always ready to talk, to provoke thought by questions, and to counsel. I passed up accepting admission to Princeton, which had been in the forefront of my thinking from those first weeks in high school, and instead enrolled at Amherst College, where one of my debating colleagues had preceded me the year before. Mr. Davis never tried to push me to a particular decision but always challenged my assumptions, forcing me to think things through. I was fortunate to have other good teachers whom I remember well for their excellence generally and also for specific unforgettable lessons.[11] Mr. Davis in particular has always been for me the prime example of the impact a good teacher can have on a young person's life.

My college preparatory course schedule and intention to go to college became a source of conflict with my father. Although Dad had done all the right things to place us in an environment where we could aspire to achieve anything, he never fully grasped that potential. With his background, not having gone to school beyond the fourth grade and certainly never having a thought of completing grade school or going on to high school, he had no experience with higher education, no understanding that it would or should be something attainable for me, and no base from which to assume it would provide economic security in the future. For at least the first three years, he argued that it was important for me to "learn a trade" in high school and to do so by taking classes in wood- and metal-working and other practical shop courses. He repeatedly said he regretted that he did undertake such training, claimed that he suffered economic disadvantage because of this lack, and thought that I should pursue the security of "having a trade" to fall back on.[12]

I did not accede to his wishes, of course. I continued to take all those college preparatory courses and none of the shop classes. He was nevertheless proud to see me graduate from high school, as he also was upon my brother's high school graduation two years later.

Shortly before I finished high school, Dad suffered a series of heart attacks that disabled him from continuing to work. His and my mother's roles changed: Dad stayed at home and Mother went to work. He had always done some food preparation, particularly making Italian sausage that we hung to dry in the attic and preparing pizza and various sausage dishes. He began to take a more wide-ranging role as he prepared our meals. He and my sister, Nancy, became much closer. Dad had always especially loved his baby girl, and his confinement at home gave him much more time with her. It seemed that Mother became resentful of their closeness, which she apparently thought created a separation from her. When she and Nancy lived alone after Dad's death, there were frequent tensions between them.

My father and my grandfather Balma also established an interesting rapport in their late years. I have no idea how they got along and felt about each other immediately after my parents' marriage that had been so opposed by Mom's family; as a child I never particularly noticed interactions between my father and grandfather. However, after the Balmas' Narragansett Street house was sold in 1949, Grandpa Balma lived with his children, rotating for periods of three months or so among the homes of those who lived in the Chicago area. When he was living at our house, Grandpa and Dad were left alone for long days together. Politics became a point of mutual interest and camaraderie between them because of their shared displeasure with Democrats—in particular, Harry Truman, first, and later Adlai Stevenson. Dad and Grandpa were both avid daily readers of Colonel Robert McCormick's *Chicago Tribune*. Nourished by the colonel's rabid conservatism, they commiserated about the world's state of affairs and fumed about the Democrats.

As with high school, when I entered college in the fall of 1953 I felt that my father had reservations about the practicalities of what I was doing and did not understand why I needed to go off to a small, expensive college in New England. He did not express any criticism, however, and I think he grew much more comfortable with the notion when he heard praise from others for the path I had chosen.

I completed college in four years, the first at Amherst and the last three at Wheaton College in Illinois. The year after my graduation in June 1957, an event my parents both very proudly attended, I stayed on at Wheaton for a year teaching political science and taking a few courses in the graduate school of theology. Meanwhile, my brother had enrolled at Wheaton in the autumn of 1955. He followed a pre-med course, graduating in June 1959, again with our proud parents in attendance.

By the time of our college graduations, Dad's health was deteriorating. Brother Jim married June Kastein in December 1958, during his senior year at Wheaton. Dad was still somewhat robust at that time. He weakened considerably, however, by the time of Jim's graduation in June. My wife, Jan, and I were married a month later, on July 11, 1959. Dad was unable to remain through to the end of our afternoon wedding reception at the Western Springs Baptist Church parlors and had to be rushed home to rest in bed. He continued to weaken throughout the remainder of the year.

Meanwhile, the same deterioration was occurring with Grandpa Balma, who was then living at Uncle John's home in Des Plaines, Illinois. He died there on October 11, 1959, at age eighty-eight. Jan and I were working in Fairfield County, Connecticut, at the time. I felt a great sadness when Grandpa Balma passed on, and also a sense of warmth and satisfaction. I thought of him as a straight-shooting pioneer. He had stood firmly and steadfastly for what he believed and pushed those around him to straight talk and straight behavior.

When Jan and I returned to the family home in Western Springs for Christmas 1959, the bad state of my father's health was apparent. He was unable to lie down because of his congestive heart condition. Forced to sit up in a living room chair all night, he endured the long hours with little complaint but was weary, in pain, uncomfortable, and unhappy. Jan and I returned to Connecticut at New Year's, but before the end of January we came back to Western Springs after Dad was taken to Hinsdale Hospital in critical condition. I was pleased to be able to remain with him the last twenty-four hours until he died of congestive heart failure early on the morning of January 25, 1960, at age sixty-one. His funeral and burial services were conducted by the Reverend Lloyd Fesmire of the Western Springs Baptist Church, who also was a neighbor. Dad liked Lloyd, and in his last years had become close to him as a pastor and friend.

Francesco Cicero had traveled far from his roots in tenements in Buffalo and Chicago. With little formal education, he had provided economic sufficiency for himself and his family and abundant opportunity for his children. Occasionally in later years my mother would revisit the "might have beens" and the affluence and economic independence she dreamed the aborted business venture in 1945 would have provided. My father, however, was realistic in accepting his accomplishments and abilities. Having barely survived a massive heart attack later in 1945—an event that both he and my mother attributed in part to the pressures surrounding the business venture—he had lived a generally comfortable life for another fifteen years. In that time he had experienced the joy of adding a beloved daughter to the family and had seen his two sons finish college on their way to becoming accomplished professionals. He was not one to conclude that his life might have been better rather than ending much sooner if he had endured the stress of running his own business.

My mother and sister were by themselves after my father's death. In less than three months, my mother at age fifty-one had lost the only two men who ever were really important to her. Both her father and her husband were strong-willed, wanting things their way. She was the same. She was dependent on them and did not confront them on important matters on which she disagreed; confrontation would have risked either an open breach or subjugation. Instead, while appearing to acknowledge and acquiesce in what they wanted, she worked silently and at times underhandedly to subvert their will and get her way.

I saw this pattern numerous times. Such behavior surrounded her marriage to my father, when she did not openly challenge and risk a break with her father over the issue of marrying Frank but instead worked out a way to carry out her plan. Similarly, on the few occasions she and I talked about her "agreement" with my father about their future as a Protestant household and her children being raised non-Catholic, her description of events was always vague. No specific discussion or agreement between them was ever referenced; rather, they "sort of understood" what would happen.

After Dad's death, Mother continued to work but in the early years also took time off for significant trips. The first summer—1960—she spent several weeks as a volunteer at Camp Awana in Wisconsin, which Nancy was attending. The next summer she took a five-week cruise to Europe, a trip sponsored by Wheaton College. In 1965, when my brother, Jim, by then a doctor, was stationed in Germany, she made a Christmastime trip to visit him and his family.

Following her graduation from Wheaton College in 1968, Nancy worked two years in Paris and Lyon for the Evangelical Alliance Mission. Mom took advantage of Nancy's presence there to visit France in the summer of 1970. During a trip by car from Lyon down the Italian peninsula to Naples and back, they made a point of meeting up with the only relative in Italy Mother knew about. Her cousin, Guido Balma, son of Grandma Balma's brother, Giosuè, was a professor of French and French history at the University of Rome. Mom and Nancy spent time with Guido and his family in Rome. Unfortunately, they did not visit the large Waldensian church where Guido and his family were members, nor did they seek out the Balma's ancestral home in the Waldensian valleys of Piedmont.

Mother worked most of the rest of her life after Dad's death. She continued to live in Western Springs the first thirteen years; three in the family house on Johnson Avenue and then a decade in an apartment two blocks away. In 1973, she moved to Shell Point Village, a Christian and Missionary Alliance retirement community in Florida where her sister Helen and brother-in-law Hank were working. She lived there twenty years, working full-time outside the village at first and later doing book-keeping for other residents of the retirement community. She enjoyed the conservative evangelical Protestant doctrine of that community, which was squarely in the tradition she had known at the Waldensian Presbyterian churches, at Moody Church, and later in the Bible and Baptist churches we attended.

Mary Balma Cicero died at Shell Point Village on July 18, 1993, three weeks after suffering a stroke. She was buried in Hinsdale, Illinois, beside my father on July 24, 1993, the day before her eighty-fifth birth-day. She was the oldest and the first to die of the last four children born to Marguerite and James Balma. In a marvelous turn of events, after James and Marguerite had lost their first five children with only one reaching his fourth birthday, the next, Mary, lived until her mid-eighties, and her three younger siblings thrived into their nineties.

* * *

Later in the year 1960, after my father died, I finally made it to Princeton University. I enrolled in a two-year graduate program at the Woodrow Wilson School of Public and International Affairs, receiving a master's degree in public affairs in 1962. As a further step in an intended career in government and politics, I followed Princeton with enrollment at the University of Chicago Law School, receiving my JD degree there in 1965. Law school led me to a different full-time career. For more than forty years, while I continued an active involvement in politics and pub-lic affairs, my professional life has been as a trial and appellate lawyer in courts across the United States and tribunals in Europe.

My brother, Jim, finished his medical education at Northwestern University Medical School. An ROTC graduate, he served a tour as a doctor with the U.S. Army in Germany. In civilian life, he signed on as medical director of the maximum security prison in Stillwater, Minnesota, and then began a long career as one of the pioneers in emergency medical practice in St. Paul, Minnesota.

Grandchildren of four Italian immigrants, Jim and I were the first in the third generation not only to finish college but also to attain professional degrees.

Nancy graduated from Wheaton College in 1968, majoring in psychology. After a tour as a Protestant missionary working with young people in France, she pursued a career as a college educator concentrating in student affairs and counseling and eventually serving as dean of students at Gordon College, in Massachusetts.

Although it was never a matter we discussed, I am quite sure that my father as well as my mother would never have dared to hope, when they planned their marriage and the education of their children, that we would all graduate from a distinguished high school in a distant western suburb of Chicago or that we would go on to college and postgraduate degrees and careers as a lawyer, a doctor, and a college dean. In a real sense, however, these happy outcomes are precisely what they were striving for and unknowingly dreaming of in the ways they conducted their lives for their children.

Two cardinal principles ruled their lives. The first—as with millions of other first- and second-generation immigrants—was that we were going to be raised as Americans. Thus, they and we did not speak anything but English at home, a fact that I regretted as I grew older. They did not talk of the old country, attend ethnic events, affiliate with Italian-American groups or social clubs, or focus on our ethnic background. That non-Italian emphasis was undoubtedly facilitated by the fact that we were not raised Catholic. Identifying with a parish or a Catholic school, attending parish celebrations, saint's festivals, or other events were not part of our world.

The second guiding principle—intermingled with the first in its practical working out—was that we were going to be raised and educated in places and schools that were apart from any insular Italian heritage. Thus we moved. From resettling in the far western reaches of Chicago when I was less than a year old until our last new home on the far western edge of Cook County when I reached high school age, our moves were made for access to better schools in more thoroughly American neighborhoods and communities.

15

Those Who Stayed Behind

As a child and youth, I heard little about family members who remained in Italy. On the Balma side, my understanding was that no siblings or other close relatives of my Balma grandparents had come to America, and I recall hearing only a few vague references to family who remained in Italy. In contrast, on the Cicero side, there were in Chicago numerous close relatives of my father who had immigrated from Sicily, but I recall hearing nothing about any who stayed in Sicily.

BALMAS

As an adult, when I began to inquire about the Balmas' religious and family origins, I learned a little about my grandparents' siblings. There were a few. Although some had moved from their remote home villages of Rodoretto and Prali, they remained rooted in the region that for centuries had been the homelands of their Waldensian ancestors.

James Balma's ten-years-older sister, Marie Madeleine, married Jean Etienne Bertin, a native of Torre Pellice whom she had met in Waldensian church activities. They established their household in Torre Pellice, where their four children were born. The oldest child, Marie Adele, married a Swiss man named Constance Buvelot. Adele and Constance emigrated to Chicago in 1907, three years after her uncle and aunt, my grandparents James and Marguerite, arrived there. Within the Balma family in Chicago, Adele always was referred to in French as *la cousine* (the cousin). The two Buvelots were very close to the Balma family and were customarily present at family events.

Grandpa James Balma's younger sister, Catherine, who was a young girl at home in Rodoretto when he was serving in the Italian army—James recounted his welcome home by her in his 1947 tape-recorded interview—married Grandmother Marguerite Balma's older brother, Jean. Such marriages of siblings of one family to siblings of another were not uncommon in the Piedmont valleys, with their small population and even smaller pool of like-minded Waldensians. Catherine and Jean eventually also moved to Marseilles, where they raised two daughters and lived out their lives.

As with millions of other families, during World War II there was little communication between the Balma family in Marseilles and the Balmas in Chicago. Adele and Constance Buvelot's son, Albert, who was serving in the American army, visited his great aunt, Catherine, in Marseilles after that city was liberated. There was also correspondence in 1945 and 1946 thanking the Balmas in Chicago for CARE packages they had sent. Apart from that, I have no information about the Jean Balma family.

The only other sibling of my Balma grandparents about whom I have any knowledge is Marguerite's four-years-younger brother, Giosuè, born in the Waldensian valleys in 1879. At some point he moved down valley to Pinerolo with his wife, Ausonia Malan. Like many born in the valleys, he and his family returned to the mountain villages to spend summers at an old family home in Rodoretto. Giosuè was a high school teacher in Pinerolo; Ausonia, who pursued advanced academic studies and earned a PhD, was also a professor.

Giosuè and Ausonia had four children, two sons and two daughters. Their oldest child, Guido, earned his doctorate and became a professor of French and French history in Rome. Guido and his family, whom my mother and sister visited in 1970, were members of the large Waldensian church on Via IV Novembre just off the Piazza Venezia in the center of Rome.

An explanation in part for the little I heard of Balma relatives in Italy, and an insight into Grandpa James's personality, is furnished by postwar correspondence between James and Marguerite's sister-in-law, Ausonia, and my aunt Kay (Catherine). From 1946 to 1948, Ausonia carried on an active correspondence with her niece, Catherine Balma Allshouse. Ausonia wrote in excellent English of Giosuè's and her lives, the education and lives of their children—including Guido, later the professor in Rome—and events involving Waldensian friends. Then Ausonia inquired whether it might be possible for Aunt Kay to have one of Giosuè and Ausonia's daughters live for a time with Kay and her family in Western Springs and, perhaps, to find employment for the young woman. According to Aunt Kay, Grandpa, upon hearing of the request, asserted that it showed all the old country relatives wanted was to take advantage of the prosperity of the Americans and forbade Catherine having any further communications with Ausonia. While James's position is interesting, it also is telling that Catherine obeyed and discontinued the correspondence.

CICEROS

As described earlier, I do not recall ever hearing anything within the family about relatives of my paternal grandparents in the old country; I never heard that there were any others who emigrated to America nor that any remained in Sicily. During my first trip to Montemaggiore, when I met Christine and her family and investigated old municipal records, I finally found specific information about Grandfather Giuseppe's siblings. On that occasion, sifting through record books in the town hall, I was excited to find the birth certificate of Giuseppe's two-years-older brother, Rosario. Later, I learned that in family lore Rosario was referred to as "gambler." It was said that he may have emigrated from Italy at some point. I have been unable, however, to find any explanation for that alleged nickname, any evidence to support the assertion that he immigrated to America, or any other information concerning his life.

In recent years, however, I have learned much more, principally from information possessed by my newly discovered Sicilian cousin Carmelo (1973). Carmelo is custodian of a sizeable collection of documents that have been kept over the years by the three generations preceding him. These records show that Grandfather Giuseppe had five other siblings. The oldest was a brother named Francesco. Born in the late 1840s, he was thus six or seven years older than grandfather Giuseppe. Francesco was studying to be a priest when he died young, at age twenty-one.

Giuseppe also had a four-years-older sister, Maria, who was born in Montemaggiore in 1850. Although there is also family lore that Maria immigrated to Buffalo around 1890, three years before Giuseppe, I have been unable to find any evidence to support that assertion. Nor have I been able to learn anything concerning how long she lived or what her life may have been in Sicily.

After Giuseppe's birth in 1854, his parents' next child was another son, Andrea, who was born in 1856 in Montemaggiore. He is said to have . died at an early age.

The most remarkable information revealed by Carmelo from his trove of documents related to Giuseppe's two youngest siblings, Marina and Salvatore Francesco. Different from anything I had ever known, these documents showed two remarkable things. First, another Cicero family, headed by Marina, had emigrated to Buffalo seventeen years after my grandparents and their large family, including my father, had departed Buffalo for Chicago. In addition, and even more remarkable to me, a second Cicero family—Carmelo's line—had descended from my grandfather's brother, Salvatore Francesco, had remained in Sicily, and still lived there.

Marina was born in February 1866. Her mother, Angela Nicosia, was then forty-four years old. Angela had given birth to five children, one every two years until 1856, and then ten years passed before the birth of Marina, her next—but not last—child. Five years later, days before Angela's forty-ninth birthday, Salvatore Francesco was born in April 1871.

Marina lived in Montemaggiore most of her life. She was twenty-seven years old when my grandfather Giuseppe left Montemaggiore for Buffalo in April 1893, leaving behind his wife, Maria Castiglia, and their four children. In the late 1880s, Marina had married Giuseppe Parisi, also of Montemaggiore. Marina and her husband had a seven-month-old daughter when her sister-in-law, Maria, died in May 1893, a few days after Giuseppe passed through Ellis Island and reached Buffalo. Marina, with her husband and their infant daughter, moved into Giuseppe's house on Via del Collegio in Montemaggiore to raise her four motherless nieces and nephews—who ranged in age from thirteen to five—along with her own family.

Other Cicero family who remained in Montemaggiore with Marina included her mother, Angela Nicosia, and her younger brother, twenty-three-year-old Salvatore Francesco. Seventeen years younger than my grandfather, the youngest of his generation, Salvatore Francesco was within just a few years of some of his older nephews and nieces. They were his playmates and companions during the many years they lived together in Montemaggiore.

Salvatore Francesco lived in Montemaggiore for twenty-five years. He married Rosaria Marchese of Montemaggiore in the mid-1890s, soon after his brother immigrated to Buffalo and his sister-in-law died. Salvatore Francesco and Rosaria stayed on only three more years. In July 1896, he went to work for the Italian National Railroad and moved from Montemaggiore, leaving his mother, Angela, with Marina and her children and Giuseppe's children as the only family members remaining in their ancestral town.

Marina and her husband had five more children before he was killed in June 1911 in an accident on the railroad where he worked. Their six children ranged in age from four to nineteen years when their father died. Marina was said to have been strongly impacted by her husband's death. It was not to be her last painful loss, however. The very next year, her twelve-year-old daughter, Angela, died unexpectedly. And the following year, in June 1913, Marina watched her oldest child, Maria, depart for Buffalo with her new husband, Gaetano DiPasquale.[1]

Marina remained in the Via del Collegio house for another eight years. In addition to the care of her children, she also was charged with caring for her mother. Marianna Angela Nicosia, my great-grandmother, was said to be strong and vigorous, tending the animals, caring for the olive and fruit orchards, and maintaining a household until late in her life. She died in Montemaggiore on April 1, 1920, a few days before her ninety-eighth birthday, leaving Marina and children the only family members remaining in Montemaggiore.

Nine months later, in February 1921, at age fifty-five, ten years widowed but relieved of the care of her mother, Marina immigrated to Buffalo with her three youngest children, Carmelo (later Charles) Parisi, who was twenty years old at the time, Giuseppina (Josephine) Parisi, age seventeen, and Rosaria (Sarina) Parisi, age thirteen. The four had an adventurous voyage. Their steamship from Palermo, originally bound for New York, was unable to discharge its passengers there because of congestion in the port. After several days waiting for a berth, their ship was diverted to Philadelphia, where they finally debarked two weeks after they had sailed, and then traveled on by rail to Buffalo. Marina's older son, Gaetano (Tom) Parisi, had emigrated from Montemaggiore two years earlier at age twenty-three, traveling directly to Chicago, where a friend had arranged employment in a foundry and mill. Tom later joined his mother and siblings in Buffalo.

With the departure of Marina and her children, none of my grandfather Giuseppe's siblings or descendants remained in Montemaggiore. The next year, in March 1922, almost thirty years after his own departure for America and twenty years after his children had followed him, Giuseppe and his direct heirs, the children of his long-deceased first wife, Maria Castiglia, signed a power of attorney before a notary in Chicago authorizing Salvatore Francesco, his brother who remained in Sicily, to sell "the family house" on Via del Collegio in Montemaggiore.[2]

Salvatore Francesco and the Ciceros Remaining in Sicily. It has been most intriguing to learn about family that remained in Sicily. The idea itself—unknown and undreamed of by me for many decades—was a novel and exciting one. It also has been interesting to learn that there were in fact many communications and relations between family members in Sicily and those in America, including my father, aunts and uncles, and cousins. In addition, it is revealing to observe how each generation lived in Sicily and in America. Americans commonly believe very simply that in each generation those who immigrated to America and their descendants had much better lives than their counterparts in the old country. For some, this assessment may hold true, but not for all in every generation.

While my grandfather Giuseppe struggled for several decades to find work as a laborer in Buffalo and Chicago, his youngest brother, Salvatore Francesco, held a steady job with the Italian National Railroad for some twenty-seven years in various office positions. He was promoted regularly and transferred frequently. He and his family moved to live in a dozen different towns and cities in north, central, east, and southeast Sicily.

Salvatore Francesco and Rosaria had two sons, Carmelo, born in 1899, and Salvatore, born in 1903. The boys grew up in frequent contact with their six cousins in Montemaggiore, who overlapped in age. In the early years, Salvatore Francesco's family lived in towns near Montemaggiore.

Even when they moved farther away, with good railroads and a father who worked for the company, they saw their aunt Marina and their cousins often, spending family holidays, feast days, and summer vacations in Montemaggiore.

The two cousins closest in age were Salvatore (later Sam) Cicero, born on March 3, 1903, and Marina's daughter Giuseppina (later Josephine) Parisi, born March 18, 1904. They were playmates and close friends for sixteen years in Sicily.

Salvatore (Sam) immigrated to Buffalo in 1920, two months before his aunt, Marina, and her children, including Giuseppina (Josephine), arrived after their delayed trip through Philadelphia. His father, Salvatore Francesco, made notes concerning his son's emigration process in a meticulously kept diary that I had the opportunity to read at Carmelo's home in Ispica. He notes that Salvatore (Sam) first departed Ispica for America on May 5, 1920, at age seventeen but had to return to Ispica just four days later because his papers lacked the necessary financial guaranty. The diary further records that, after months spent curing the problem, Salvatore left again on December 5, 1920. He traveled by boat from the Sicilian port of Patti, near Messina, to Naples, then left Naples on December 8 on a trans-Atlantic steamship that arrived in New York two weeks later, on December 22, barely two months before Marina and her children would arrive.

Lifelong friends from infancy, Josephine Parisi and her cousin Sam Cicero married in June 1925, four years after their arrivals in Buffalo. They lived full and long lives. Sam worked as a barber; he died in 1978 at age seventy-five. Josephine lived to age 102; she died in Buffalo in 2006.

Meanwhile, back in Sicily, Carmelo, Salvatore Francesco's older son, had gone to work in the small towns in central Sicily where the family lived. He established himself in a trade, the course my father wished for me when I was taking those college prep courses in high school. Carmelo, a self-taught mechanic with exceptional aptitudes and instincts, distinguished himself in Sicily. He became a licensed expert and surveyor in mechanics, electronics, industrial optics, and other fields. He was also an inventor who held patents for an advanced faucet as well as other water handling devices. In 1927, shortly after his marriage to Giuseppa Demauro, they established their residence in Ispica, in the province of Ragusa, near the coast in southeastern Sicily.

In 1923, Salvatore Francesco was terminated from active service with the railroad. A convinced and known antifascist in an era when such beliefs were not looked upon with favor by Mussolini and his administrators, he was required to take early retirement. He and his wife, Rosaria, also moved to Ispica, where Carmelo lived with his family and where the next two generations have continued to live.

Shortly after they settled in Ispica, in 1927 Rosaria Marchese died. Two years later, as described above, Salvatore Francesco made his only trip to America, traveling to Buffalo and Chicago in the fall and winter of 1929–30. He died in Ispica in 1946.

Through good fortune, as noted before, I was introduced to descendants of Salvatore Francesco—the only line of relatives that remained in Sicily—when a letter from his great-grandson Carmelo was forwarded to me in Chicago in May 2007. With the letter came my first knowledge that there were relatives in Sicily. Subsequently, I learned much from Carmelo about several generations of Ciceros in Sicily and also about the family in Buffalo that I did not know existed.

In March 2008, I enjoyed my first visit to Ispica, where I met the grandson of Salvatore Francesco (1871), also named Salvatore Francesco. Born in Ispica in 1931, Salvatore Francesco was my generation, my second cousin.[3] An educator and high school teacher, he loved literature and philosophy and was also a poet. I was privileged to receive from him two books of poetry; they are collections of reflective, highly personal verse written over the years. I am most thankful that I had the occasion to meet Salvatore Francesco in Ispica. He was suffering from cancer at the time of my visit and died within the year, in February 2009.

Salvatore Francesco (1931) married Giovanna Barone in February 1972. Giovanna taught art history for many years, retiring shortly before I was first introduced to the family. They had three children. The oldest, Giuseppina, was born in 1972; she is married and has two sons. Their second child is Carmelo, my correspondent, born in 1973. Carmelo is a chemist and quality control analyst at a paint and chemical company. He and his wife, Simonetta Guarella, have two young sons, Salvatore and Lorenzo. Carmelo's younger sister, Rosalia, born in 1976, is a graduate of the Academy of Fine Arts at Catania, where she studied art history and metal restoration. She works in Bologna.

Carmelo's collection of documents is invaluable. Accumulated over more than 150 years by the three preceding generations, many are legal documents, including, for example, the contract regarding Giuseppe's share of the estate of his father, Carmelo (1824), the power of attorney Giuseppe gave to his brother, Salvatore Francesco (1871), to sell the Via del Collegio house in Montemaggiore, and a number of papers relating to Marina's affairs, particularly as she was undertaking to immigrate to Buffalo in 1921. To my knowledge, none of the family of the same generations in America kept any such records. I have enjoyed studying them with Carmelo, all the more because they brought me back to Buffalo.

Marina, Salvatore Francesco (1871), and the Ciceros in Buffalo. I remember thinking as a child it was rather exotic that my dad was born in Buffalo and not in Chicago, as were my mother and numerous aunts and uncles. I never heard that there were any relatives in Buffalo, however, and I had no curiosity to visit there. Moreover, apart from a high school field trip to Washington, DC, I never had traveled east of Michigan until I went off to Amherst, Massachusetts, for college, and I felt no compulsion to visit Buffalo—which had a reputation then as an old, grimy, industrial city.

In my college years and immediately after I had numerous opportunities to visit Buffalo but never thought to bother. As a freshman I became a good friend of a classmate from Jamestown, New York, some seventy miles south of Buffalo. I and others from the Chicago area drove through Jamestown and stayed overnight at his home several times on our way to and from Amherst. We bypassed Buffalo every trip.

In retrospect—having become interested in my heritage and the role Buffalo played in it and even more having learned that there were relatives in Buffalo all along—I especially regret the fact that I did not seize the opportunity to explore the city and meet distant family members the two summers after my college graduation. During both I worked as a bellboy on the cruise ship SS *North American,* which made weekly trips from Chicago to Buffalo and back. Early every Tuesday morning the ship docked in Buffalo, and it remained in port until dinnertime so that passengers could spend the day visiting Niagara Falls. At the time, the lakefront and dock area were occupied by railroad tracks and cargo handling facilities and built up with warehouses and industry. I and my coworkers would walk the five or six blocks to the downtown center for lunch if we did not make the bus trip to the falls, but I had no curiosity to visit the old Sicilian neighborhood, St. Anthony of Padua Church, St. Joseph Cathedral, Niagara Square, or other sites that I now know were only a few blocks away.

I regret these near-misses now, of course, but it was not until decades later when I began to research my family history that I developed any curiosity about relatives in Buffalo or my own grandparents' time there. My cousin Carmelo in Sicily was the source of the revelation that from the 1920s to the present there had indeed been Cicero relatives in Buffalo. In one of his early letters, Carmelo explained generally how my grandfather's younger sister, Marina, had remained in Montemaggiore, married Giuseppe Parisi, had children there with him, and later immigrated to America, bringing with her sons and daughters who in turn married and had families that continued to live in Buffalo.

The revelation that nieces and nephews of my grandfather and cousins of my father had lived in Buffalo for decades reminded me of missed opportunities to seek out family over the years. I did not want any more time to pass. To start, the only family names I knew were Cicero and Parisi. Males, of course, would continue to carry their family names; female relatives with new married names could be difficult to find. I discovered that, after several generations, there were Parisis, there was one Parisi who became a Cicero—Josephine, when she married Sam and reclaimed her maternal grandfather's family name, a reacquisition that was temporary since their daughters later married and brought new names into the family—and there were numerous other new family names.

I learned that there had been a network of relatives in Buffalo since the second decade of the twentieth century. Indeed, only eight years after my grandfather Giuseppe had moved his family out of Buffalo to Chicago, other relatives came in. The first was Marina's oldest daughter, Maria Parisi, when she arrived with her husband, Gaetano (later Thomas) DiPasquale, in July 1913. Their immigration record shows that a sister and other family of Tom DiPasquale had been in Buffalo for more than a decade.[4] Seven years later, Marina herself arrived with her three children, a few weeks after her nephew Sam Cicero came from Sicily. Some two years later, Marina's oldest son, Gaetano (Tom) Parisi, moved from

Chicago to Buffalo, where he married and raised a family. Marina died in Buffalo in 1929. Descending from her four children and Sam, son of Salvatore Francesco, numerous cousins of three more generations—cousins who have the family names Parisi and others, but no Ciceros—live on in Buffalo and elsewhere in America.

My sister, Nancy, and I visited the Buffalo cousins in the summer of 2008. The personal connection gave us much additional information about the family and about our grandparents' life in Buffalo. Old city directories, maps, and photographs, all in the public library or the Erie County Historical Society, as well as documents from official civil sources and records from St. Anthony of Padua Church filled in much of what was recounted above.

The second cousins with whom we met also disclosed that there were correspondence, many telephone calls, and even visits between some of my aunts and uncles in Chicago—my father's brothers and sisters—and Josephine and Sam Cicero and the Parisi cousins in Buffalo. My uncle Benny and aunt Jenny had visited Buffalo on several occasions. Indeed, the Buffalo cousins said that Benny Cicero, living in Chicago, and Sam Cicero, living in Buffalo, had great affection for each other, a close relationship that went back to the time they were children together in Montemaggiore.

Although there were many contacts among the Chicago and Buffalo cousins who knew each other from Montemaggiore, none of the Buffalo relatives with whom we met, nor my sister and I, knew of any contacts by Buffalo cousins with my father or his siblings, the children of Giuseppe's second marriage. They in Buffalo were as ignorant of the children and grandchildren of Antonina Panepinto as I was of them. We all agreed, however, that we wanted to strengthen our newfound connection.

The urgency of that wish to remain in contact, and the losses of passing time, are well illustrated by the fact that two of the second cousins whom I met for the first time in 2008 died within a few months thereafter. In February 2009, as stated earlier, my second cousin, Salvatore Francesco Cicero, grandson of Salvatore Francesco, died in Ispica, Sicily. A month later, in March 2009, Sarah Cicero Fiorella, granddaughter of Marina and daughter of Josephine Parisi Cicero, whom Nancy and I met in July 2008, died in Buffalo.

Epilogue

SICILY IS NO LONGER THE MOON. I have been there. Numerous times. I have walked the streets of the towns where my grandparents lived, as did their ancestors—and mine—for centuries before. I have gained some sense of what their lives must have been and why they felt they had to leave while others stayed behind. I have made friends in Montemaggiore and Valledolmo, walked, talked, joked, and laughed with them, visited in their homes or offices, and learned what lives there are like now. Guided by the irrepressible Benny, I have also come to know many cities and villages—small and smaller—all over the island but particularly in the interior, where many tourists never visit.

The largest island in the Mediterranean, Sicily has a rugged beauty dominated by Mount Etna in the east—the largest active volcano in Europe—and rugged hills and valleys across the island to the west. Ancient towns perch on high hillsides, many with views of the sea. Situated in the center of the seaway between the Atlantic and the eastern reaches of the Mediterranean, Sicily was a crossroads of the ancient world. Reminders are everywhere of the more than three millennia of history and the people and cultures that have occupied it. Beginning with the pioneering Phoenicians, followed by the Carthaginians, then the Greeks, the Romans, and the Byzantines, followed by the Arabs, who ruled for centuries, only to be displaced by the Normans and later the Spanish—each culture left its mark on the island, in the spectacular ruins and other archeological sites as well as in the cuisine, customs, religion, and attitudes of the people.

I have found Sicily to be fascinating and have visited often. The sense I had for many years that Sicily is an unreachable, an alien, and somehow a very mysterious and different place is gone. There are still mysteries, but the place itself is comfortable and welcoming.

Sicily has changed in the three decades I have traveled there. In the early 1980s, in the interior particularly, most Sicilians spoke only the local dialect and many fewer spoke standard Italian. Many were suspicious and wary of foreigners—even of Americans with Italian names. Some of the comfort and warmth I have come to feel is undoubtedly because I now speak Italian, but most, I am sure, is due to television, with its use of standard Italian and its bringing of the world to living rooms and kitchens, and, among the young in particular, the Internet.

In addition, of course, discovering in the last two years—through a magnificent stroke of good luck—that there are cousins in Sicily who are eager to share their lives and to know their relatives in America has added a new dimension and a great deal of information to my knowledge of the island. I am continually excited by the discovery of family in Sicily, as are my children and their families. Carmelo, his wife Simonetta, and their sons, Salvatore and Lorenzo, are equally thrilled that they have learned of cousins in America. Carmelo's deceased father, Salvatore, felt the same way, as do Carmelo's mother and his siblings.

I am also grateful to Carmelo for taking the initiative to seek out family in Chicago with a broadside letter to all the Ciceros he could find—a list that did not include me. And, of course, I am hugely grateful to Susan Cicero for her thoughtfulness in making the effort to send Carmelo's letter on to me. But for her initiative, I would have remained as ignorant of a great deal of family history as I was before being introduced to Carmelo and his father and their trove of documents.

In learning from Carmelo and his father of the lives and careers of the three generations of family descending from my grandfather Giuseppe's brother, Salvatore Francesco, I have seen the richness of the lives of those who stayed behind, at least of this one line of one family. In "the second generation," Carmelo (1899), my father's first cousin, lived a full life as a mechanic, expert surveyor, engineer, inventor, and patent holder who was at least as accomplished as any of his cousins—the same generation—in the United States. Carmelo's son, Salvatore Francesco, my generation and my second cousin, was a respected educator. A lifelong student of philosophy, he was also a poet who published two collections of thoughtful, very personal poems. I am grateful that I had the opportunity to visit him in his home in Ispica less than a year before his death. His son, Carmelo, my children's generation, is a chemical analyst with a large corporation. In addition to productive careers, these men with their families have lived in lovely surroundings close by the sea in southeastern Sicily.

Exploration of my roots in Sicily and the lives of those who came from there to America has acquainted me with my paternal grandparents. I still do not know how they met or whether they ever formally were married. Also, my picture of Giuseppe Cicero is incomplete. He apparently was a hard worker. He is described as gruff and irascible, a man of few words. Not given to outward displays of tender emotions, he nevertheless loved his children and family. He certainly lived all his life surrounded in close quarters by a great number of them. Grandmother Antonina Panepinto has a warmer and more endearing image in my mind. Having buried at least two infants and her husband in Italy in the space of ten years, she understandably was ready to escape Valledolmo for Buffalo, where almost all her family members and hundreds of other Valledolmesi had preceded her. In a short time, she assumed a much larger family when she joined with Giuseppe Cicero and promptly added five more children to their brood. She is described by those who knew her as a warm and caring person. She and my father were very close. She was welcoming and became equally close to my mother.

My travels to Piedmont over the last three decades, intertwined with the vastly greater knowledge I have acquired of the area's civil history as well as the religious roots of my Balma family's Waldensian protestant faith, have also yielded exciting and remarkable discoveries. The rugged mountains and valleys where my grandparents, their fellow Waldensians, and their ancestors lived and were sheltered for centuries are strikingly beautiful. They are green and narrow, with steep mountains and formative rivers the conspicuous features. Many of the small towns and villages nestle alongside their rivers. Others are perched high on the valley sides, over-looking the few broad valleys or up and down the steeper river courses. In many of the villages, the Waldensian "temples"—some dating to the sixteenth century—are on conspicuous sites offering tremendous views. The splendid isolation of these Waldensians makes it easier to understand why so many persisted for almost 850 years, nurtured and, when necessary, defended their faith, and not only assured its survival but carried forward a vibrant, active church centered in their ancestral valleys.

The tiny and remote cluster of a few stone huts high in the Italian Alps against the French border, barely big enough to call a hamlet, from which my Balma grandparents emigrated, has been remarkable to come to know. Seeing Balma and the nearby village of Rodoretto, visualizing the rigors of life in harsh surroundings, the absence of paying work and the poverty, it is easy to understand why they would have decided to leave. It is also difficult to comprehend what the impact must have been on them of the contrast between their ancestral home in the Alps and the congested, turbulent life of Chicago.

Coming to know Piedmont has been interesting in numerous other ways. Geographically, it is varied and productive, ranging from the broad, fertile, agriculturally rich plains of the Po Valley, across renowned wine growing hillsides, to beautiful mountains. Turin surprised me. Knowing that it is one of Italy's largest industrial areas, the home base of the storied Fiat automobile company, a city that drew tens of thousands of immigrants from central and southern Italy in the years after World War II to work in its factories, I expected to see a grimy industrial city.[1] To the contrary. Graceful and historic palaces of the Savoy dynasty, broad piazzas fronted by public and private buildings with finely crafted facades against the background of beautiful mountains, it is a most attractive city. I have come to love it.

The long and influential history of the Savoy dynasty must, of course, be a principal element of any discussion of Piedmont and the lands of my maternal ancestors. Straddling what is now the French/Italian frontier, the historic territory of the counts, then dukes, and later kings of the House of Savoy included what is now French Savoie, comprised of the departments of Savoie and Haute-Savoie, the city of Nice, and what are now the Val d'Aosta and Piedmont regions in Italy. The dynasty survived centuries of political and military maneuvering among France, Spain, the empire, and the papacy to become ultimately the key force in Italian unification in the middle decades of the nineteenth century, a process that at least one scholar calls the "Piedmontization" of Italy.[2]

My ancestors, of course, were in no way players or even interested, and likely not even aware over the centuries of the maneuvering, intrigues, growth, and expansion of their Savoyard rulers, except of course—and probably unknowingly—as those activities brought reprisals against them because of their reform beliefs.

As noted above, for much of my life I knew very little of the basis of our Protestant faith other than that we were something called Waldensians, from Piedmont, which distinguished us from the Catholics based in Rome. In recent years, I have learned much more about the faith and how its history intersected with that of the Savoy dynasty. The Waldensian faith and the church survive and prosper in Italy, based in the village of Torre Pellice in the Pellice River valley. There are also active Waldensian communities and churches in South America. In the United States, the Waldensian heritage is carried on through partner denominations, including the Presbyterian Church (U.S.A.) and the United Methodist Church, and in the programs and outreach of the Waldensian Presbyterian Church, founded in 1893, in Valdese, North Carolina.

In Chicago, while the differences between Piedmont and Sicilian origins are of interest to me—and undoubtedly have led to contrasts in temperament, culture, cuisine, and mores—the key difference between my mother's and father's families was that of religion. It was the primary obstacle to my parents' marriage. It has remained the key difference between the two sides of our family.

Mary Balma and Frank Cicero's marriage bridged the ancient schism of their families' religions and cultures, but, apart from their own descendants, it did not alter the historic differences between their two families. I and my siblings and our descendants, like the descendants of my mother's siblings, have been and are almost without exception Protestant, conservative, and evangelical, with a faith fundamentally that of the Waldensians. Several have been Protestant missionaries, some even returning to practice their faith and to evangelize in or near the lands where the Waldensian reform was nurtured over the centuries. Thus, two of my uncle John's children, Sherry and Tom, returned to "the old country" and lived their adult lives as missionaries in France and Italy, respectively—Sherry in Paris suburbs and Annecy in Haute-Savoie; Tom in Florence—raising their children as Protestants who attended the local schools and spoke the local language. My sister, Nancy, spent her first years after college as a Protestant missionary among French young people in Lyon, the city where Valdesius instigated the Reform some eight hundred years earlier. Similarly, my mother's sister, Helen, spent much of her adult life as a missionary in the hills of eastern Tennessee, evangelizing in the schools and after-school Bible classes, as did her daughter, Marguerite, in several locales.

On my father's side, his siblings all married Catholics or, in one case, a woman who converted to Catholicism. Their children have been raised as Catholics, many attending Catholic elementary and high schools—unlike their parents, who could afford only to go to public schools—and some also enrolled in Catholic colleges and universities. They have lived and practiced the Catholic faith of their ancestors.

The fact that I was raised in a family that in many respects was bicultural, with exposure to very different religious traditions, affected my own attitudes. There were many mysteries about Catholicism—for example, the Latin mass, transubstantiation, and purgatory—but I never felt any hostility toward Catholicism or Catholics. I had and have great affection for my Catholic cousins; their religion is in no way an issue. My attitude is reciprocated by them. All my life and to this day, my Catholic cousins made it clear that they did not and do not understand but instead find somewhat strange the fact we are something else. And yet, we are family.

My siblings and I were raised to be "Americans." Neither the Italian language nor either of my parents' local tongues was spoken at home. We moved residences regularly to live and attend school in nonethnic communities. Apart from cuisine, we did not generally celebrate matters Italian. I did not think of myself as an Italian-American. I was not ashamed of my Italian roots. In fact, to the extent I thought of the matter, I rather liked them. Italian seemed better than any other ethnic background I could think of. Moreover, the surname *Cicero* gave my Italian origin a classic touch. I was rather proud of that. It was not until I became a lawyer—and eventually one who was fairly well known—and for a time an elected official that I experienced any effort to have me join Italian-American ethnic societies. I signed on to some to give my support as a member, but I was never an activist nor out celebrating my participation—to do so is simply not my style, either as a person or as a lawyer.

I have great admiration for those who emigrated and for the immigrant experience. No matter how bad conditions may have been in Italy, it still took great courage to leave home and strike out, make the difficult trip across the ocean, and start over. All four of my grandparents undoubtedly were motivated by the general objective of seeking a better life. But there were other catalysts among them. My maternal grandparents, Giacomo and Margherita Balma, were leaving the poverty and difficulty of life in a place not only where they had buried their first three children but also where the prospect of raising a healthy family in the future was very doubtful. In addition, they were going where many friends and co-religionists had preceded them. Giuseppe Cicero, similarly, was motivated to travel to Buffalo either to establish a place to bring his family to or to earn in America and provide for them at home. In Sicily's benign climate and living conditions, there was not the same jeopardy to his family's future health and survival that there was in the Piedmont mountains. My paternal grandmother, Antonina Panepinto, had remnants of family in Valledolmo, but after losing her loved ones she undoubtedly was ready to seek a happier life in Buffalo, where many family, neighbors, and friends already lived.

Having reached America, my grandparents and my parents' generation worked hard and saved to provide for their families, but in general they were not particularly entrepreneurial. They did not create organizations or strive to build businesses, nor did they have a vision that included the need for higher education. Those ambitions came in time, thanks to the junior high and high schools we attended as a result of the residence moves.

Looking back, I see some differences in attitude between the Sicilian side and the Piedmont side of my family, perhaps fostered by culture but probably also by religious differences. Waldensians have always been a small minority, embattled, periodically persecuted savagely, but, at least what I saw in the Piedmont variety, they are not downtrodden and despairing or pessimistic. Piedmontese have proud attitudes; that is why the Savoyards had the confidence and temerity to push and maneuver and fight for power, eventually ruling all of Italy. My grandparents were not of the ruling class—they likely were not even aware of those attitudes—but perhaps fostered by their reform faith—and the conviction that they knew the truth and the correctness of the path others should follow—they were optimistic and confident. Sicilians, on the other hand, with their millennia-old tradition of domination by outsiders, perhaps combined with their superstition-infused version of priest-dominated Catholicism, have a darker and more pessimistic outlook. As one writer, who describes herself as proud to be called Italian (Sicilian) American, has observed, "Sicilians feel they are outsiders both in Italy and the United States."[3]

I am not boasting in writing this account. To the contrary, I am humble about where I am and grateful to the grandparents and parents who got me here. I recognize that I am a latecomer to Italian history and to the medieval reform and religious history I have recounted here. I truthfully can say that I wish I had started earlier. For one, it would have been much easier to collect facts: many people have passed on whom I would like to have interviewed. I would love to have discussed with them where they were and how they got here. But I've enjoyed the process, learned a great deal, and found a lot of people who wanted me to record my experience.

MAPS, PHOTOS, FAMILY TREES

Valdesius (Waldo) of Lyon depicted in a monument to the Reform at Worms, Germany.

Monument in meadow at Chanforan in the Angrogna Valley commemorating meetings held there in 1532 among leaders of the Waldensians and of the Swiss reform movement that would later bear Calvin's name. Photo by author.

Sculpture of Pastor Henri Arnaud on the grounds of the Tavola Valdese, the Waldensian church headquarters, in Torre Pellice, Piedmont, Italy. Arnaud led the Glorious Return from Switzerland in 1689. To regain their valleys, the Valdese émigrés fought several battles against the Duke of Savoy's troops, reflected in Arnaud's unsheathed sword, perhaps unique among statues of Protestant clerics. Photo by author.

Rodoretto in the 1890s. The large white structures in the upper left corner of the town are the Waldensian church, on the left, where Margherita and Giacomo Balma were married in 1896. The Catholic church with its imposing bell tower is the large structure just below and to the right. Cultivated fields on the steep meadows of the Germanasca River valley surround the town. Waldensian Photo Archives; Torre Pellice.

Rodoretto and the Germanasca River valley, before 1920. The Waldensian temple and manse are visible at the top of the town on the right, the Catholic church with its tower stands in the center. The hamlet of Balma is some two miles up the trail toward the rear of the photo, and the border with France is six miles away, beyond the ridge of snow-capped mountains. Balma/Cicero family collection.

The small cluster of stone huts named Balma, high above the Germanasca River, where Margherita and Giacomo Balma made their home from the time of their marriage in 1896 until their emigration in 1904. Four miles away, the Italian-French frontier stretches along the mountain ridgeline. Photo by author.

The stone buildings and the large rock outcropping—the *balma*—that gave the hamlet its name and afforded protection from the frequent winter avalanches. When the author, his wife, and daughters first visited Balma in July 1983, the buildings were abandoned and substantially collapsed, with no roofs, windows, or doors and fallen walls. They were purchased and renovated later that decade by residents from towns down the valley. Photo by author.

Contemporary views of Montemaggiore (top) and Valledolmo (bottom), Sicily. Photos by author.

Immigrant passengers, crowded on the steerage class deck, arriving in New York in the early 1900s. Courtesy Library of Congress.

Buffalo viewed along Erie Street with the Erie Canal and Lake Erie in the background in the 1890s, YEAR?. The five-story tenement building in which the Cicero family lived is at the intersection with the diagonal street on the left side of Erie Street, just above the center of the photo. The Buffalo & Erie County Public Library, Buffalo, New York.

Looking toward Court Street, port of Buffalo, with Erie Canal barge and ship traffic, 1890s. Giuseppe Cicero lived at 271 Court Street, some two hundred yards from the canal, from 1893 until 1898. The Buffalo & Erie County Public Library, Buffalo, New York.

Mansions of former president Millard Fillmore (above) and Samuel
Wilkeson (below), primary promoter of the Erie Canal, on Niagara Square
as they appeared at the turn of the twentieth century. Niagara Square was
the most fashionable residential district in Buffalo at the time. The neighborhood where many Sicilian immigrants lived was immediately behind
the Wilkeson mansion. The bell tower of St. Anthony of Padua Church,
the home church for generations of Sicilian immigrants, is visible at the
right behind the Wilkeson homestead.

St. Anthony of Padua Roman Catholic Church, Buffalo. Photo by author.

St. Anthony church viewed from Court Street, with the Buffalo City Hall, built in 1931 on the former site of the Wilkeson homestead, looming to the east. Photo by author.

Giacomo Balma in the uniform of the Third Alpine Regiment, c. 1893–94. Balma/Cicero family collection.

A busy Chicago street near the Balma and Cicero homes: Clark Street, look-ing south from Randolph, 1890s. Transport by street railway was clearly not speedy: a dozen or more streetcars are visible in a four-block stretch. Courtesy Krambles-Peterson Archive.

Gridlock at nearby Dearborn and Randolph streets, Chicago, c. 1909. The con-trast in living conditions between Chicago and Balma in the Piedmont moun-tains could hardly have been greater. Courtesy Krambles-Peterson Archive.

Balma Giacomo 28 maggio 1871
Balma Margherita 4 dicembre 1875
Balma Giovanni Stefano 21 febraio 1897
Balma Giovanni 11 febraio/aprile 1899
Balma Paolo 18 luglio 1901
Balma Elena 17 novembre 1903
Balma Emma 8 febraio 1906
Balma Maria Margherita 25 Luglio 1908
Balma Caterina Emma 15 luglio 1910
Balma Elena Luisa 27 Giugno 1912
Balma Giovanni 10 Septembre 1915

Balma James — Oct. 11, 1959
Balma Margherita 21 Jan. 1942
Balma Giovanni Stefano 10 dicem. 1898
Balma Giovanni 21 aprile 1903
Balma Paolo 5 feb. 1903
Balma Elena 6 feb. 1907
Balma Emma 6 sep. 1907

Family birth and death dates recorded by Giacomo Balma in the Bible purchased at the time of his marriage and kept by him until his death. The births and deaths of five infants before the age of four are memorialized in Giacomo's handwriting. Balma/Cicero family collection.

James (Giacomo), Mary, and Marguerite Balma, c. 1910. Mary, the author's mother, was the first child to live beyond infancy. Balma/ Cicero family collection.

Catherine and Mary Balma, c. 1911–12 (left), and Helen, Catherine, and Mary Balma, c. 1913 (below). After the deaths of five infants, one can visualize the parents' pride and gratitude as they arranged periodic portraits of their growing family. Balma/Cicero family collection.

Girls' club, perhaps at Erie Neighborhood House, c. 1922–24, each member with her homemade doll. In the front row, Catherine Balma, second from left, and Mary Balma, second from right: the Balma girls were not permitted to cut their hair. Balma/Cicero family collection.

Mary, Catherine, and Helen Balma, c. 1925. Balma/Cicero family collection.

The author's great-grandmother Angela Nicosia. Balma/Cicero family collection.

FORMATO GABINETTO

Angela Nicosia posed with her daughter Marina's children. Giuseppe Cicero requested and held this photograph of his mother on his deathbed, December 23, 1929. Balma/Cicero family collection.

The Santa Maria Addolorata Church at Peoria and Grand avenues, Chicago. The five-story tenement building at 466 North Peoria where the Cicero family lived for thirteen years after their arrival in Chicago in 1904 is visible at the rear of the church. The Montefiore School on Grand Avenue, attended by the younger Cicero children, is partly shown at right beyond the church school. Santa Maria Addolorata Parish, 50th Anniversary 1903–1953, Souvenir Book (Courtesy Casa Italia Archives, Melrose Park, IL).

The church survived the great Chicago fire in 1871 but was destroyed by another conflagration in 1931. Santa Maria Addolorata Parish, 50th Anniversary 1903–1953, Souvenir Book (Courtesy Casa Italia Archives, Melrose Park, IL).

Inscription inside the rear cover of Giuseppe Cicero's prayer book, bought for fifty cents in 1905 from the Santa Maria Addolorata Church:

Libro Riscattato Dalla Chiesa Dolorata Chicago Ill; 50 soldi 1905

Cicero Giuseppe fu Carmelo Da Montemaggiore Belsito provincia Palermo

Italia

"Book ransomed [sic] from the Dolorata Church Chicago Ill 50 cents 1905. Giuseppe Cicero son of the deceased Carmelo of Montemaggiore Belsito province of Palermo Italy."

Grandfather Giuseppe Cicero on the sidewalk in front of the apartment building at 1108 North Central Park Avenue, to which the Cicero family moved in 1922. He died there on December 23, 1929. Balma/Cicero family collection.

Grandmother Antonina Panepinto in the garden of the apartment building at 1108 North Central Park Avenue, c. 1935. Balma/Cicero family collection.

Brothers Carl, Benny, Frank, Tony, Ross, and Joe Cicero at their father's funeral, December 1929. Balma/Cicero family collection.

Grill and Berger wholesale produce house at the Randolph Street Market, c. 1931–33. Mary Balma is at right. Balma/Cicero family collection.

LaMantia Bros. Arrigo Co. at the Randolph Street Market, c. 1931–33. Frank Cicero is the second person from the left. Soon Mary Balma joined the staff at LaMantia Bros., where she and Frank met. Balma/Cicero family collection.

St. John's Presbyterian Church at Harrison and Hoyne, where Mary Balma and Frank Cicero were married on Saturday morning, February 2, 1935. A Story of St. John Presbyterian Church, pamphlet printed 1936, folder Chicago History Museum.

The Reverend Pasquale R. De Carlo, pastor of St. John's. Reverend De Carlo was a successful businessman in his native Italy, where he was converted from Catholicism by a former Catholic priest. Following his immigration to the United States, he quit his business ventures, became an ordained Presbyterian minister, and assumed the pastorate of a small mission outpost of the First Italian Presbyterian Church on Taylor Street in Chicago's largest Italian district. By the 1930s he had built the renamed church into the largest Protestant congregation serving Italians in Chicago. Reverend De Carlo agreed to perform the marriage service of Mary Balma and Frank Cicero when ministers of the churches Mary had attended refused. A Story of St. John Presbyterian Church, pamphlet printed 1936, folder Chicago History Museum.

Cook County, Illinois, certificate of the marriage of Frank Cicero and Mary Balma on February 2, 1935. Balma/Cicero family collection.

The Presbyterian denomination marriage book filled out and signed by Reverend De Carlo. The book was also inscribed at the wedding by the only witnesses, Mary's close friend Nida Richard and her nineteen-year-old brother, John. It was signed later by four other friends and Mary's sister, Helen. Balma/Cicero family collection.

The author's grandmother, Antonina, father Frank, and the author in their home at 1108 Central Park Avenue, Chicago, 1936. Balma/Cicero family collection.

The rear and side yards of the Balma family home at 3422 North Narragansett Avenue in Chicago. (Left) John, Catherine, Marguerite, and James Balma with the very young author, c. 1937–38. Balma/Cicero family collection.

The author in his beloved cherry tree with his father, Frank, and mother, Mary, c. 1938–39. Balma/Cicero family collection.

Acknowledgments

THIS BOOK WOULD NOT EXIST were it not for the contributions of many people. First, of course, were my mother's siblings, my aunts and uncle Catherine Balma Allshouse, Helen Balma Molter, and John Balma and his wife Cleo Ellis Balma. Their recollections and their varied collections of documents and photographs were invaluable in recounting the Balma family story. Similarly, on the Cicero side of my family, the early genealogies and notes assembled by my cousins Robert and Dan Thelen, comprising their own research as well as the recollections of their mother, my father's sister, Mary Cicero Thelen, were not only a valuable source of information but also an inspiration to me to research and elaborate as much of the family history as I could. Helpful information and encouragement were provided also by cousins on both the Balma and Cicero sides and, especially, by my sister, Nancy, and my brother, Jim.

My good friends of many years, Crocetta (Christina) Pasquale, her brother, Vincenzo (Vince) Pasquale, and their parents—whom I met by chance in the first minutes of my initial trip to Montemaggiore in 1980—taught me much about life in Sicily and assisted me in research in the municipal archives of Montemaggiore and Valledolmo. Years later, in Torre Pellice at the far other end of Italy, Gabriella Ballesio, archivist, scholar, and editor at the *Centro Culturale Valdese* and the *Società di Studi Valdese,* and her friendly and helpful volunteers dug out otherwise unavailable genealogical information about my Balma ancestors as well as factual information about the faith and lifeways of Waldensians in Italy and elsewhere. Closer to home, Professors Geoffrey Symcox of UCLA and

Edward Muir and Robert Lerner of Northwestern University provided information, encouragement, and inspiration.

Even with all these sources, however, this story would have been much shorter, with many fewer characters and much less history, were it not for the initiative of my previously unknown cousin, Carmelo Cicero, in the previously unheard-of town of Ispica, Sicily. His effort three years ago to find relatives in America by sending dozens of letters to Cicero names—not including mine—in Chicago telephone directories started an improbable process that led to me and eventually to much important information about generations of relatives in Buffalo and Sicily. For that result Carmelo, his now deceased father, my second cousin Salvatore Francesco Cicero, and I give credit and thanks to Susan Cicero of Chicago. Susan received Carmelo's letter and, after determining that she was not a relative, forwarded it on to me, whom she had heard about in our profession-in-common, the law, but had never met. Susan's thoughtfulness opened new windows on history to many Cicero relations on both sides of the Atlantic. We are all grateful.

I owe thanks in addition to many who helped shape this material into this book. First, to my wife, Jan, especially, and to our daughters, Erica and Caroline. Sounding boards, critics, "suggesters," they gave advice on many critical points. My thanks go also to Norma Madsen and Wayne Whalen, old friends and wise critics, who read the entire manuscript and made many suggestions that greatly improved the story. Laura Czukla, Mary Beth Kamraczewski, and other coworkers at my law firm provided helpful support. Of them, David Sokol, in particular, created designs and images that were invaluable to the final project. Shannon Pennefeather of St. Paul improved the text substantially with her careful editing and advice.

Finally, much credit for the content of this book is due also to my Italian teacher, Alessandra Visconti. She patiently but with rigor and discipline brought me from knowing only a few phrases to oral, reading, and writing fluency without which I would have learned much, much less of the history and lives recounted in this book.

My thanks go to all.

Notes

NOTE TO PROLOGUE

1. Tourn, *Les Vaudois.*

NOTES TO CHAPTER 1

1. Avondo and Peyronel, *Cît Paris,* 69–77.

2. Balma was the family name of both my grandfather Giacomo and my grandmother Anna-Margherita. The word *Balma* in Italian, or *Balme* in French, means an "overhanging rock forming a shelter." A common name for locations in the Italian and French Alps, it was also the name given to the hamlet where my grandparents lived because the stone huts were sheltered behind a large rock outcropping, a balma. The use of Balma, Balmas, or Balme as a family name was documented in these Piedmont valleys as early as 1265 and in Rodoretto specifically in 1451.

   The names of thirty-seven Balmas were listed among the banished in the First Exile from the Waldensian valleys in 1687; the name also appeared on the list of banished in the Second Exile in 1687. The Waldensian synod minutes of 1889 listed forty-three Balma families. In 1974, 115 persons of that name were listed in parish records in the valleys. See Coisson, *I nomi di famiglia.*

3. Watts, *Waldenses in the New World,* 3. The commune—*comune* in Italian—is the basic local government in Italy, as it is also in France. The rough equivalent of a municipality in American polity, it is also similar to townships as they exist in many American states in that it covers a geographical area that may include more than one city, town, or urban settlement as well as rural areas.

4. *Valdese* is the Italian word for Waldensian. The town of Valdese, North Carolina, founded in 1893, was settled predominately by émigrés from Rodoretto, Prali, and a few neighboring communes.

5. Avondo and Peyronel, *Cît Paris,* 72.

6. *La Savoie,* ship manifest, Ellis Island Archives.

7. *La Savoie,* ship manifest.

8. *La Savoie,* ship image records, Ellis Island Archives.

9. Bolino, *Ellis Island Source Book,* 63–65.

10. Bolino, *Ellis Island Source Book,* 9–12; Coan, *Ellis Island Interviews, passim.*

11. Years later, Giacomo described the afternoon he arrived in Chicago and his first day at work:

> I was such in a hurry to make my living that in the afternoon I went out first thing to buy a bed to sleep in and I went out to the hardware store with my friend and buy a shovel.
>
> The next morning I started out on the Ogden Avenue streetcar and come as far as Twenty-second and Cicero—but I know the place now but in those day I don't know it—and we were changing at the Twenty-second Street car and going to La Grange down there, went out at far as Lyons to work out there.
>
> I tell you I worked so hard and I was so disgusted with America that in the evening I had the price to buy a ticket and I pay a ticket and I decided I go back. Anyway I got the practice and by and by I worked, I worked pick and shovel until I was sixty-two, sixty-three years old.

Giacomo (John) Balma, interview by Herbert Allshouse, Chicago, Apr. 25, 1947.

12. *La Lorraine,* built in France in 1899, was 11,146 gross tons, 580 feet long, and 60 feet wide. It carried 1,112 other passengers with Margherita and Elena: 446 in first class, 100 in second class, and 550 other passengers in steerage (third) class.

NOTES TO CHAPTER 2

1. See note 3 above for a discussion of the commune in Italy.

2. With respect to the House of Savoy, see generally Bocca, *I Savoia;* Symcox, *Vittorio Amedeo II.*

3. Giacomo Balma, *Libretto Personale; Foglio di Congedo Illimitato,* Sept. 9, 1894.

4. Giacomo (John) Balma interview.

5. Giacomo Balma, *Libretto Personale.*

6. *Foglio di Congedo Illimitato,* Sept. 9, 1894.

7. Giacomo Balma, *Libretto Personale*, 4–5.

8. *Foglio di Congedo Illimitato,* Sept. 9, 1894.

9. Giacomo (John) Balma interview.

10. Giacomo (John) Balma interview.

11. Giacomo (John) Balma interview.

12. In addition to giving the name *Margherita* to innumerable baby girls for generations, the queen also allowed her name to grace a famous pizza. In 1889, during a holiday visit to Naples, the royal couple called to their palace one of the city's most popular pizza chefs, who brought an array of pies prepared specially for the occasion. The queen liked best the one made with mozzarella, basil, and tomatoes in the red, white, and green colors of the Italian flag. The chef dedicated that style to the queen and called it *pizza margherita,* a name that has been used for well over a century.

13. Giacomo (John) Balma interview.

14. Their first child, Giovanni Stefano Balma, was born February 21, 1897. He died on December 10, 1898, shortly before his second birthday. A second son was born April 11, 1899. His parents also named him Giovanni. Paolo joined him two years later, on July 18, 1901. However, the family included two children for just over a year and a half. Then nineteen-month-old Paolo died, on February 5, 1903. A little over two months later, on April 21, 1903, Giovanni died, just ten days after his fourth birthday.

NOTES TO CHAPTER 3

1. Audisio, *Waldensian Dissent,* 6–13; Biller, "Goodbye to Waldensianism?" 23; Cameron, *Waldenses,* 11–16; Merlo, *Eretici ed eresie medievali,* 49–50; Tourn, *Les Vaudois,* 11–16.

Cameron writes, "The Waldenses of the later middle ages had no very precise idea of their own origins. Some believed their movement to be as old as the apostles; some thought that it dated from the fourth century . . . (314–35). Years later, some Protestant apologists tried to argue for a similarly ancient origin, at least as far back as the ninth century and possibly before. Nevertheless, the overwhelming weight of modern opinion follows that of medieval Catholic chroniclers. These ascribed the origin of the 'Waldenses' to a citizen of Lyon called Valdesius, who lived in the late twelfth century, and after whom the movement was named." Cameron, *Waldenses,* 11, and notes cited therein. See also Biller, "Goodbye to Waldensianism?" 5.

2. Audisio, *Waldensian Dissent,* 6–13; Cameron, *Waldenses,* 2; Merlo, *Eretici ed eresie medievali,* 49–50; Tourn, *Les Vaudois,* 11–16.

3. Biller, "Goodbye to Waldensianism?" 14 and n22; Cameron, *Waldenses,* 14–15; Alexander Patschovsky, "The Literacy of Waldensianism from Valdes to c. 1400," in Biller and Hudson, *Heresy and Literacy,* 116; Merlo, *Eretici ed eresie medievali,* 51. The two clerics had no spiritual connections with Valdes and his movement. One of them, Stephen of Anse, did the translation; the other, Bernard of Ydros, took it down by dictation. Patschovsky, 113.

4. Patschovsky, "Literacy of Waldensianism," 116. Thus Patschovsky writes, "Around 1200 Bible translations appear in the dioceses of Metz and Liege, at first in the Romance language and quite soon afterwards in German. The Synods of Toulouse (1229), Rheims (1230/1), Trier (1231), Tarragona (1233) and Beziers (1246) provide similar testimony . . . Arguably, Waldensianism and the work of translating the Bible into the vernacular were virtually synonymous around the year 1200." As discussed later in the text, by this period in the early thirteenth century, missionaries from Provence had carried the Waldensian beliefs into the alpine valleys of Piedmont.

5. Gabriel Audisio, "Were the Waldensians More Literate than Their Contemporaries (1460–1560)?" in Biller and Hudson, *Heresy and Literacy,* 180; Cameron, *Waldenses,* 211–15.

6. Patschovsky, "Literacy of Waldensianism," 119–23. Durand of Osca, an early Waldensian cleric and apologist for Waldensian beliefs, wrote a treatise, *LiberAntiheresis,* about which Patschovsky states, "His quotations, references and illusions show a breadth of education far beyond the general knowledge of the clergy. He was among the first rank of theologians of his time." (Later, in 1207, Durand was persuaded by Pope Innocent III to return to the church.)

Similarly, a letter of information sent by the Poor Lombards to their brethren in Germany is "a text of considerable literary quality which is indubitably Waldensian" (121).

Patschovsky concludes, "A careful investigation of the evidence from the pens of the opponents of Waldensianism, together with the insights gained from genuinely Waldensian sources, leads us to the following overall picture of Waldensian literacy. The relationship of the Waldensian religious community as a whole to literacy turns out to be surprisingly complex, varying considerably in different times and places. Its fundamental inspiration is, of course, the Bible, and particularly the gospels and the epistles" (134).

7. Audisio, "Waldensians More Literate?" 184.

8. Cameron, *Waldenses*, 2, 33. A corollary of the belief of Valdesius and his followers that they had a mission to preach the gospel because a morally deficient priesthood was not doing so was the conviction that the same clergy and hierarchy had no right to stop their preaching. Indeed, some Waldensian theologians argued that the Catholic clergy and hierarchy were themselves committing heresy in their efforts to prevent laymen from preaching the gospel. Cameron, *Waldenses*, 33.

9. Cameron, *Waldenses*, 211–15; Merlo, *Eretici ed eresie medievali*, 49–51; Tourn, *Les Vaudois*, 64.

10. Cameron, *Waldenses*, 2–3, 33–34.

11. Biller, "Goodbye to Waldensianism?" 21; Cameron, *Waldenses*, 2–3, 165–66; Pierette Paravy, "Waldensians in the Dauphiné (1400–1530): From Dissidence in Texts to Dissidence in Practice," in Biller and Hudson, *Heresy and Literacy*, 168–72.

12. Cameron, *Waldenses*, 19–20; Merlo, *Eretici ed eresie medievali*, 51.

13. Cameron, *Waldenses*, 21. Waldensians commonly called themselves or were referred to as "brothers" or the "Poor of Lyon" as well as "Waldenses," the latter especially, more formally, by their inquisitors. Biller, "Goodbye to Waldensianism?" 19.

14. Cameron, *Waldenses*, 49–55.

15. Biller, "Goodbye to Waldensianism?" 3; Cameron, *Waldenses*, 20–22; Merlo, *Eretici ed eresie medievali*, 52.

16. Tourn, *Les Vaudois*, 42.

17. See, for example, Lerner, *Heresy of the Free Spirit*.

18. Cameron, *Waldenses*, 70–92.

19. Cameron, *Waldenses*, 36–48, 298–300.

20. Lerner, "German Waldensians," 234, 241.

21. Lerner, "German Waldensians," 247.

22. See Cameron, *Waldenses*, generally and "Conclusions and Reflections," 298–303; Merlo, *Valdesi e valdismi medievali*. But see Biller, "Goodbye to Waldensianism?" especially 17–32.

23. Biller, "Goodbye to Waldensianism?" 14 and n23.

24. In February 2006, the Val Chisone became known to the world as the site of the alpine events of the Turin winter Olympics.

25. Cameron, *Waldenses,* 151; Tourn, *Les Vaudois,* 49–50; Watts, *Waldenses in the New World,* 3.

26. Cameron, *Waldenses,* 153

27. Cameron, *Waldenses,* 152.

28. See, for example, Tourn, *Les Vaudois;* Wylie, *History of the Waldenses.*

29. See www.chiesavaldese.org (accessed July 2010). Of course, iconoclasts have described many of these sights as "patently mythical." See, for example, Biller, *Goodbye to Waldensianism,* 7.

30. Tourn, *Les Vaudois,* 52.

31. Cameron, *Waldenses,* 161.

32. Cameron, *Waldenses,* 161.

33. See generally Tourn, *Les Vaudois,* 68–70, regarding events in the fifteenth century.

34. Arché, *Le massacre des vaudois du Luberon;* Audisio, *Les Vaudois du Luberon,* 190–94; Cameron, *Waldenses,* 259–62.

35. For authority for this section, see Audisio, *Waldensian Dissent,* 164–209; Biller, "Goodbye to Waldensianism?" 3–34; Cameron, *Waldenses,* 209–70; De Lange, *Calvino, I Valdesi, e l'Italia,* 9–10 and nn2–4; Merlo, *Valdesi e Valdismi Medievali,* 109–13.

36. De Lange, *Calvino, I Valdesi, e l'Italia,* 14.

37. De Lange, *Calvino, I Valdesi, e l'Italia,* 16

38. Cameron, *Waldenses,* 270

39. De Lange, *Calvino, I Valdesi, e l'Italia,* 29, and Calvin letter dated Apr. 19, 1556, at 55–56.

40. Cameron, *Waldenses,* 267.

41. In the presbytery form of church organization, the church is governed by a small group of leading members, usually called elders or presbyters. A synod is a group of pastors of churches in a locality.

42. Audisio, *Waldensian Dissent,* 190–202; Cameron, *Waldenses,* 275; Tourn, *Les Vaudois,* 86–87.

43. De Lange, *Calvino, I Valdesi, e l'Italia,* 33 and n19.

44. Audisio, *Waldensian Dissent,* 6–13, 200; Cameron, *Waldenses,* 276–78; Tourn, *Les Vaudois,* 86–87.

45. Audisio, *Waldensian Dissent*, 200; Cameron, *Waldenses*, 274.

46. Cameron, *Waldenses*, 274.

47. Chiesa Evangelica Valdese, Union of the Methodist and Waldensian Churches, "What We Believe," http://www.chiesavaldese.org/eng/pages/beliefs/bible.php (accessed Feb. 1, 2010).

48. Cameron, *Waldenses*, 210.

49. Chiesa Evangelica Valdese, Union of the Methodist and Waldensian Churches, "Confession of Faith," http://www.chiesavaldese.org/eng/pages/beliefs/confess_faith.php (accessed Feb. 1, 2010).

50. Chiesa Evangelica Valdese website, 35; see also Tourn, *Les Vaudois*, 73–78.

51. Cameron, *Waldenses*, 292–93; Tourn, *Les Vaudois*, 115–16.

52. Audisio, *Waldensian Dissent*, 204–7; Cameron, *Waldenses*, 293–94; Watts, *Waldenses in the New World*, 6–7.

Among those who lamented the Piedmontese Easter massacre was the English poet John Milton. My Balma cousin Henry Molter recently came upon the reference to Milton in a book concerning Henry David Thoreau. See Robert Sullivan, *The Thoreau You Don't Know: What the Prophet of Environmentalism Really Meant* (New York: Colliers, 2009). The author states that Thoreau, who was fond of word play, had made a connection in his book *Walden* between the name of his pond and the Waldenses. In the chapter titled "The Pond in Winter," Thoreau writes,

Ah, the pickerel of Walden! When I see them on the ice . . . as if they were the pearls, the animalized nuclei or crystals of the Walden water. They, of course, are Walden all over and all through; are themselves small Waldens in the animal kingdom. Waldenses.

The author goes on to say that Thoreau probably knew of the April 1655 massacre from a sonnet by John Milton:

Sonnet 18

Avenge O Lord thy slaughtered Saints, whose bones
Lie scatter'd on the Alpine mountains cold,
Ev'n them who kept thy truth so pure of old
When all our fathers worship't Stocks and Stones,

Forget not: in thy book record their groanes
Who were thy Sheep and in their antient Fold
Slayn by the bloody Piedmontese that roll'd
Mother with Infant down the Rocks. Their moans

The Vales redoubl'd to the Hills, and they
To Heav'n. Their martyr'd blood and ashes sow
O're all th' Italian fields where still doth sway
The triple Tyrant: that from these may grow
A hunder'd fold, who having learnt thy way
Early may fly the Babylonian woe.

53. Cameron, *Waldenses*, 292–93; Symcox, *Vittorio Amedeo II*, 93–94.

54. Audisio, *Waldensian Dissent*, 208–9; Symcox, *Vittorio Amedeo II*, 94–95; Tourn, *Les Vaudois*, 130–37.

55. Audisio, *Waldensian Dissent*, 209–12; Symcox, *Vittorio Amedeo II*, 102–3; Tourn, *Les Vaudois*, 139–46.

56. Cameron, *Waldenses*, 294; Symcox, *Vittorio Amedeo II*, 102–5.

57. Symcox, *Vittorio Amedeo II*, 114.

58. Cameron, *Waldenses*, 295.

59. Tourn, *Les Vaudois*, 149–50.

60. Tourn, *Les Vaudois*, 150.

61. Tourn, *Les Vaudois*, 151.

62. Symcox, *Vittorio Amedeo II*, 185–87; Tourn, *Les Vaudois*, 153–55.

63. Symcox, *Vittorio Amedeo II*, 114, 184–86.

64. Symcox, *Vittorio Amedeo II*, 294; Tourn, *Les Vaudois*, 170, 175–76: Chiesa Valdese website, "The History"; Watts, *Waldenses in the New World*, 8–9.

65. The Risorgimento was the political and ideological movement that eventually freed Italy from foreign and papal political domination and brought unity and independence to the Italian peninsula. It is generally described as beginning in 1848–49, although decades of skirmishes and uprisings preceded this date. Under the political leadership of the kings of the House of Savoy and their ministers, in 1859–60 Milan and much of northern and north-central Italy as well as Sicily were annexed to Piedmont. The Kingdom of Italy was proclaimed in March 1861, with its capital initially in Turin and later in Florence. The Papal States in the center of the Italian peninsula, with other areas of central and southern Italy, remained under French domination. In 1870 the French were ousted, and the pope fled to the Vatican. The Papal States, including Rome, and the remainder of the Italian peninsula were brought into the unified Italy under the Savoy kings. The capital moved to Rome.

66. Cignoni, *I protestanti a Roma nell'Ottocento.* At dawn the morning of September 20, 1870, immediately after royal troops entered the city, six *colporteurs*—roving peddlers of Bibles and Protestant literature, two of whom were Waldensians, two Methodists, and two members of the Free Church—entered Rome with a dogcart full of literature and began distributing it to the population.

67. Chiesa Evangelica Valdese website.

68. Watts, *Waldenses in the New World,* 11–16.

69. Watts, *Waldenses in the New World,* 17–34.

70. The word *Waldenses* is widely used by scholars and by most European writers in the English language to describe Waldensians. I will use *Waldensians,* the word more commonly used in America, to describe the Waldenses in the United States.

71. Watts, *Waldenses in the New World,* 163–70.

72. Watts, *Waldenses in the New World,* 175. The correct name of the church was the First Italian Presbyterian Church of Chicago.

73. Watts, *Waldenses in the New World,* 175.

74. Watts, *Waldenses in the New World,* 175.

75. Watts, *Waldenses in the New World,* 79.

76. Watts, *Waldenses in the New World,* 79.

77. Watts, *Waldenses in the New World,* 85, 96, 98.

78. Watts, *Waldenses in the New World,* 91.

79. Watts, *Waldenses in the New World,* 95, 127–28; Waldensian Presbyterian Church, *History and Heritage.*

80. Watts, *Waldenses in the New World,* 95, 127–28; Waldensian Presbyterian Church, *History and Heritage.*

81. Watts, *Waldenses in the New World,* 91.

82. Watts, *Waldenses in the New World,* 112, 151.

83. Watts, *Waldenses in the New World,* 152.

84. Watts, *Waldenses in the New World,* 157 and n344, quoting Morganton *News-Herald,* Nov. 17, 1933.

85. Tourn, *Les Vaudois,* 12.

NOTES TO CHAPTER 4

1. Pliny the Younger writing to Tacitus, quoted in Touring Club of Italy, *Italy: From the Italy Experts* (2002), 109.

2. Michelin & Co., *Green Guide, Italy* (1981), 187.

3. Michelin & Co., *Green Guide, Italy* (1981), 187.

4. Carlo Levi, *Christ Stopped at Eboli* (Turin: Einaudi, 1945, 1965, 1990).

5. Murat was a distinguished officer in Napoleon Bonaparte's army. Named marshall of France, married to Napoleon's sister Caroline Bonaparte, he reigned as king of Naples and Sicily from 1808 to 1815. After fighting at Napoleon's side during the Hundred Days, Murat fled to Corsica following Napoleon's second fall. Attempting to regain his throne in Naples by means of an insurrection in Calabria, he was arrested during a landing near Pizzo by forces of his rival, Ferdinando IV. Quickly tried by a military court, he was handed over to a firing squad. An exceedingly handsome and dashing figure, he is remembered for his last words, after refusing to accept a chair or allow his eyes to be bound: "Save my face. Aim for the heart. Fire."

In an epilogue on Murat's fate, his brother-in-law, Napoleon, expressed a succinct judgment, "Murat tried to reconquer with 250 men the territory that he had not succeeded to hold when he had at his disposition 8000." Rizzoli Larousse, *Il Piccolo Larousse* (2004), 1583–84.

6. Although numerous writers and artists are celebrated in Taormina, the most illustrious by far is D. H. Lawrence, who lived with his wife, Frieda, in Taormina from January 1920 to February 1922. While Lawrence enhanced his reputation as a writer, a drinker, and the center of a circle of homosexual friends, his wife, the Baroness Frieda Richthofen, made her reputation as a free spirit and an ardent taker of lovers. Of particular celebrity was her passionate months-long affair with Peppino D'Allura, a mule driver in the employ of a very rich English divorcée who became Frieda's close friend. Friend "Betty" had a magnificent villa at Castelmola, a picturesque village nine hundred meters above the sea behind Taormina, with spectacular views over the commune, the sea, and Mount Etna. Peppino was assigned by Betty to descend to the Lawrence house in Taormina and provide carriage on his mule for Frieda on the long climb to and descent from Castelmola. They soon became involved in a passionate affair in the fields and woods between Taormina and Castelmola and, for periods of time, in Betty's guesthouse there.

Lawrence apparently not only became aware of the affair between Frieda and Peppino but solicited from Frieda accounts of her time with him. In 1928, Lawrence published his celebrated novel *Lady Chatterley's Lover*. Although set in

England, it is said to be based largely on the events that unfolded in the countryside between Taormina and Castelmola. See G. Saglimbeni, *Lady Chatterley e il Mulattiere* (Armando Siciliano Editore, 2003) and *I Peccati e Gli Amori di Taormina* (Armando Siciliano Editore, 2006).

7. The Greek colony was founded and the temples built in the sixth century BC. The temples were partially destroyed by the Carthaginians in 406 BC. Restored by the Romans in the first century BC, they have experienced seismic damage and pillaging in the millennia since, but their grandeur and beauty are still remarkable. Larger and more concentrated in one place than any temples in the Greek homeland, they can fairly be described as true examples of "second city" ambitions at work: the settlers in Sicily far outdid their compatriots back in the Greece homeland in the size and beauty of the structures they erected.

There is an additional array of ancient Greek ruins a short distance away in the old city of Agrigento. Together with the temples in the valley, it is said that "nowhere else on earth, not even in Greece, will you see so many sacred buildings in one place." The imposing row of temples at the valley is, however, the most remarkable site. Visitors can walk along the temples, going into each one in turn, touching their stone, marveling at their presence, their past, their spectacular size, and how well they are preserved. See Touring Club of Italy, *Italy: From the Italy Experts* (2002), 132–44.; Michelin, *Green Guide, Sicily* (2007), 121–25.

NOTES TO CHAPTER 5

1. The Italian custom, particularly strong in Sicily, was and still is to name sons after their grandfather and daughters after their grandmother or the feminine form of their grandfather's name. To minimize confusion among persons having the same name, I will often attach the birth year to the name. Thus, for example:

    Carmelo (1824) is my great-grandfather, husband of Marianna Angela Nicosia

    Carmelo (1886) is his grandson, Giuseppe's son

    Carmelo (1899) is also Carmelo (1824)'s grandson, son of Salvatore Francesco

    Carmelo (1973) is grandson of Carmelo (1899)

2. See note 2 above regarding the name *Balma*. When I next visited Balma almost twenty years later, the stone huts had been restored and expanded. Graced with satellite dishes, a fenced-in grassy yard with swing set and benches overlooking

the valley, and the adjacent ruin of a residential hut converted into a chapel, the cluster of stone houses had ended the twentieth century as summer homes for residents of down-valley towns. A later visit revealed that the chapel is now, ironically, a consecrated Catholic church.

3. Norwich, *Normans in Sicily.*

4. I have made several trips to Montemaggiore in recent years, as the Pasquale/ Manzella family are friends I enjoy seeing. Three generations still live in the same house I first visited on Via Sant'Isidoro. I was pleased to see Christine's father on two visits before he died. Christine's mother, Marianna, is now in her eighties; Nino is retired from the telephone company. Christine continues to be a vibrant and active housewife and mother. I have become well acquainted with Christine's two daughters. Maria Concetta was born one month after I first met Christine; I can always fix how old she is in reference to my first visit to Montemaggiore. She is now a graduate of the University of Palermo, where she studied jurisprudence and law and achieved top honors in Sicily in the final examinations for her degree. Arianna, two years younger, is a bright, vivacious student, living at home.

5. Yans-McLaughlin, *Family and Community,* 26–27, and sources noted therein.

6. Carmelo and Angela would have experienced the only historical event I have ever seen mentioned with reference to Montemaggiore in the great deal that has been written about Sicily's place in Italian history. In her significant study of Sicily and events relating to Italian unification in the middle of the nineteenth century, historian Lucy Riall writes that programs for the partition of land provoked dramatic conflicts between peasants and landowners, including violent uprisings in Montemaggiore and elsewhere. Riall, *Sicily and the Unification of Italy,* 91.

7. Nelli, *Italians in Chicago,* 4–5; Caroli, *Italian Repatriation from the United States,* 37.

8. Caroli, *Italian Repatriation from the United States,* 37.

9. Caroli, *Italian Repatriation from the United States,* v., table 16, 41.

10. Carmelo and Angela had three children in addition to Giuseppe (1854), Marina (1866), and Salvatore Francesco (1871). Their first child was a son named Francesco, born in the late 1840s. Francesco was training for the priesthood when he died in his early twenties in 1869 or 1870. Their next child, a daughter named Maria, died shortly after her birth. The third child, Giuseppe's older brother, Rosario, was born in April 1852, a birth record I found during my first visit to Montemaggiore. I know little of him, except that he came to

be known by the nickname "Gambler," which may have been a reflection of his occupation or attitude toward life. I do not know whether he was still living in 1893 and, if so, where. Giuseppe was the next child, followed two years later by another son, Andrea (1856), who also died in infancy.

NOTES TO CHAPTER 6

1. It is always interesting to me to observe dates at which events have occurred contemporaneously in different places. Thus, the founding of the Monreale Cathedral at Palermo by the Normans was just four years prior to the initiation of the Waldensian reform by Valdesius in Lyon in 1176.

2. I was particularly interested to see the small city of Cinesi, home of a youth named Peppino Impastato, where the events portrayed in the film *Cento Passi*—"A Hundred Paces"—occurred. Peppino, while still a teenager, had drawn great attention to himself by very publicly rebelling against and ridiculing the mafia culture of his father and uncle. He was murdered for his efforts. His courage is commemorated with a plaque on his home.

3. Late April and early May is my favorite time to travel to Sicily. The hills and fields are fresh and green. The orchards of orange trees and the jasmine that borders them are in bloom, their fragrance strong even while driving past on the roads. The hot summers turn everything straw colored. Although the weather is cooler again in late September and October, the fields, hills, and orchards remain brown until spring.

4. The Parrocchia di Valledolmo, officially named the Church of the Immaculate Conception, is the chiesa madre of the parish. The present church was built in the early 1700s. It succeeded the smaller Church of the Holy Spirit that was built in 1645 and elevated to the rank of archdiocese in 1650. See *Parrocchia Immacolata Valledolmo; Catalogo delle opere d'arte di proprietà della Parrocchia* (Comune di Valledolmo, n.d.); Orazio Granata, *Valledolmo; dall'origine ai giorni nostri* (Comune di Valledolmo, 1982).

5. Office manager, interview, Parrocchia di Valledolmo, May 2, 2005.

6. Yans-McLaughlin, *Family and Community,* 17.

7. Goldman, *High Hopes,* 180. Yans-McLaughlin, *Family and Community,* cites a different authority and states that "by 1947 a total of eight thousand Valledolmesi had settled in Buffalo" (17, n1).

8. Yans-McLaughlin, *Family and Community,* 25.

9. All figures in this paragraph, Yans-McLaughlin, *Family and Community,* 36.

10. A year later I returned to the commune offices in Valledolmo to seek additional information about my grandmother's family. Assisted by a very willing and helpful staff member, Sara Pizzolanti, and another visitor, I searched more than two decades of birth records and found the birth certificates of three siblings of my grandmother. An older sister, Teresa Panepinto, was born on November 14, 1859. Antonina's birth followed on February 9, 1862. The family was filled out with the birth of a brother, Francesco, on November 19, 1864, and a sister, Rosalia on October 4, 1867. The certificates record that all four babies were baptized at the chiesa madre. The vagaries of record keeping in these communes is shown in the details—probable estimates—of the ages of the parents, Antonio Panepinto and Rosa Guzzetta, at the time of the babies' births. Antonio's age is recorded as thirty-seven in 1859, forty in 1862, and thirty-two in 1864. Rosa's age is more consistent: twenty-five in 1859, twenty-seven in 1862, and thirty in 1864. I found the same type of inconsistencies when I examined birth records of my grandfather Giuseppe Cicero and his brother during my first visit to Montemaggiore.

NOTES TO CHAPTER 7

1. Sarah Cicero Fiorella remembers as a child helping her father, Sam, who was for many years secretary of the Montemaggiore Club, prepare announcements for meetings and going to the post office with him late at night to deposit them in the mail. Interview, Sarah Fiorella, July 13–15, 2008.

2. St. Anthony of Padua Roman Catholic Church, "Weekly Bulletin," July 13, 2008.

3. Yans-McLaughlin, *Family and Community,* 119; St. Anthony of Padua Roman Catholic Church, *Guidelines for Research at St. Anthony's* (2006).

Efforts to organize an Italian national parish had begun in Buffalo in 1887 as a mission of St. Joseph's Cathedral. A group met in a chapel of the cathedral. By 1889 a fundraising effort to establish a separate church had collected enough money to buy the property on which the church still stands at Court and Elmwood streets. In October 1890, a Scalabrinian missionary arrived from Italy to become the church's first priest. The Scalabrinian Order had been founded four years earlier in Milan by Bishop Giovanni Battista Scalabrini specifically to minister to the needs of immigrants. The new church was completed in 1891 and dedicated on August 2 to St. Anthony of Padua. Brown, *Scalabrinians in North America,* 47.

I have found no explanation of the reasons the new Italian church was dedicated to St. Anthony of Padua. It is interesting to speculate whether it is related to the fact that St. Anthony is the patron saint of Valledolmo, the Sicilian town from which an influx of immigrants had been arriving in Buffalo.

4. Certificates of Baptism, St. Anthony of Padua Church, Buffalo, NY.

5. Martin Ederer, interview, July 13, 2008. Mr. Ederer is a lecturer in history and social studies education at Buffalo State College. He has been a devoted volunteer at St. Anthony for years, serving as an altar boy, deacon, and historian and in numerous other roles. He is the author of two books on Buffalo churches: *Buffalo's Catholic Churches: Ethnic Communities and the Architectural Legacy* (digital@batesjackson LLC, 2003) and *A Colorful Bouquet of Saints* (Buffalo: E. T. Nedder, 2004).

Ederer relates that the two floors were crammed into the upper space of the church because the basement, now the location of the church school and other facilities, was in the early days too damp and cold to be used for meeting spaces.

6. Ederer interview. As part of my effort to find evidence of a marriage between grandparents Giuseppe and Antonina, I reviewed microfilm of the cathedral records regarding marriages. Well in excess of 95 percent of the unions in the years 1896–1905 were between two persons of Irish descent and only two were of Italian couples.

7. Courier Company, *The Buffalo Directory* (Buffalo, NY: The Company, 1904).

8. Thus Antonio Scalia's younger brother Pietro arrived in New York at age thirty-two on May 26, 1889, aboard the SS *Burgundia*. Younger brother Leonardo arrived in New York at age thirty-five on May 26, 1891, aboard the SS *Victoria*. Following them, the youngest sibling, Rosaria, arrived in New York at age thirty-one on July 21, 1892, aboard the SS *Olympia*. Ships' manifests.

9. SS *Bolivia,* ship manifest, line no. 126–29.

10. Ancestry.com, "New York Passenger Lists, 1820–1957" (Provo, UT: The Generations Network, Inc., 2006).

11. U.S. Federal Census, 1900, Buffalo Ward 19, p 26–27.

12. Certificates of Birth and Baptism, St. Anthony of Padua Roman Catholic Church, Buffalo, NY.

NOTES TO CHAPTER 10

1. Young, *Chicago Transit,* 1; Chicago History Museum, et al, *Electronic Encyclopedia of Chicago.*

2. Vecoli, "Chicago's Italians Prior to World War I," 159 and n72.

3. Vecoli, "Chicago's Italians Prior to World War I," 163.

4. Vecoli, "Chicago's Italians Prior to World War I," 164–65, and sources cited therein.

5. The difficulty is compounded by the fact that both the Peoria and Grand and the Curtis Street locations where the Cicero family lived, as well as the 800 block of West Ohio Street, home of the Balmas, were demolished in the 1950s to build major expressways.

6. Vecoli, "Chicago's Italians Prior to World War I," 168–69.

7. Nelli, *Italians in Chicago,* 31–34; Schiavo, *Italians in Chicago,* 37; Vecoli, "Chicago's Italians Prior to World War I," 168.

8. Chicago Department of Health, *Biennial Report, 1895–96,* 29, 38; Chicago Commons, "The Neighborhood About Chicago Commons"; Taylor, "Who Will Stand Between Life and Death?"; Taylor, *Chicago Commons,* 47 ; John D. Robertson, "Chicago's Tuberculosis Problem," in Chicago Municipal Tuberculosis Sanitarium, *Annual Report, 1917* (Chicago, 1918), 108–13, 116, cited in Vecoli, "Chicago's Italians Prior to World War I," 69n95.

9. Vecoli, "Chicago's Italians Prior to World War I," 176.

10. Vecoli, "Chicago's Italians Prior to World War I," 177.

NOTES TO CHAPTER 11

1. Renumbered to 810 West Ohio Street by ordinance effective September 1, 1909.

2. Giacomo (James) Balma interview.

3. Giacomo (James) Balma interview.

4. Giacomo (James) Balma interview.

5. James Balma, conversations with author.

6. Giacomo (James) Balma interview.

7. Giacomo (James) Balma interview.

8. Giacomo (James) Balma interview.

NOTES TO CHAPTER 12

1. The *session* is the board of directors of a Presbyterian church. Although they generally serve terms of limited duration, its members, entitled *elders,* are ordained for life.

2. Register, First Italian Presbyterian Church of Chicago, Vols. I and II, Archives of the Presbyterian Historical Society, Philadelphia; Reverend William Lankton, archivist, correspondence with author and summary of records of Presbytery of Chicago.

3. Register, Vol. I, Feb. 14, 1910, and *passim.*

4. Ghigo, *Provencal Speech of the Waldensian Colonists,* ix–xvii.

5. Franz L. Braun, handwritten memoir of visit to Chicago, 1910, Chicago Historical Society.

6. Braun memoir.

7. Braun memoir.

8. Braun memoir.

9. Braun memoir.

10. Candeloro, *Chicago's Italians,* 16.

NOTES TO CHAPTER 13

1. Funeral and burial records, invoice, Wold & Wold Funeral Directors, Sept. 5, 1907, receipts, Mount Olive Cemetery, Feb. and Sept. 1907.

2. U.S. Department of Commerce and Labor, Bureau of the Census, *Thirteenth Census of the United States: 1910 Population.*

3. Giacomo (James) Balma interview.

4. Register, Vol. I, Feb. 14, 1910.

5. Giacomo (James) Balma interview.

6. Molter, *My Heritage.*

7. Molter, *My Heritage.*

8. Certificate of Naturalization, No. 362083, July 18, 1913.

9. My paternal grandparents, Giuseppe and Antonina, never became citizens.

10. Catherine Allshouse, Helen Molter, and John Balma, interviews by author.

11. Frank Cicero, letter to Mary Balma, July 24, 1934; Frank Cicero, telegram to Mary Balma, July 28, 1934.

12. Undated summary; Manger memo, c.1939, both Erie Chapel 1905–21, folder, Chicago Historical Society.

13. Manger memo.

14. Minutes of the session, Third Presbyterian Church, Vol. 5, Chicago Historical Society.

15. Nieves, "Erie Neighborhood House," 56–57.

16. Erie Chapel, Annual Report, April 1917–March 1918, folder, Chicago Historical Society.

17. Erie Chapel, 1933 brochure, folder, Chicago Historical Society.

18. Vecoli, "Chicago's Italians Prior to World War I"; Candeloro, *Chicago's Italians;* Nelli, *Italians in Chicago.*

19. Candeloro, *Chicago's Italians,* 18.

20. Register, Vol. II, Jan. 5, 1915.

21. Helen Molter, telephone interview by author, June 14, 2003.

22. Giacomo (James) Balma interview.

23. Giacomo (James) Balma interview.

24. Deed to grantees James and Marguerite Balma, Mar. 26, 1924; John Balma, interview by author, Breckenridge, CO, June 9–10, 2003.

Three years after buying the Narragansett house, James purchased two residential building lots in the northwestern suburb of Des Plaines. He had invested in a real estate development of the Home Builders of America at about the time of the Narragansett Street house purchase. The development, called Homerican Villas, was planned to provide several hundred building lots. In 1927, however, Home Builders was unable to carry through on the project and went into default. The principal lender, the Foreman Trust and Savings Bank of Chicago, foreclosed and offered investors the opportunity to purchase lots by investing funds to complete the roads, utilities, and other necessary infrastructure. James had saved enough money to take advantage of the offer. He purchased two lots at a total price of $3,422. Payment was $1,500 cash and a mortgage loan of $1,932 to be paid over two years in monthly installments of $34.32. On August 15, 1931, the mortgage was paid off as originally scheduled.

James held the lots for almost twenty years. He continued to pay the taxes and went out to inspect the properties every summer. In 1948, John purchased the lots from his father and began construction of a new house for his family. The John Balma family lived there until 1996, when John retired; they sold the house, and he and Cleo moved to Colorado.

25. Catherine Allshouse interview; John Balma interview.

26. Register, Waldensian Presbyterian Church.

27. Forty years later, on May 14, 1967, the Waldensian Presbyterian Church merged with the Erie Chapel Presbyterian Church to form the Erie Waldensian Presbyterian Church. Thus were joined the two institutions that had served Italian Protestants for so many years virtually side by side on Erie and Ohio Streets. Erie Waldensian Presbyterian Church was dissolved in 1975. Register, Erie Waldensian Presbyterian Church.

28. Program, the Waldensian Presbyterian Church and the Samaritan Neighborhood House, c. 1931–32.

29. Reverend William Lankton, interview by the author, Chicago, May 14, 2003.

30. Nelli, *Italians in Chicago,* 183; Moody Church, "The History of the Moody Church," http:///www.moodychurch.org/information/history.html (accessed July 17, 2009).

In 1910, volunteers from Moody Church organized the Moody Italian Mission as a separate meeting place to minister to the Italian immigrant population that lived nearby and to carry on and expand Italian language Bible and Sunday school classes that had begun at Moody Church in 1906. The Moody Italian Mission was one of at least fourteen Protestant churches or missions that were organized in the years after 1892, when the First Italian Presbyterian Church opened at 71 West Ohio Street. It was also one of the more successful, with an active ministry in the Italian community for decades. In the 1930s, the Italian Mission (later Moody Italian Church) acquired a former Swedish Lutheran church at Elm and LaSalle Streets, where it continued to hold Italian language worship services into the 1940s. Starting in the 1940s, under the names Elm/LaSalle Church and later LaSalle Street Church, it also began to serve low-income families in nearby public housing projects. It continues an active ministry to this day. The senior pastor from 1961 into the 1980s was William Leslie, a friend and college classmate of the author. Helen Balma and Henry Molter were married at the Moody Italian Church on November 20, 1937. http://www.lasallestreetchurch.org/pages/ourstory.php (accessed July 25, 2009).

31. Helen Molter, telephone interview; Molter, *My Heritage.* The Moody Bible Institute occupies a large urban campus comprised of several buildings at LaSalle Street and Chicago Avenue on the site that Moody Church occupied for forty years before moving a mile north to LaSalle Street and North Avenue. The institute is often described as one of the most successful world centers for missionary training. It was founded in 1889 under the leadership of Dwight Moody. In the twentieth century, the institute became known for its conservative fundamentalism and its opposition to liberal theology and the

social gospel. Chicago History Museum, et al, *Electronic Encyclopedia of Chicago* and bibliography cited therein (accessed June 6, 2009).

32. John Balma interview.

33. John, then nineteen years old, remembers the drive home in the brand-new car as a somewhat harrowing one. There were no licensing requirements to drive. For years, as a youth riding public transportation, John had simulated driving by watching the bus driver and mimicking his actions as he shifted gears. He had driven a car only a couple of times. The new Ford was much more powerful than anything he had experienced, causing him anxious moments as he made his first trip home on city streets. The '34 Ford was eventually totally destroyed when an inattentive driver crashed into it while it was parked in front of the Narragansett house.

34. See, for example, Candeloro, *Chicago's Italians,* 14.

35. Letter, General Laundry Machinery Corporation, Chicago, Aug. 21, 1930.

36. Archdiocese of Chicago, *History of the Parishes of the Archdiocese of Chicago,* 563–67; Brown, *Scalabrinians in North America,* 385–86; Martin Ederer to Frank Cicero, July 18, 2008.

37. Sanborn Maps. All the buildings on Peoria Street were "tenements"—low-rent, multifamily dwellings. The Chicago building code defined a tenement as any building housing three or more households living independently. Garb, "Regulating Urban Living," 5–6.

38. Stabilmenti Benziger & Co. S. A., *Prayer Book,* inside back cover.

39. *Chicago Tribune,* Feb. 25, 1907.

40. Archdiocese of Chicago, *History of the Parishes of the Archdiocese of Chicago,* 565.

41. Baptism index, 1903–15, Santa Maria Addolorata, Archdiocese of Chicago.

42. Although Stanislau (*Stanislao* in Italian) is not a common Italian name, it was the name of the father of Antonina's first husband. In 1883, she and Antonino Scalia named their first child Stanislao after the child's grandfather. That son died in infancy. It obviously was important for Antonina in 1905 to name her last son after his long-deceased half-brother.

43. Chicago City Directory, 1917.

44. U.S. Department of Commerce and Labor, Bureau of the Census, *Fourteenth Census of the United States: 1920.*

45. Chicago History Museum, et al, *Electronic Encyclopedia of Chicago,* 244, 1135.

46. Chicago History Museum, et al, *Electronic Encyclopedia of Chicago*, 244, 1135. By 1900 there were more than one hundred settlement houses in America. Fifteen were in Chicago. Approximately half nationwide had religious sponsors.

47. Carmelo later told me he sent twenty-five letters to persons in Chicago named Cicero. Susan Cicero was the only recipient who responded in any way to his request.

48. U.S. Department of Labor, Immigration Service, "Application for Reentry Permit."

49. Interestingly, among the documents Carmelo sent me early in our correspondence were two photographs of Giuseppe's sons—one of Carmelo (1886) and the other of Benedetto (1888)—taken on July 4, 1928, apparently in Chicago. Their uncle, Salvatore Francesco, whom of course they had known well in Montemaggiore, must have acquired them during his 1929 trip or by some other means; passed down to his descendants in Sicily, they are the only known copies of those photographs.

50. Mary Thelen, Christmas card to Salvatore Francesco (1871) Cicero, Dec. 23, 1929.

51. Ben Cicero, Western Union telegram, Dec. 23, 1929.

52. Antonina Panepinto Cicero letters. There were letters as well from other family members in Chicago to Uncle Salvatore Francesco. Margaret Monteleone, wife of my father's half-brother, Carmelo (1886), who was herself also from Montemaggiore, also corresponded with her uncle in Sicily.

    In addition to correspondence, Josephine Parisi Cicero and her husband Sam had visited his brother, Carmelo (1899) in Ispica, Sicily in the early 1950s. There had been correspondence back and forth among those brothers and their spouses over many years.

53. The children in the photo were identified by Carmelo (1973) and his father, Salvatore, as Angela's grandchildren, Giuseppina (Josephine) and Gaetano (Tom) Parisi, children of Marina Cicero Parisi, who had remained in Montemaggiore until 1921. Great-grandmother died in Montemaggiore in 1927, six years after the departure of her daughter Marina and family. Our Buffalo cousin also showed Nancy and me a similar photograph of Angela Nicosia with two other grandchildren.

NOTES TO CHAPTER 14

1. Helen Molter, telephone interview by author, June 25, 2005; Molter, *My Heritage.*

2. *Marriage Service from the Book of Common Worship,* Board of Christian Education of the Presbyterian Church in the U.S.A., Philadelphia, Marriage 2nd of February, 1935; *Marriage License,* State of Illinois, Cook County, license issued Jan. 29, 1935, certificate by minister Feb. 2, 1935.

3. Candeloro, *Chicago's Italians,* 46–48; "A Story of St. John Institutional Church, Chicago," pamphlet, Chicago History Museum Archives.

4. Register, June 6, 1905, Mar. 13, 1908, and other dates.

5. "A Story of St. John Institutional Church."

6. *Market Newspaper.*

7. Room receipt, Feb. 3, 1935, Palmer House Chicago.

8. The porch was not large. We lived out there in the summertime. Our folding card table was set up for dinner every day, and also for lunch on the weekends. Sleeping "outside" on the porch was an imperative to my father. Early in the evening, he took out his folding canvas army cot and made up the bed. He left for work at the market at about three o'clock every morning. Because it was still light in the evening and rainstorms often blew in, he devised a system of folding canvas awnings that hung down over the screens. They had draw cords and pulleys so they could be pulled up entirely or let to hang down fully, or they could be folded horizontally in half to let in more air, with the folded canvas pulled up to cover the top half and shield a light rain or let down to cover the bottom for more privacy.

9. I take the reference to having "faithfully carried out her tasks here" as a pastoral encomium to her devotion to her family and faith rather than a reference to specific works.

10. Within a few years, Benny moved to Los Angeles, where he worked in the Central Farmers Market. Ironically, in recent years I have visited the Los Angeles Farmers Market many times with my younger daughter, Caroline, and her family, who live in that city. The farmers market is now an upscale, highly fashionable, and popular shopping mall, with stores such as American Girl, the Disney Store, Prada, and several expensive restaurants and cafes. Some of the original structures of the 1950s market remain; they house a food court that has many small cafes and ethnic food counters, some of which claim to trace their existence back to the old farmers market.

11. I have never forgotten, for example, the very first day in Miss Allen's first-year English class. When we entered the classroom, she had the words *all* and *right* printed in chalk at opposite ends of the blackboard that extended across the front of the room. Nothing was said about those words, which remained there until some days later, when it became clear that use of the common misspelling *alright* was, figuratively speaking, a capital offense to Miss Allen.

12. An irony I have often thought about is the fact that I became an accomplished lathe and drill press operator during college. After I transferred to Wheaton College near my home in Illinois, primarily for financial reasons, I worked thirty hours or more a week for more than three years in a machine shop in nearby Glen Ellyn. The pay was excellent, I have good mechanical abilities, I acquired the skills quickly, and I enjoyed the work. Although I thought about those past conversations with my father concerning shop courses, I never mentioned the subject to him. If the thought of our earlier discussions ever occurred to him, he never mentioned the matter either.

NOTES TO CHAPTER 15

1. S.S. *Moltke,* Alien Passenger Manifest, Ellis Island Records.

2. *Procura Generale.*

3. Named Salvatore Francesco (1931), as was his grandfather, he was first introduced to me as Salvatore, the name he often used familiarly. His two collections of poetry and reflections published in recent years, *Anabasi dal Deserto,* in 2003, and *Verso il Nadir,* in 2008, used Salvatore Cicero, but his inscriptions to me were signed Salvatore Francesco.

4. S.S. *Moltke* manifest, p.17, lines 10–11. Manifest records stated that he had a sister and father living there. Tom had been in Buffalo before: 1900 passenger records show that he came at age twenty-three. Apparently he had returned to Montemaggiore and married before returning to Buffalo in 1913.

NOTES TO EPILOGUE

1. Berta, *Mirafiori,* 45–48; Cardoza and Symcox, *History of Turin,* 248–53.

Cardoza and Symcox state:

> While Turin had already become a magnet for immigration from other areas of Italy before World War II, this earlier phenomenon paled in comparison to the massive influx of southerners into the Piedmontese capital after 1950. The city, which had a population of 719,300 in 1951, mushroomed a decade later to 1,102,600 and then to 1,124,714 by 1967, a rate of growth that far exceeded that of the other major cities, Rome,

Milan, and Bologna, in these years. The areas on the periphery of the industrial metropolis grew at an even faster rate, over 80%, between 1961 and 1967. The population in the zone around the Mirafiori [Fiat] plant, for example, skyrocketed from 18,700 to 141,000 in two decades, while the historical center actually lost population. Such demographic change was due almost exclusively to the influx of immigrants, with southerners accounting for nearly half all new arrivals by the early 1960s. By the end of the decade, Turin had emerged as the third largest "southern" city in the country, behind only Naples and Palermo (249).

Fiat's huge, technologically advanced Mirafiori factory, inaugurated by Mussolini in 1939, grew at a rapid pace in the 1950s and early '60s. From 16,000 workers in 1953, 18,000 in 1956, 21,000 in 1959, and 32,000 in 1962, the labor force reached 46,000 by the end of 1967. Berta, *Mirafiori*, 45.

2. Riall, *Sicily and the Unification of Italy,* 118.

3. Giunta, *Writing with an Accent,* 72.

Sources

PRINCIPAL SOURCES OF INFORMATION for this book were interviews with family members, in particular my mother's siblings, Catherine Balma Allshouse, Helen Balma Molter, and John Balma and his wife, Cleo; my cousins Elaine Cicero Kolovitz and Gerald Cicero; my recently discovered cousins in Buffalo, Sarah Cicero Fiorella, Carmela Parisi Orazi, and Helen Parisi Vaux, and my recently discovered cousins in Sicily, Carmelo Cicero (1973) and his father, Salvatore Francesco (1931). Carmelo and Salvatore Francesco were particularly helpful in supplying me copies of family documents, including legal documents, correspondence, and photographs, from a trove kept in their branch of the family going back more than 130 years to my great-grandmother Angela Nicosia.

The primary, and by far most valuable, source of information about my Balma grandparents and early family life is the recording made on a wire recorder on April 14, 1947, of a conversation with my then seventy-six-year-old grandfather, James Balma, conducted by my uncle Herbert Allshouse. I and numerous members of the Balma family have long been grateful to our gadget-loving Uncle Herb for testing his new recorder by sticking a microphone in front of a modest and reluctant grandfather during a family gathering on a Sunday afternoon.

My way also was paved by the work I have referred to as the Thelen Genealogy: this combination of genealogy and other family lore was prepared in 1993 by my cousins Robert and Dan Thelen based primarily on recollections of their mother, my father's sister, Mary Cicero Thelen, the only daughter of my grandparents Giuseppe and Antonina, as well as cousins Mary and Elaine Cicero, and Sara Pagliaro Cicero, second wife of my father's brother Joe.

Other sources are listed below.

BOOKS AND MONOGRAPHS

The Archdiocese of Chicago. *A History of the Parishes of the Archdiocese of Chicago, Published in Observance of the Centenary of the Archdiocese 1980.* Chicago: The Archdiocese, 1980.

Arché, Guy-Jean. *Le Massacre des Vaudois du Luberon.* [Paris:] Curandera, 1984.

Audisio, Gabriel. *Les Vaudois du Luberon: une minorité en Provence, 1460–1560.* Aix-en-Provence: Curandera, 1984.

_____. *The Waldensian Dissent: Persecution and Survival, c.1170–1570.* Translated by Claire Davison. Cambridge: Cambridge University Press, 1999.

Audisio, Gabriel, ed. *Inquisition et Pouvoir.* Aix-en-Provence: Publications de l'Université de Provence, 2004.

Augeron, Bonnin, et. al. *La Rochelle: capital atlantique, capital huguenote.* La Rochelle: Monum, 1998.

Avondo, Gian Vittorio, and Ettore Peyronel. *Cît Paris . . . in Val Chisone; L'emigrazione nel pinerolese tra '800 e '900.* Effatà, 2006.

Berta, Giuseppe. *Mirafiori.* Bologna: Il Mulino, 1998.

Bevilacqua, Paola, and Fabrizio Zannoni. *Mastri da muro e piccapietre al servizio del Duca; Cronaca della costruzione delle gallerie che salvarono Torino.* Turin: Giancarlo Zedde, 2006.

Biller, Peter, and Anne Hudson, eds. *Heresy and Literacy, 1000–1530.* Cambridge: Cambridge University Press, 1994.

Bocca, Claudia. *I Savoia.* Roma: Newton and Compton, 2002.

Bolino, August C. *The Ellis Island Source Book.* 2nd ed. Washington, DC: Kensington Historical Press, 1990.

Brown, Mary Elizabeth. *The Scalabrinians in North America (1887–1934).* New York: Center for Migration Studies, 1996.

Cameron, Euan. *Waldenses: Rejections of Holy Church in Medieval Europe.* Oxford: Blackwell Publishers, Inc., 2000.

Candeloro, Dominic. *Chicago's Italians: Immigrants, Ethnics, Americans.* Charleston, SC: Tempus Publishing, Inc., 2003

_____. *Italians in Chicago: Images of America*. Chicago: Arcadia Publishing, 1999.

Cardoza, Anthony L., and Geoffrey W. Symcox. *A History of Turin*. Turin: Accademia delle Scienze di Torino and Giulio Einaudi editore, 2006. Simultaneously published in Italian under the title *Storia di Torino*.

Caroli, Betty Boyd. *Italian Repatriation from the United States, 1900–1914*. New York: Center for Migration Studies, 1973.

Chessex, Jacques. *Portrait des Vaudois*. Bienne, Switzerland: Editions de l'Aire, 1982.

Chicago History Museum, Newberry Library, and Northwestern University. *Encyclopedia of Chicago*. 2005. http://encyclopedia.chicagohistory.org

Coan, Peter Morton. *Ellis Island Interviews: Immigrants Tell Their Stories in Their Own Words*. New York: Barnes & Noble Press, 1997.

Coisson, Osvaldo. *I nomi di famiglia delle Valli Valdesi*. Torre Pellice: The Historical Committee of the Waldensian Presbyterian Church, 1975.

De Lange, Albert. *Calvino, I Valdesi, e l'Italia*. Torino: Claudiana-Torino, 2009. Monografia Edite in Occasione del 17 febbraio.

_____. A Cura di Albert De Lange. *I Valdese: Un Epopea Protestante*. Firenze: Giunti, 1989.

Ghigo, Francis. *The Provencal Speech of the Waldensian Colonists of Valdese, North Carolina*. Valdese, NC: Historic Valdese Foundation, 1980.

Giunta, Edvige. *Writing with an Accent: Contemporary Italian American Women Writers*. New York: Palgrave, 2002.

Goldman, Mark. *High Hopes: The Rise and Decline of Buffalo, New York*. Albany: State of New York Press, 1983.

Grundmann, Herbert. *Religious Movements in the Middle Ages*. Translated by Steven Rowan, with an introduction by Robert E. Lerner. Notre Dame, IN: University of Notre Dame Press, 1995.

Lang, Jack. *Francesco I; Il sovrano Francese che s'innamorò dell Italia*. Paris: Librairie Academique Perrin, 1997; Rome: Mondadori, 1999.

Lerner, Robert E. "The German Waldensians, A Case of Religious Counter-Culture," *The American Scholar* 55 (1986): 234–47.

_____. *The Heresy of the Free Spirit in the Later Middle Ages*. Berkeley: University of California Press, 1972.

Lupo, Salvatore. *Storia della Mafia; dalle origini ai giorni nostri*. Roma: Donzelli editore, 1993, 1996, 2004.

Merlo, Grado Giovanni. *Eretici ed eresie medievali*. Bologna: Il Mulino, 1989.

_____. *Nel nome di san Francesco: Storia dei frati Minori e del francescanesimo sino agli inizi del XVI secolo*. Padova: Editrici Francescane, 2003.

_____. *Valdesi e Valdismi Medievali: Itinerari e proposte di ricerca*. Torino: Claudiana, 1984.

_____. *Valdesi e Valdismi Medievali II: Identità valdesi nella storia e nella storiografia; studi e discussioni*. Torino: Claudiana, 1991.

_____. *Valdo: L'eretico di Lione*. Torino: Claudiana – Torino, 2010.

Nelli, Humbert S. *Italians in Chicago 1880–1930: A Study in Ethnic Mobility*. New York: Oxford University Press, 1970.

Norwich, John Julius. *The Normans in Sicily*. London: Penguin Books Ltd., 1967, 1970.

Paravy, P. *De la Chrétienté romaine a la réforme in Dauphiné*. 2 vols. Rome: Collection de l'Ecole Francaise de Rome, 1993–94.

Rambaud, Pascal. *L'île de Ré; terre protestante*. La Rochelle: La Découvrance, 2007.

Riall, Lucy. *Sicily and the Unification of Italy: Liberal Policy and Local Power 1859–1866*. Oxford: Clarendon Press, 1998.

Schiavo, Giovanni E. *The Italians in Chicago: A Study in Americanization*. Chicago: Italian American Publishing Co., 1928.

Smith, Denis Mack. *Italy and its Monarchy*. New Haven, CT: Yale University Press, 1989.

Stille, Alexander. *Excellent Cadavers: The Mafia and the Death of the First Italian Republic*. New York: Vintage Books, 1996.

Symcox, Geoffrey. *Vittorio Amedeo II: L'assolutismo sabaudo 1675–1730*. Torino: Società Editrice Internazionale, 1989; originally published: *Victor Amadeus II: Absolutism in the Savoyard State 1675–1730*. London: Thames and Hudson, 1983.

Tourn, Georges. *Les Vaudois: L'étonnante aventure d'un peuple-église*. Torino: Claudiana, 1980.

Vray, Nicole. *La Rochelle et les Protestants du XVI au XX siècle*. La Crèche, France: Geste, 1999.

Waldensian Presbyterian Church. *History and Heritage of the Waldensian Presbyterian Church, 1883–1893*. Valdese, NC: The Church, 1993.

Watts, George B. *The Waldenses in the New World*. Durham, NC: Duke University Press, 1941.

_____. *The Waldenses of Valdese.* Valdese, NC: The Author, 1965.

Wylie, J. A. *History of the Waldenses.* 2nd ed. London: Cassell, Petter, and Galpin, 1882.

Yans-McLaughlin, Virginia. *Family and Community: Italian Immigrants in Buffalo, 1880–1930.* Ithaca and London: Cornell University Press, 1977.

_____. *Immigration Reconsidered: History, Sociology, and Politics.* New York: Oxford University Press, 1990.

Young, David M. *Chicago Transit: An Illustrated History.* DeKalb: Northern Illinois University Press, 1998.

JOURNALS AND ARTICLES

Biller, Peter. "Goodbye to Waldensianism?" *Past & Present* 192 (August 2006): 3–34.

Garb, Margaret. "Regulating Urban Living." *Chicago History* 35.3 (Spring 2008): 4–29.

Kneupper, Courtney. "Reconsidering a Fourteenth-Century Heresy Trial in Metz: Beguins and Others." *Franciscana; Bolletino della Società internazionale di studi francescani* 8 (2006): 187–227.

Lerner, Robert. "Book Review: Quellen zur Geschichte der Waldenser von Strassburg (1400–1401)," *The Catholic Historical Review* (April 2009): 331–32.

Nieves, Esther. "Erie Neighborhood House: Providing Hope and Responding to Community Change Since 1870." *Church and Society* (January/February 2003).

Vecoli, Rudolph J. "Contadini in Chicago: A Critique of The Uprooted." *Journal of American History* 51.3 (1964): 404–17.

_____. "Prelates and Peasants: Italian Immigrants and the Catholic Church." *Journal of Social History* 2.2 (Spring 1969): 217–68.

UNPUBLISHED SOURCES

Chiesa Evangelica Valdese: Union of the Methodist and Waldensian Churches. Tavola Valdese: Torre Pellice, Italy. http://www.chiesavaldese.org/eng/pages/beliefs/bible.php.

Cignoni, Mario. *I protestanti a Roma nell'Ottocento.*

Molter, Helen Louise Balma. *My Heritage.* Unpublished memoir, 1992.

Vecoli, Rudolph John. "Chicago's Italians Prior to World War I: A Study of Their Social and Economic Adjustment." PhD diss., University of Wisconsin, 1963.

Index

Index

About the Author

Frank Cicero is a trial and appellate lawyer. He has tried and argued a wide variety of civil and criminal matters in courts at all levels in the United States as well as in international arbitrations and litigations. He is a member of numerous professional societies, including the American College of Trial Lawyers and the *Società di Studi Valdesi*.

Frank's accomplishments and cases he has tried have been discussed in various publications, including *Who's Who in America; The Best Lawyers in America; Superwreck* by Rudolph Chelminski (William Morrow & Co., Inc.); *The Man Who Beat Clout City* by Robert McClory (Swallow Press, Inc.); *L'Affaire Amoco* by Yvon Rochard (Editions ArMen); and *Le procès de l'Amoco Cadiz* by Alphonse Arzel (Édilarge S.A.–Éditions Ouest-France). Frank holds a J.D. degree from the University of Chicago, a Masters degree in Public Affairs from Princeton University, and a B.A. from Wheaton College (Illinois). He is a senior partner with the law firm of Kirkland & Ellis LLP, based in Chicago.